Blueprint for Green Management

Blueprint for Green Management
Creating your company's own environmental action plan

Dr Georg Winter

McGRAW-HILL BOOK COMPANY

London · New York · St Louis · San Francisco · Auckland
Bogotá · Caracas · Lisbon · Madrid · Mexico
Milan · Montreal · New Delhi · Panama · Paris · San Juan
São Paulo · Singapore · Sydney · Tokyo · Toronto

Published by

McGRAW-HILL Book Company Europe

Shoppenhangers Road, Maidenhead, Berkshire SL6 2QL, England
Telephone: 01628 23432
Fax: 01628 770224

British Library Cataloguing in Publication Data

Winter, Georg
  Blueprint for Green Management: Creating Your Company's Own Environmental Action
Plan
  I. Title
  658.408

  ISBN 0–07–709015–2

Library of Congress Cataloging-in-Publication Data

Winter, Georg,
  Blueprint for green management: creating your company's own environmental action plan /
Georg Winter.
     p. cm.
  Includes index.
  ISBN 0–07–709015–2
  1. Environmental policy – Handbooks, manuals, etc. I. Title.
GE170.W56 1994
658.4′08–dc20   94–32037
                                               CIP

12345 CL 98765

Typeset by Computape (Pickering) Ltd, North Yorkshire
and printed and bound in Great Britain by Clays Ltd, St Ives plc

Printed on permanent paper in compliance with ISO Standard 9706 and from a sustainable
forest resource, the paper is neutral sized. No elemental chlorine is used in the bleaching process
and the paper bears the Nordic Swan Environmental label.

Contents

Preface

Public pressure on companies is mounting in parallel to public awareness of environmental damage. There is dynamic growth in demand for green products, manufacturing processes and services.

Many international companies are now embarking on a greening process – for example, their Quality Assurance people are increasingly demanding green product variants from suppliers. This may force small and medium-sized enterprises (SMEs) as well as the large ones in the supplier chain to take action.

Many companies are voluntarily going onto the offensive, launching ecological alternatives which are driving competitors from the market. They have found that they can boost their profits by making and marketing products that give savings in water, raw materials and energy, and by reductions in waste disposal cost.

Another alarming factor for companies is the increased risk of being held liable for environmentally harmful products or failure to meet emission levels. There are many companies that can no longer get a bank loan without prior inspection of their factory sites for soil pollution.

The book is intended as a practical guide showing how companies can increase opportunities and reduce risks by environmental action. It is distilled from many years of practical experience.

A great deal of this experience comes from Ernst Winter & Sohn, a company run by me and my brother Ernst Michael Winter, that made environmental protection one of its corporate goals as early as 1972 and later developed the Integrated System of Environmental Management.

Since then, many companies throughout the world have contributed to the development of environmental management. Tribute is paid in the 'Acknowledgements' to all co-authors who have provided inputs from their academic or practical knowledge to the material in the checklists.

Situations and opportunities for progress towards environmental management in business enterprises vary throughout the world. To highlight this I asked eight experienced personalities to contribute a resumé of how things stand in their particular country.

I would also like to thank Tom Peters for his Foreword. In one of his videos, he describes me as his 'favourite crazy'. I hope one day to prove worthy of this compliment.

Worldwide environmental problems are brewing up to a major storm for the business community. Companies great and small will need a good helmsman. This book is a compass for the navigating bridge, and a tool kit for the engine room.

Many companies that do lasting damage to the environment will become extinct; the environmentally conscious will inherit the earth's markets.

Georg Winter
Hamburg, September 1994

Acknowledgements

The author would like to thank the following people and organizations who have contributed to the contents of this book.

Mr C M Andreas, Checklist 14; Mr F Blom, Checklists 7, 8 and 11; Prof Dr H-J Ewers and Dr C Maas, Checklist 9; Dr M Gege, Checklists 5, 18, 22 and 23; Prof Dr R Hackstein and Dr F J Heeg, Checklist 21; Mr R Jöekel and Dr R Stiefel, Checklist 12; Dr W G Jocher, Checklist 10; Mrs H Jung, Checklist 17; Mr H Klemp, Checklist 16; Mr V Hoffman and Dr A. Weescamp, Checklist 24; Dr P C Mohr, Checklist 26; Mr H Schilling, Checklist 27; Mr W Dahnz and Mr K P Thevessen, Checklist 28; the organizations Jauch & Huber for Checklist 25 and GRIPS for Checklist 6. I would also thank Prof Dr V Stahlmann for his contribution to the chapter on Eco Controlling, and Mr Troy Davis for his contribution to the chapter on INEM.

The author would like to thank those companies and organizations whose activities have been used as examples of good practice and codes of conduct.

The information for examples of successful good practice at the end of Chapters 5–10 were collected from various sources by BAUM (the German Environmental Management Association). The information for the UK examples was noted in the ENDS Report and publications of *Business and the Environment*.

A final thanks to Dr M Gege for his advice in the development of the checklists and his contribution to the design of the Winter model, and to Mr C Sutherland for editing the German content and adapting the text to a global English edition as well as the material on environmental policies and reporting.

Foreword by Tom Peters

Georg Winter first presented his ideas to the general public in 1987, with the original edition of *Das umweltbewußte Unternehmen*, followed by the English version *Business and the Environment* (McGraw-Hill Book Company, Hamburg). The text has subsequently been translated and published in nine languages.

This new book, *Blueprint for Green Management*, building on the original, is a superb and helpful guide for management, demonstrating how to conserve natural resources and the environment, while at the same time attaining profit goals. Clean and green stands for growth, profit and long-term competitive advantage. That is the unmistakable message of this book.

The 'Winter Model', which is the concept behind this book is a comprehensive ready-to-use approach of environmental management available.

Its key messages are:

- Environment becomes a top-of-the-agenda issue for company management. Concern for the environment—from noise abatement to energy conservation—penetrates every aspect of company activities. The Winter Model perceives the company as a 'living organism'. The environmental approach is decisive for company organization and company strategy.
- This holistic approach focuses attention both on production processes and on products. No aspect of company activity is neglected in the search for environmental excellence.
- Helping all employees to develop 'environmental intelligence' is part and parcel of the process.
- Continuous improvement counts more than any 'big bang'. The key to success lies in involvement of everyone, moving forward inch by inch, rather than in multi-million dollar breakthroughs.
- Implementation calls for a step-by-step programme. And this is exactly what Georg Winter has produced in his highly readable new book. The detailed programme of action is indispensable. But, as always, what matters at the end of the day is the basic mental approach. At the same

time, this is an approach which opens up new markets, boosts market shares and makes profits.

It amounts to an encouraging message to those of us who are concerned about the environment in general; and it is equally encouraging to those who have to do the sums and the books to keep company finances in good shape.

September 1994

Tom Peters is co-author of *In search of Excellence* (Harper & Row, 1982), *A Passion for Excellence* (Random House, 1985); author of *Thriving on Chaos* (Knopf, 1987), *Liberation Management* (Knopf, 1992), and *The Tom Peters Seminar*.

Introduction

A DECADE OF CHANGE

Environmental management by business enterprises has made great advances in the late twentieth century.

In the 1980s, some larger companies, which had very much to gain or lose, considered the environment and used certain approaches and techniques in daily operations.

Where the job title existed, the environment manager was often a more junior staff member, frequently with scientific training, monitoring regulations, testing air emissions, and confirming water purity. Medium and smaller business were rarely involved, although some were quite innovative.

Public awareness of the impact of business on the environment was still low, except when major ecological disasters occurred. Even in developed countries, overall environmental legislation had yet not been enacted.

Now, however, we see businesses:

- recognizing environmental issues as important elements in product design, manufacturing, packaging, and transportation, and, indeed, in some enterprises' continued existence
- using excellence in environmental management as a means of promoting their product, the company, and their presence in the community
- raising the status and importance of the environment to Board level
- reporting to the public on environmental performance and having their environmental impacts and performance independently verified.

At international and national level, during this time we have seen:

- supra-national groupings, such as the European Union and its national governments, introduce much more stringent environmental directives, laws and regulations, and standards of quality, such as those of the International Standards Office

- the 1992 Rio Summit, at which world leaders gave their active support to promoting environmental good practice by business
- the formation of federations of business associations, International Network of Environmental Management (INEM) and the initiatives of the International Chamber of Commerce (ICC) to promote and develop good practice in environmental management
- workers' associations and trade unions taking an active interest in ensuring that more exacting Health and Safety regulations are adhered to
- continuing and successful efforts of pressure groups to monitor the conduct of businesses and government regarding environmental issues
- the beginnings of a profession, with the formation of Institutes of Environmental Managers.

We have also had Chernobyl and other major and minor environmental disasters, which highlight the consequences of failing to have proper environmental management and procedures.

THE PURPOSE OF THIS BOOK

These changes have brought environmental issues into the working lives of many managers who have had little training or experience in this field. They remain good managers, but with something new to manage—'the environment as impacted by my company's activities', has been added to their job description.

In addition, medium- and small-sized businesses have found themselves under local community or market pressure to address the environment as an issue.

The objective of this book, therefore, is to assist these new environmental managers in the task of setting realistic objectives and making things happen.

The author and his colleagues introduced an integrated system of environmental management into the medium-sized company, Ernst Winter and Sohn, owned by himself and his brother, Ernst Michael Winter. This initiative started in 1972 and, over the years, a philosophy and model of how to manage an environmentally aware organization, were developed. Another objective of this book is to pass on this experience.

A NOTE ABOUT THE ENVIRONMENTAL POLICIES AND EXTRACTS FROM COMPANY STATEMENTS REPRODUCED IN THIS BOOK

Throughout this book are examples of actual environmental policy statements given to us or extracts from those made public by the companies listed below. The home country of the company is also given here to highlight the international nature of environmental management. All these companies, of course, follow their policies wherever they do business.

Amoco Corporation	USA
ACRO Chemical	USA
American Express Company	USA
Eskom	South Africa
Fudjita	Japan
IBM Corporation	USA
ICI	UK
Kraft General Foods	USA
Mohndruck Graphische Betiebe	Germany
Monsanto Company	USA
National Westminster Bank Ltd.	UK
Noranda Minerals Inc.	Canada
Rohm and Haas Company	Europe
Philips	Netherlands
PowerGen	UK
Rhône-Poulenc	France
Thorn/EMI	UK
Union Carbide Corporation	USA

Business and the environment around the world

AUSTRALIA

By John Cole, Chief Executive Officer, Environment Management Industry Association of Australia, Queensland

Against a deepening recession and growing anxiety about the nation's economic prospects, early in 1992 Prime Minister Keating began to rewrite Australia's environment agenda to align it with job creation and economic development.

Four years previously, an Australian government discussion paper on ecologically sustainable development concluded 'there are considerable benefits potentially available to countries and companies that move quickly to develop and market the technologies that can meet these demands'.

Then, the talk was of 'technologies'. Today, the talk is of an 'environment management industry,' for two reasons. First, critical mass was given to the 'industry network' by the establishment of a national industry association, The Environment Management Industry Association of Australia (EMIAA). Second, because the answers to problems go beyond technologies—to research and education, new ways of doing things, and, above all else, to the development of systematic approaches, often involving the 'software' of engineering and workplace culture as much as the 'hardware' of technology.

The Environment Management Industry Association of Australia has over 200 corporate members and, as a young but fast-growing organization, represents the leading quarter of the industry.

An ANOP (Australian National Organisational Polling) survey undertaken for DASET (Department of Arts, Sport, Environment and Territories) towards the end of 1991 on community attitudes to the environment revealed that 91 per cent of Australians placed high priority on encouraging industries that helped the environment.

The poll also revealed that 53 per cent of Australians believed that the most effective way to encourage protection of the environment by industry was to emphasize incentives for research and development to find safe solutions.

Taxation and fiscal measures supporting environmental performance also rated significantly at 33 per cent, as did guidelines and regulations, at 38 per cent.

Looking to the future, international cooperation between the Australian Environment Minister and regional counterparts, the Inter-governmental Agreement on Environment and the constructive approach of the recently formed Commonwealth Environmental Protection Agency (CEPA) are central planks in the development of a competitive Australian environment management industry.

Once offshore, Australian environment management companies and organizations face stiff competition in the market-place, particularly from the Germans, Japanese, Canadians, and Americans.

We know that growth in environment management exports depends particularly on how effectively the public and private sectors collaborate to ensure Australia further develops and *demonstrates* competitive examples of best practice in environmental management in industry, technology, and infrastructure.

In a country like Australia, which has public rather than private ownership of community infrastructure and a limited industrial base, good environmental standards and public sector administrative and procurement policy determine primarily the viability of a nation's environmental industries.

Better integration of industry and environmental goals will provide three key benefits

■ a cleaner and better conserved environment
■ a more competitive (that is, efficient) manufacturing industry
■ a 'first division' environmental management sector.

Environmental policy must reward the innovator, ensure the polluter pays and acknowledge the cost of environmental degradation in community resource and economic strategies.

A practical approach is required, one that focuses on targets and outcomes in a specified time frame and capitalizes on the demand for environmental quality with the generation of jobs and growth in exports.

CANADA

By David W. Conklin, National Centre for Management Research and Development, Western Business School, The University of Western Ontario, Canada

There has been no precise jurisdictional division of responsibility for environmental issues between Canada's federal and provincial governments. The provincial governments have traditionally been responsible for resource management, while the federal government has played a leading role in international matters and those that have involved cross-border dimensions. The diversity of laws and regulations within Canada has created considerable uncertainty for businesses, and the establishment of national standards continues to be a contentious subject. For many decades, the Great Lakes have received special attention. Their position between Canada and the United States means that international coordination of programmes and regulations has been necessary.

Canada's provincial governments have established air and water effluent standards for various types of corporate activities, and they have played an active role regarding the development of sewage systems and landfill sites. Rapid changes in scientific information and technological capabilities have meant that standards have been changing rapidly and it is likely that the pace of these changes will continue. New methods of government monitoring, new enforcement procedures, and higher financial penalties will command the attention of corporate managers.

The Canadian Institute of Chartered Accountants (CICA) has been legally empowered to set accounting standards in Canada, and it is currently changing the ways in which corporate financial statements reflect the environmental obligations created by new laws. For example, Section 3060 of the CICA Handbook now requires that financial statements must include explicit estimates of the future costs and liabilities that will be involved in providing for site restoration.

Many of Canada's environmental laws place a responsibility on organizations to inform appropriate government representatives about certain corporate activities. This means that the corporate structure must be designed to ensure that the organization does communicate as required and that these communications are well considered.

There is an increasing trend in the law to impose personal liability on corporate directors for environmental matters, and so they must follow new procedures to ensure that their organization complies. Financial institutions are now responsible, in certain cases, for costs that their clients incur in connection with environmental matters. A lender's security depends on the ability to obtain title to real property in the event of default. If the borrower has violated environmental laws, or if the borrower is open to law suits from customers, employees, or the general public, then the lender may find that its security is worth less than it anticipated.

Throughout 1989 and 1990, Canada's federal government developed an active dialogue with Canadians in order to establish a consensus concerning new steps to achieve a healthy environment. As a result of this process, the federal government issued a Green Plan, which outlines the government's goals and key initiatives. Canada's federal and provincial governments have established permanent 'round tables' on the environment and the economy in each jurisdiction in Canada as a means of continuing dialogue on how to achieve sustainable development practices.

HONG KONG AND CHINA

By Stephen W. Lam, Executive Director, Private-sector Committee, Environment Centre, Hong Kong
Hong Kong initiated its pollution control institutions and legislation in the late 1970s and early 1980s. Control mechanisms similar to those of the UK and most Western countries are used in administering its water, air, waste, and noise issues. The government institution dedicated to the environment in Hong Kong was formed initially as a small unit in 1976, and this was subsequently enlarged, forming an agency, in 1981. Finally, in 1986, it became the fully fledged Environmental Protection Department of today, and the number of staff has grown from a handful at the start to more than 1200.

Environmental groups in Hong Kong include those introduced by international bodies, such as the World Wide Fund for Nature (WWF), Friends of the Earth, as well as those established by local organizations, such as the Conservancy Association and Green Power.

The Government established an advisory body, the Advisory Council on Environment (formerly the Environmental Pollution Advisory Committee), appointing non-government members. The Committee provides consultation to government on major policy matters regarding the environment.

Major advances in governmental commitment to environmental issues in a policy paper released in June 1989, presented as a ten-year blueprint for pollution control and containing about 100 initiatives with an estimated worth of US$ 2.5 billion (1988 price, adjusted upwards later in several occasions). As shown in Figure 1.1, the total yearly spending by the Government on the environment was set on an up-trend ever since—from US$ 66.7 million in 1989 to US$ 418.3 million in 1993—with an average increase of about 40 per cent per year.

In the arena of environmental equipment and services, which will be of most concern to businesses, the Government earmarked US$ 2.56 billion in the 5 years leading up to 1996–7 for sewerage, sewage, and solid waste infrastructure alone. The corresponding need estimated for private investment in the same period is US$ 1.9 billion (as estimated by the Environmental Protection Department in October 1992), in which particular requirements are for compacted and package-type pollution control equipment that is appropriate for space-constrained high-rise industrial premises.

These figures represent a total annual requirement of an average of US$ 0.9 billion for environmental equipment and services. It is estimated that 80 per cent of the requirement will be filled by foreign-sourced products and services, making Hong Kong a sizable imports market.

The People's Republic of China (PRC) commenced a comprehensive legislative provision for environmental protection, and this was written into the constitution in 1982. In the 1980s, an emphasis on 'management and planning' was adopted, and the limited resources were then allocated to the setting up of legislation and instituting it.

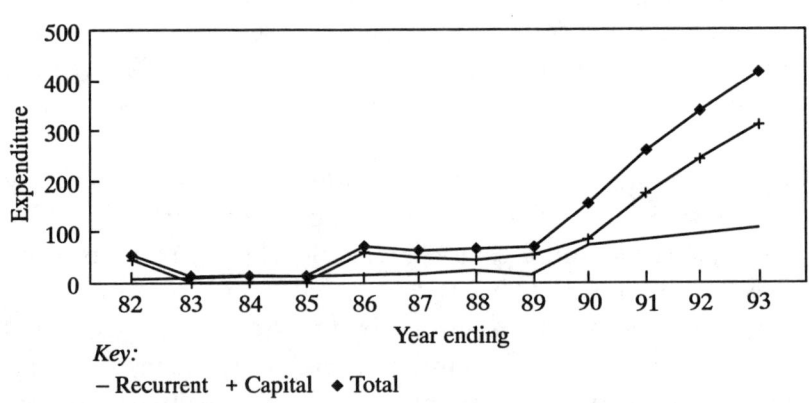

FIGURE 1.1 THE HONG KONG GOVERNMENT'S EXPENDITURE ON THE ENVIRONMENT (IN MILLION US$)

The most senior state body entrusted with the responsibility of making policies regarding the environment is the State Council on Environmental Protection Commission. The National Environmental Protection Agency is a separate agency under the State Council responsible for planning, drafting laws and standards, and advising on policy. The enforcement of policies is left to local environmental protection bureaux, which are formed separately at three different levels:

■ the province/municipality/autonomous region level
■ the prefecture/city level
■ the county level.

Major efforts towards developing pollution abatement policies and an infrastructure to implement these came in the 1990s, resulting from China's economic progress. In early 1992, the conference of the Environmental Protection Commission of the State Council passed the Ten-Year Programme and the Outline of the Eighth Five-year Plan (1991–5) for National Environmental Protection, and budgeted US$ 9.5 billion in 1991–5 to upgrade its environmental infrastructure. China spends US$ 2.3 billion on environmental protection annually, accounting for 0.7 per cent of its gross national product. This figure is greater than that of any other developing country in the world. However, what needs to be spent as a result of environmental degradation in China, is estimated to be more than US$ 11.5 billion per annum, approximately 5 times the environmental spend at the moment.

Capital for these investments mainly comes from multilateral funding institutions, such as World Bank and Asian Development Bank, and bilateral cooperation, particularly with Japan. There is a significant support mechanism established in China for financing environmental investment, in the form of tariffs and pollution fees charged to the public and enterprises.

The flourishing environmental market in Hong Kong, China, and South East Asia (South East Asia's envirotech market size is estimated to be, collectively, at US$ 6 billion, and growing at 16 per cent annually) is the focus for an international transfer of trade and technology.

Hong Kong is the crossroads of Asia and the 'window' of China. Being a major regional financial and communication centre, Hong Kong is a key location for entering the envirotech market in Asia. It is essential that commensurable business facilitators be set up in Hong Kong to serve as the information clearing house, and technology transfer services and marketing centre for the regional envirotech market.

The Private Sector Committee Environment Centre (PSCEC) is a non-profit organization, established by the Private Sector Committee on the Environment (PSCE), which consists of 23 of Hong Kong's leading business conglomerates, collectively representing 65 per cent of the Hong Kong Heng Seng Index stock market capital. PSCEC serves as the executive arm of PSCE and pools the collective resources and efforts, with the aim of providing appropriate environmental technologies, training, and information to business and industry, and mobilizing them to take on a more proactive environmental stance.

The Centre currently implements several major programmes, namely Industry Technical Assistance Services, Technology Cooperation Services, Environmental Database, Waste Exchange/Recycling Information Services, and Communications. As a major privately funded initiative, a 40 000-square foot Centre building is being designed for PSCEC, scheduled for completion in 1995. The Centre, once completed, will include a 15 000 to 20 000 square foot exhibition area for environmental hardware and product display and envirotech business incubation, a 5000 square foot technology demonstration area, a 200-seating capacity training auditorium, and an information/database centre. In the longer term, PSCEC will become a one-stop environmental information clearing house, resource and training centre, and a major facilitator for the environmental technologies and services used in Hong Kong, China, and, perhaps, the Asia region.

IRELAND

By Norbert Gallagher, Irish Productivity Centre, Dublin

What are the environmental issues affecting business managers in Ireland?

The Irish Productivity Centre (IPC) has carried out extensive investigations into the issues affecting business managers, under its Environmental Business Management programme. A major problem for managers can be their difficulty in considering what they personally or their company can do regarding the environment while remaining competitive. Analysing the benefits and risks in business terms not only provides them with a pathway to action, but also the realization that this action is necessary if their business is to survive and thrive.

Irish companies are becoming involved in environmental business management in order to gain market advantage and cost savings, assess environmental implications for the organizations, support compliance to legislation, and eliminate pressure from parent companies.

The companies foresee the following benefits as a result of implementing an environmental business management programme:

■ market advantage and gaining of new customers
■ confidence, stemming from compliance with legislation
■ reduction of waste production
■ economic survival
■ improved working conditions and company image
■ reduced danger of pollution and potential for liability to third parties
■ reduction of costs.

What is the impact of local legislation?

Environmental law is one of the largest growth areas as far as legislators are concerned, with new legislation expected in the areas of waste and planning. The body charged with the growing responsibility for environmental protection is the Environmental Protection Agency (EPA). Indeed, it is a requirement of the emerging environmental standards that companies make provision for continually updating their Register of Regulations. These considerations, as well as the anticipated start-up of the licensing function of the EPA and increasing legislation stemming from the European Union (EU), mean that the environmental field is one that will continue to see many changes over the coming years. These changes will probably continue to happen gradually, with a general tightening up of existing quality controls, and an emphasis on waste reduction and recycling.

This is a challenging time for manufacturers, but the environment is a nettle that must be grasped, and, preferably, grasped early. The alternative—companies not paying attention to these matters early enough—could be disastrous, not only from a legal point of view, where potential fines for environmental breaches are growing all the time, and, in some cases, are astronomical (up to £10 000 000 in the case of sea clean-up costs), but, also, there are concrete signs that customers are no longer prepared to risk dealing with environmentally unfriendly companies.

What actions has the business community taken?

A number of positive actions have been taken in the Irish business community. In 1991, Printech International PLC established an Environmental Works Committee to make sure everybody in the company has a say on environmental issues. This has led to continuously improving waste recycling figures, and greater use of vegetable-based inks. The Department of the Environment (DoE) provided a wide range of awards to small and large industries for both awareness-raising and practical on-the-job initiatives. One Irish-based international company, Yamanouchi Ireland Co. Ltd., won a prestigious award out of a field of 175 European competitors.

Which are the key national environmental organizations and what are their activities?

In addition to the DoE, which provides an excellent bulletin on developments in environmental protection, the key organizations include the following: The DoE Environment Information Service (ENFO) operates a public information centre with an extensive reference library and provides public access to national and international databases on environmental topics. The new Environmental Protection Act (establishment) Order 1993 means that both the private and public sectors are subject to the control of the Environmental Protection Agency (EPA). The National Centre for Environmental Management (NCEM) is an independent umbrella organization set up to monitor international trends in environmental management and promote good environmental management practices in Irish industry. A full list of organizations involved in environmental issues can be obtained from the NCEM.

What are the future trends?

Future trends of note include such existing initiatives as the development of Contingency Environmental Management Models for private manufacturing firms, service companies, and the public sector. This innovative programme is being developed through the combined efforts of the NCEM, the Irish Productivity Centre, and Trinity College Dublin's Engineering Department with the support of the EPA under the European Commission's LIFE initiative (L'Instrument pour le Financement de l'Environment).

In the light of consumer concerns and the growing demand for greener products, the Irish Productivity Centre is setting up a green product advisory line ('Green PAL') telephone service with help of the European Commission. This service will provide advice and information to consumers and small industries on a variety of environmental concerns.

THE PHILIPPINES AND SOUTHEAST ASIA

By Corazon P. B. Claudio, Philippine Business for the Environment, Manila

In pursuit of rapid economic growth, many Asian countries have disregarded the environment, resulting in severe pollution of air, water, and the destruction of natural sites. In many countries in this region now, however, there is a growing awareness of the need for environmental management, in particular on the part of small- and medium-sized enterprises. Unfortunately, capacity, resources, and manpower to make improvements are extremely limited. Therefore, one of the greatest needs of the region is capacity building, not only through the creation of professional firms that can assist local industries to strengthen their technical capacity, but also of public agencies, in particular local governments.

The Environmental Improvement Project (EIP) is now being promoted in the ASEAN countries with a grant from the US Agency for International Development. The challenge is to tap this environmental opportunity. The task for the developing countries is to provide opportunities for international financing that can enable them to undertake environmental projects and environmentally sound economic development.

Typical of the situation in many South East Asian countries is the case of the Philippines, which is described below.

In response to the growing array of environmental problems in the Philippines, the Ramos administration has created an environmental programme. The two main aims of this are pollution abatement, and the promotion of private-sector investment in pollution control technologies. The private sector faces not only increases in this kind of government action, but also increasing environmental advocacy from the more than 1500 NGOs (Non-Governmental Organizations) in the Philippines. The rising costs of electricity and water, which are due to frequent shortages, also have a crippling impact on the ability of local industries to be competitive.

However, there have been positive signs, together with a trend in industry to try to work hand-in-hand with the government. In the Philippines today, there is a growing awareness of the environment, and of the idea that the environment has a cost. Some business leaders are beginning to take voluntary initiatives, one of which was the creation of the Philippine Business for the Environment (PBE) in 1992—a non-profit association to assist the business community in addressing environmental issues and concerns.

The PBE cooperated with the Philippine Science Technical Committee (PCCI) to create the Philippine Business Charter for Sustainable Development, which aims to stimulate enterprises to commit to the improvement of their environmental performance, develop common standards for environmental management, and to demonstrate that business is taking its environmental responsibility seriously.

One of the PBE's key interests is the promotion of private investment in pollution control. One method for doing this is to raise awareness among investors and insurers about the risk of the insufficient pollution prevention measures of their clients. The PBE received a grant from the ASEAN EIP to prepare and conduct a two-day seminar for the financial and insurance sectors in the Philippines. In addition to sections on risk management and avoidance and investments in industrial waste prevention, management case studies were used to demonstrate that investments in clean production can avoid liability costs and improve profitability.

Basic compliance with environmental laws is often lacking because of poor government control and low consumer awareness. To help create competitive advantages for those companies that comply with or go beyond existing legislation, the PBE is working to introduce eco labels and other ways of approving positive environmental performance in the Philippines.

SOUTHERN AFRICA

By Jonathan Hobbs, Director, Industrial Environmental Forum of Southern Africa, and Chief Consultant (Environmental Policy) ESKOM, Johannesburg

In the recent past, apartheid, sanctions, disinvestment, political uncertainty, and violence have taken their toll on the economies and environments of the southern African region. The full consequences of the new dispensation have yet to be realized, but the creation of a political system in South Africa that allows for the participation of all citizens and the normalization of relations with neighbouring countries has met two fundamental prerequisites for effective sustainable development. The end of international ostracization of South Africa means that the whole region can now work more effectively as partners in fulfilling international commitments to environmental protection.

The motivational forces driving the business community of southern Africa towards improved environmental performance are, however, quite unique. The overriding requirement is to balance the need to curb the excesses of affluence (and remove associated inefficiencies and wastage) on the one hand with the need to alleviate abject poverty on the other. In southern Africa, supermarket customers who discriminate in favour of environmentally preferred products are few and far between, while people forced by their impoverished circumstances to ignore the sustainability of the resources around them are commonplace. The necessity of ensuring short-term survival does not encourage long-term perspective regarding resource utilization.

More traditional pressures on business do exist. Environmental legislation increases annually. Even Mozambique, one of the world's poorest countries, has over 40 pieces of environmental legislation, but enforcement of it is minimal and punitive measures taken against transgressors are no real deterrent. This is true of the region as a whole. Concern exists that it could become a haven for footloose polluters from countries with stricter legislative controls.

As South Africa returns more fully to international markets, it is conscious that the environmental rules of the game have changed during its enforced absence. Having been disadvantaged by political sanctions, it is not about to substitute these with environmental sanctions. The South African business community is taking its environmental commitments very seriously.

In many parts of the region, business survival—not growth—is the priority. Investors and commercial banks pay only lip-service to adding environmental criteria to the conditions of lending policies for fear of crippling business with one more burden. However, increasingly, environmental conditions are being attached to aid packages. The governments of the region can no longer trade ideological allegiances for assistance from the West or the Soviet Union and its satellites. The World Bank has recently given Mozambique a tight deadline to develop a National Environmental Action Programme if aid is not to be curtailed. The implications to the Mozambican business community, already struggling to produce goods with obsolete equipment (that gives little consideration to pollution prevention and control) and infrastructure ravaged by years of civil war, are obvious.

In such circumstances, considerable responsibility falls on the business community to demonstrate the efficacy of self-regulation as a major contribution to environmental protection. The role of business and environmental associations in mobilizing a common business awareness and commitment to this responsibility is of great significance.

The foresignt of a small group of South African business leaders in 1989 resulted in the establishment of such a forum—the Industrial Environmental Forum (IEF) of Southern Africa. A visit by Dr Georg Winter, during which he discussed his expriences in founding the German business organization BAUM with local business men and women proved catalytic. The IEF has grown to become a cross-sector network of over 70 business leaders.

The IEF's active regional programme has resulted in sister organizations being established—the Environmental Forum of Zimbabwe (1993), and the Namibian Business Forum for the Environment (1993). The IEF has also been assisting interested business leaders and United Nations agencies to develop further forums in Botswana, Swaziland, and Mozambique. A comprehensive regional network is evolving.

The region's business and environmental associations have two main focal points: continuously improving business understanding of, and commitment to, environmental demands being made of them by stakeholders while also providing a high-level business voice to be considered by those formulating national environmental policies and emerging international environmental standards. Developments are critically reviewed to gauge their cost-effectiveness and relevance to African business circumstances. In a spirit of openness and partnership, business peers share experiences, trials and tribulations. A platform is provided for members and recognition given for their achievements.

The forums of southern Africa are led by senior executives from major companies and multinationals, many of whom have access to in-house environmental expertise. A major programme of the future must be to mobilize the skills in larger companies to assist smaller businesses in developing their awareness and capabilities in environmental management. The cumulative impacts of these small-scale entrepreneurs may eventually match the impacts of major corporations.

Recent turbulent political times in southern Africa could easily have eroded the business community's commitment to environmental performance until it became a low priority. That this has not happened can be attributed to the realization that there can be no political stability without sound economic growth and no economic growth without wise environmental management. A prosperous and sustainable economy cannot be developed on a bankrupt environment; the environment cannot be the trade-off for economic development.

The resumption of foreign investment in appropriate environmentally and economically sustainable growth is crucial to the ongoing reconstruction and development of the region and to meeting the high expectations that have been created by the political changes.

THE UNITED KINGDOM

By Tom Chalmers, Environmental Coordinator, EEF East Midlands Association, Leicester

The UK was late to effect environmental legislation, only bringing in its Environmental Protection Act in 1990. The timing could not have been worse for industry, coming as it did in the middle of one of the worst recessions since 1930. It was further complicated as far as industry was concerned in two ways. First, because the Environmental Protection Act involved phasing various measures in over a period of years. Although this was meant to *help* industry, it did cause confusion. Second, because of the number of authorities that were involved—The Department of the Environment, Her Majesty's Inspector of Pollution, Local or Municipal Authorities, various water boards, with differing requirements, and the National Rivers Authority.

The problem was further complicated by the fact that there was not always consensus among these authorities as to who was dealing with what. Those in charge attempted to resolve this problem by merging some of the powers of these various bodies into one organization, but, so far, this does not seem to have worked.

All this has caused industry great concern as companies have not been sure who is responsible for what. They have not always been encouraged to ask these authorities where they stand, because the only ones they can ask are the ones that can level heavy fines against them if they are breaking the law. The large companies have no option but to comply because they are so visible. Small- to medium-sized companies (fewer than 500 employees) which, in most cases, because of the recession, have been in financial difficulties, just have not wanted to know if they are breaking the law, because if they are, there is nothing they can do about it. Thus, hitherto, the legislation has not had a great effect on the small- to medium-sized companies; they have kept their heads stuck firmly in the sand, and the enforcing authorities, not having the necessary manpower to police the legislation, have been unable to do anything about this. However, the pressure from both consumers and purchasers is changing things and will increasingly change things as time goes by. The early 1990s have seen various moves in this regard, the most dramatic of which came in the form of the implementation of the Montreal Protocol. UK industry were busy discussing this in March 1993 when letters started arriving from their North American customers requiring them to confirm that just four weeks from receipt of the notification, they would stop using CFCs or they could no longer be considered a supplier. This focused the attention of companies very quickly on dealing with an environmental issue, far more so than the legislation had, and it is obvious that this is the way forward—you pass your environmental requirements down your supply chain.

This pressure, plus the growing influence of Total Quality Management (TQM) ideas, which calls for fewer but preferred suppliers, is going to be the vehicle that forces small- to medium-sized companies into line regarding the environment. If we look to the future, we can see that there will be a lot fewer of these companies around. The ones that survive will be those that are doing the right thing in terms of quality and the environment. This will also mean that the British habit of putting things into separate compartments—'everything in its place and a place for everything'—will have to change. We have to start to see things more holistically, as companies are doing in places like Germany and the USA. TQM, International Standards Organization 9000, British Standard 7750, Health and Safety legislation, and the environment should all be looked at as one issue, and systems and procedures be introduced to govern all of these areas. Some of the best companies in the UK are already doing this, but the company that wishes to survive should follow their example.

THE UNITED STATES OF AMERICA

By Robert D. Shelton, Director, Technology and Environmental Management, SRI International, Menlo Park, California
US businesses, environmental activists, governments, and communities have about 20 years of experience in dealing with the realities of environmental management. The unique US experience provides several historical and current observations regarding the health and direction of businesses' environmental management initiatives.

- In the early phase, companies react to external stimuli regarding environmental management, these primarily taking the form of regulations and public demands. The companies' responses are often confused and, typically, have a technical orientation, focusing on the end of the pipe.
- These early, reactive strategies are inherently defensive; management believes that it is under siege from regulatory and public scrutiny. Many companies in the US are still in this reactive mode.
- In recent years, a small group of leading companies have developed proactive strategies to gain control of the situation, lift the siege, and construct a sustainable corporate environmental management programme. Proactive strategies use systems approaches to integrate

environmental concerns into business practices and are less technology-dependent.

■ Proactive strategies provide many benefits—both measurable and unmeasurable. However, in times of corporate downsizing, restructuring, financial constraints, and intense competitive pressures (all of which are realities in today's business climate), the programmes are often perceived as costing too much and diverting necessary resources from crucial non-environmental business activities. This is providing new impetus for even more effective environmental programmes.

■ As a result, a new form of interactive environmental strategy is currently emerging in selected leading companies. It stresses innovative, tailored approaches that focus on developing a sustainable environmental programme within the corporate structure. The interactive model stresses cost–benefit assessments and small, highly leveraged teams to a much greater extent than previous strategies that relied more on central environmental health and safety organizations. Both proactive and interactive strategies are corporate innovations in response to the failures of reactive strategies.

■ Policymakers and businesses are currently attempting to design and implement new market-based regulations as an alternative to traditional command and control regulations. The jury is still out on whether this approach will be successful.

■ Even after 20 years of effort, US citizens, lawmakers, and business managers still have no clear, common understanding of the term 'environment'? Among the public, the definition of environment appears to be based on deeply held personal and ethnic/cultural values—a situation that helps explain the slow progress made in 'improving the environment' over the past 20 years and one that portends a lengthy debate on the meaning of the concept of 'sustainable development'.

■ Environmental activism in the US has recently entered a new phase that emphasizes collaborative solutions, along with the traditional confrontational tactics. In addition, there is growing friction between many environmental groups as to the appropriateness of collaboration with business.

■ The two decades of US experience with environmental management indicate that the greatest challenges that businesses face have not been predominantly technical, but have required large strategic and organizational reorientations—developing organizations that are able to integrate corporate resources to achieve cost-effective solutions and foster innovation and collaboration.

The US faces continuing challenges with regard to environmental management, not the least of which is the sustainable integration of environment into business and policy decision making. The job is far from over. Based on experience, the greatest resource the US has to meet these challenges is the innovativeness of industry, policymakers environmental activists, and communities.

Environmental Business Management

THE CHALLENGE

Determining the financial cost of environmental destruction is not an easy calculation to make. However, scientists have tried and estimated that financial losses are up to 6 per cent of the gross domestic product of any nation. This measure includes:

- atmospheric pollution and its direct cost on human health, damage to buildings, growing crops, and forests
- water pollution and the impact on groundwater, rivers, and the seashore
- soil damage, such as the costs of 'inherited pollution', habitat and species conservation costs, not forgetting the direct cost in many countries of the cleaning up involved after such disasters as Chernobyl
- noise pollution, including the costs of noise deflection, loss of residential values, loss of productivity and noise-induced welfare payments to workers.

This estimate, though, does not include a number of other factors, either because they do not lend themselves to quantification or because we lack the ecological know-how to attempt the exercise. Examples of these involve:

- pollution-induced effects on the quality of life, such as the ugliness of waste tips, and smell, dust, and noise pollution
- the long-term effects of noxious substances released into the environment
- the importance that people attach to certain areas of land being left untouched or to certain plant or animal species being conserved
- loss of natural habitats of animal and plant species.

Today, the world is a victim of a major destruction process. The pollution of the air we breathe and the contamination of our soil and water may be less conspicuous than the ruined cities of Europe after the World Wars, but the long-term effects are on much the same scale. The current market economy and business are identified by society as being responsible for much of this loss.

The business community is thus facing a historical challenge: to maintain an acceptable standard of living for all people, while conserving or restoring the viability of the natural environment and, hence, the very basis of human life. This means meeting the needs of the present generation without compromising the abilities of future generations to meet their own needs.

This challenge can be taken up by adopting an environmentally aware approach to management, whether in the public or private sector. As we hope to prove in this book, adopting an environmental philosophy is in each firm's own immediate and long term interest. The experiences incorporated within the checklists will help companies identify the issues and opportunities involved, and develop environmental policies and practices appropriate to society's expectations of the twenty-first century.

CHANGING ATTITUDES

Society is not unaware of these issues. Attitudes to the environment have changed rapidly in recent years, altering the setting within which business operates. These changes are evidenced in:

- the findings and trends of public opinion polls and special surveys covering areas with which business is most directly concerned
- the rise in active and financial support for environmental interest and pressure groups
- more and stricter global, regional, and national laws, and regulations on activities that have an impact on the environment.

Independent surveys regularly show that the vast majority of the population consider the environment a very important issue and support moves for stronger environmental laws and regulations. Many buy only ecologically sound products and favour those made of recycled materials. They avoid products from companies with a poor environmental reputation and an increasing number contribute time or money to environmental interests or pressure groups. Children at school are now taught the importance of the environment and how their actions can influence it for better or worse, which will make future generations even more aware of the issues.

This change creates economic threats for vulnerable enterprises, but opportunities for companies adopting positive policies and practice regarding environmental matters.

THE BUSINESS OPPORTUNITY GROUPS

Businesses are in direct contact with society through employees, customers, suppliers, banks and insurance companies and the public authorities. Their presence and activities also bring them into contact with neighbouring businesses and residents, pressure groups of various sorts and, where a story is surfacing, the media. Figure 2.1 illustrates this relationship.

Each of these groups can help or hinder the economic success of the

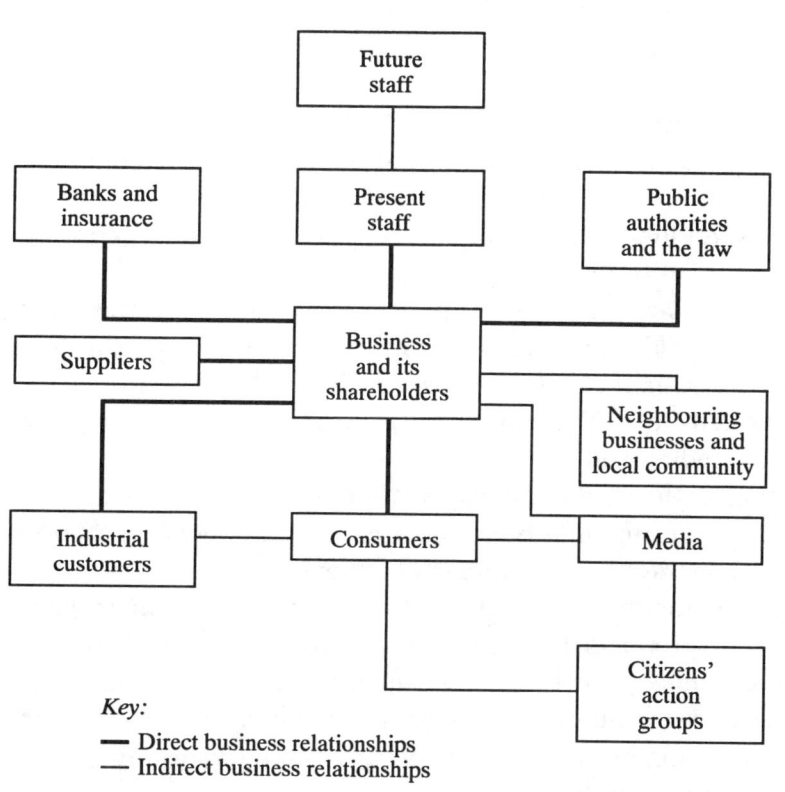

Key:
— Direct business relationships
— Indirect business relationships

FIGURE 2.1   BUSINESS RELATIONSHIPS

company, depending on its approach to their shared environment. Let us look at some of the issues arising with regard to each of these groups.

Employees

When they arrive for work in the morning, employees do not leave their environmental awareness at home. If they feel that their company is not environmentally aware, they will be faced with a loyalty conflict and are likely either to resign inwardly or may actually leave the company.

Those who are employed in work that is known to create environmental problems, such as that at nuclear power plants, will be exposed to potential conflict with family and friends unless their employer takes an active and committed stance on safeguarding the environment.

The attitudes of young executives will be important, if a shortage of well-qualified and motivated staff exists. Job applicants, do now enquire about the environmental record of companies they are interested in joining. Thus, companies that take a positive approach to their environmental responsibilities find it easier to recruit well-qualified people. Their efforts also enhance the motivation and commitment of their current staff.

Customers and consumers

'Green consumerism' is growing fast. As noted earlier, in many countries a majority of consumers are now environmentally proactive, that is, they look for environmental soundness in the products they buy. They are even willing to pay higher prices in order to do so.

German consumers are particularly green. An example of this is the market share of household cleaners made using an acetic acid base, a 'green' cleaning agent. In a stagnant market, the 'green' brand increased its market share from 0.9 per cent in 1987 to 8.0 per cent in 1990, with annual growth rates sometimes exceeding 100 per cent.

Phenomena such as this and the collapse of sales of shampoos containing dioxane, show that environmental issues in consumer products can boost or destroy a company's market and threaten its very existence.

Environmental soundness is rewarded by a positive consumer response. The same applies to products bearing authoritative 'eco labels'. Although these emblems only indicate relative environmental soundness (that is they show that some aspect of the product is environmentally more acceptable than the products of competitors), it has now become an important selection criterion for the environmentally sensitive.

More and more information is becoming available on the environmental soundness of products. For example, this becomes known through green consumer magazines or when some environmental criterion is added to conventional product testing. Many green product guides are now available, and green catalogues are available from specialist mail-order houses.

Normally, the impact of advertising declines over time, but, focusing the advert on environmental aspects can assist it to continue achieving high attention levels.

Citizens' action groups in Europe are now beginning to run campaigns to boycott environmental offenders—a method that is familiar in the USA. An example of this type of action was when copies of a letter were sent by Greenpeace to medical practitioners in Germany, appealing to them to stop prescribing the products of two named chemicals companies because these companies refused to immediately stop producing CFCs. The letter included a list of alternative products from other manufacturers, containing the same active substances or achieving the same effect as the offending products, but without the use of CFCs.

Such campaigns may threaten the very existence of companies, especially smaller ones. Defending oneself through the established legal channels is a long process and often has a poor success rate.

Industrial customers
Buyers of semi-finished products are also becoming more environmentally sensitive. They are now insisting on accurate details of the substances and concentrations of the input materials they buy to eliminate problems at source. They are also concerned about environmental aspects of their suppliers' products and wish to avoid inheriting their environmental problems as these might be passed on, affecting their customers. In part, this is due to the interdependence of today's industry, with its extreme division of labour and just-in-time delivery methods.

Suppliers
Likewise, suppliers are becoming more sensitive to green issues. Many of them want to take full advantage of their production processes and products for environmental soundness. However, they are often faced with obstacles in the form of the established environmentally unfriendly standards of their customers.

Banks and insurance companies
Financial institutions are involved with business and commerce as lenders of funds, insurers of assets, investors in businesses, and sponsors of activities.

Banks granting loans to companies are now aware that major environmental problems could jeopardize the borrower's sales and earnings and, therefore, this threatens such a borrowers creditworthiness. Loans for land or property that might subsequently be found to be polluted, for example, could dramatically reduce the security of the investment. Indeed, in many European countries, there are estimated to be up to 100 000 contaminated sites. Many existing mortgages may therefore be worth much less than their face value. If the real estate has to be repossessed in the event of a company insolvency, the expense of cleaning up the contaminated site could wipe out the value of the property.

Insurance companies are now reviewing their existing business liability insurance policies, some of which still cover the risk of environmental liability, often without extra charge. They are re-evaluating the risk of policies on a more realistic basis to include 'Environment Impairment Liability'. They also have had to revise their contract conditions to include recent amendments in the law of liability for environmental damage as this liability is no longer conditional on intent or negligence. In addition, the issue of gradual pollution, rather than sudden or accidental pollution, is being addressed.

Banks and insurance companies are also concerned about their investment portfolio and 'ethical investments'. Astute institutions are looking to invest in organizations that either produce environmental technology or in companies that are known to be clean and green. Both these types of organization are also aware that eco-sponsorship, with a factual and commercial basis, is good for their image.

Banks and insurance companies are looking for clients' businesses that are efficiently run and operate an environmental risk management approach in their affairs.

Public authorities and the law

There are few other areas of legislation where developments are moving as fast as they are in that of environmental law. Public attitudes are influencing the movement towards stricter legislation, tougher standards, and systematic enforcement of regulations. This has already produced more forceful legislation in many areas, which will increasingly affect small- and medium-sized businesses.

The number of successful prosecutions that have been brought against environmental offenders has risen in recent years, and this parallels the number of offences reported. The main subjects of prosecutions are water pollution, environmentally harmful waste dumping, and operation of machinery and equipment without a permit.

Neighbouring businesses and the local community

The degree of environmental sensitivity of close neighbours in the local community is of vital interest to any company. Neighbours such as other enterprises and householders have become highly sensitive to the effects of continual pollution, as well as any control failures and accidents.

The smoking chimney stack, once regarded as a sign of industrial progress, is now a source of concern to those nearby. Citizens' action groups are being formed to keep a watchful eye on the 'black sheep' and to restrain their activities with all the political and legal means at their disposal.

Such action groups make use of guidelines and checklists, published in 'green' literature. These explain how to use the regulations and laws to achieve particular aims. Increasingly, they are also pressing, or assisting in the preparation of, criminal charges against environmental offenders and this explains, in part, why there has been a rise in the number of reported environmental offences coming to court.

Local authorities set environmental conditions for industrial businesses seeking sites on new industrial estates, to make such projects more acceptable to other companies, citizens, and local environmental interest groups.

The media

The media (press, radio, television) are particularly alert to and interested in ecological issues and are quick to investigate suspected or actual problems. Companies, therefore, must keep abreast of areas of public interest, and have a media policy so that they can react appropriately and positively when required.

In return, the media are often happy to report examples of good environmental practice and management. These, however, will be subjected to critical scrutiny. Only really well considered environmental solutions or policies will produce positive reporting.

THE RESPONSE TO THE CHALLENGE

Environmentally aware business is based on the belief that, without ecologically-minded companies, there will be:

■ no ecologically-minded economy, which is needed to provide a reasonable quality of life

- no consensus between the business community and the general public
- ever-reducing market opportunities, as the public will seek environmentally friendly products
- greater risks of prosecutions for environmental damage as governments enact stricter regulations
- managers who are in conflict with their own consciences and losing their pride in their work.

Environmental technology is improving all the time and can make a major contribution to meeting the challenge of being eco friendly. The free-market economy made possible the reconstruction of European economies after the Second World War. Today we again need the framework of the free market economy to help restore our ravaged environment. This can only be accomplished, however, if individual companies are prepared to accept and introduce environmental concepts when running their operations.

The attributes on which the long-term success of a well-managed company are based are:

- Quality
- Creativity
- Humanity
- Profitability
- Continuity
- Civic responsibility

See Figure 2.2. Let us look now at how environmental management concepts can be built into these six crucial principles.

FIGURE 2.2   THE PHILOSOPHY OF ENVIRONMENTAL BUSINESS MANAGEMENT

- **Quality** A product can only be considered to be of high quality if it is manufactured in a way that is compatible with the needs of the environment as well as of the business and can be used and later disposed of in an environmentally acceptable manner.
- **Creativity** The creativity of the people in a company is enhanced by environmentally acceptable working conditions, such as low noise levels, healthy levels of heat, dust, humidity and so on, ergonomic office furniture, and nourishing canteen food.
- **Humanity** The working atmosphere of the company is humane if its goals, strategies, and policies are directed not only at economic success, but also demonstrate a responsible attitude towards all forms of life.
- **Profitability** This can be increased by cost-reducing environmental measures, such as economy programmes for raw materials, energy, and water, and by using market opportunities for producing or retailing ecologically acceptable products.
- **Continuity** The continuity of the company is dependent on anticipating and managing in a climate of stricter environmental legislation and of falling demand for products that have a negative impact on the environment.
- **Civic responsibility** A sense of commitment to the community will be felt by managers and workforce only if they have strong emotional ties with their environment and this is only possible if it is a pleasant place to be, if it has not been mutilated by poor environmental practices.

There are certain advantages which larger companies have in becoming an environmentally orientated organization. These include:

- having access to important and useful information sources
- often having a wide range of skills available, which can be used on environmental pilot projects
- being able to exert direct influence on its suppliers, chambers of commerce, and other professional organizations
- the effectiveness of the management team, trained and experienced in setting targets and seeing that they are achieved, all of which can be brought to the environmental context
- a workforce (which as a representative in-house cross-section of the population) is ideally suited to undertaking environmental pilot projects, both in-house and in the community
- creativity, which can be mobilized for environmental causes
- because it is non-political, a company does not take sides and so does not suffer the usual losses of political conflicts.

The first step

The first step towards introducing an environmentally aware philosophy is to develop self-awareness. What are our strengths and what opportunities can these bring to the company? What are our weaknesses and to what risks are we exposed?

This initial evaluation process is the first opportunity to use the approach and checklists illustrated in this book.

CODES OF GOOD PRACTICE – NUMBER 1

Various recognized associations and groups have issued codes of good practice for environmental management in business. These make excellent checklists and can assist managers developing policy statements and initiating action within their organizations. Seven are reproduced in this book. The following one is from the International Chamber of Commerce (ICC) and an example of how the 16 principles in this statement can be used as a checklist is given in Chapter 4, Example 4.

The International Chamber of Commerce: The Business Charter for Sustainable Development

> *Introduction*   Sustainable development involves meeting the needs of the present without compromising the ability of future generations to meet their own needs.
>
> Economic growth provides the conditions in which protection of the environment can best be achieved, and environmental protection, in balance with other human goals, is necessary to achieve growth that is sustainable.
>
> In turn, versatile, dynamic, responsive, and profitable businesses are required as the driving force for sustainable economic development and for providing managerial, technical, and financial resources to contribute to the resolution of environmental challenges. Market economics, characterized by entrepreneurial initiatives, are essential to achieving this.
>
> Business thus shares the view that there should be a common goal, not a conflict, between economic development and protection of the environment, both now and for future generations.

Making market forces work in this way to protect and improve the quality of the environment—with the help of performance-based standards and judicious use of economic instruments in a harmonious framework—is one of the greatest challenges that the world faces in the next decade.

The World Commission on Environmental and Development, 'Our Common Future', expresses the same challenge and calls on the cooperation of business in tackling it. To this end, business leaders have launched actions in their individual enterprises as well as through sectoral and cross-sectoral associations.

In order that more businesses join this effort and that their environmental performance continues to improve, the International Chamber of Commerce hereby calls upon enterprises and their associations to use the following principles as a basis for pursuing such improvement and to express publicly their support for them.

Individual programmes developed to implement these principles will reflect the wide diversity among enterprises in size and function.

The objective is that the widest range of enterprises commit themselves to improving their environmental performance in accordance with these principles, to having in place management practices to effect such improvement, to measuring their progress, and to reporting their progress as appropriate, internally and externally.

Note that the term 'environment' as used in this document also refers to the environmentally related aspects of health, safety, and product stewardship.

The principles

1. Corporate priority

To recognize environmental management as among the highest corporate priorities and as a key determinant to sustainable development, to establish policies, programmes, and practices for conducting operations in an environmentally sound manner.

2. Integrated management

To integrate these policies, programmes and practices fully into each business as an essential element of management in all its functions.

3. Process of improvement

To continue to improve corporate policies, programmes and environmental performance, taking into account technical developments, scientific understanding, consumer needs, and community expectations, with legal regulations as a starting point, and to apply the same environmental criteria internationally.

4. Employee education

To educate, train, and motivate employees to conduct their activities in an environmentally responsible manner.

5. Prior assessment

To assess environmental impacts before starting a new activity or project and before decommissioning a facility or leaving a site.

6. Products and services

To develop and provide products or services that have no undue environmental impact and are safe in their intended use, that are efficient in their consumption of energy and natural resources, and that can be recycled, reused, or disposed of safely.

7. Customer advice

To advise, and, where relevant, educate customers, distributors, and the public in the safe use, transportation, storage, and disposal of products provided, and to apply similar considerations to the provision of services.

8. Facilities and operations

To develop, design, and operate facilities and conduct activities taking into consideration the efficient use of energy and materials, the sustainable use of renewable resources, the minimization of adverse environmental impact on the environment and waste generation, and the safe and responsible disposal of residual wastes.

9. Research

To conduct or support research on the environmental impacts on the environment of raw materials, products, processes, emissions, and wastes associated with the enterprise and on the means of minimizing such adverse impacts.

10. Precautionary approach

To modify the manufacture, marketing or use of products or services or the conduct of activities, consistent with scientific and technical understanding, to prevent serious or irreversible environmental degradation of the environment.

11. Contractors and suppliers

To promote the adoption of these principles by contractors acting on behalf of the enterprise, encouraging and, where appropriate, requiring improvements in their practices to make them consistent with those of the enterprise, and to encourage the wider adoption of these principles by suppliers.

12. Emergency preparedness

To develop and maintain, where significant hazards exist, emergency preparedness plans in conjunction with the emergency services, relevant authorities, and the local community, recognizing potential transboundary impacts.

13. Transfer of technology

To contribute to the transfer of environmentally sound technology and management methods throughout the industrial and public sectors.

14. Contributing to the common effort

To contribute to the development of public policy and to business, governmental and intergovernmental programmes and educational initiatives that will enhance environmental awareness and protection.

15. Openness to concerns

To foster openness and dialogue with employees and the public, anticipating and responding to their concerns about potential hazards and impacts of operations, products, wastes or services, including those of transboundary or global significance.

16. Compliance and reporting

To measure environmental performance; to conduct regular environmental audits and assessments of compliance with company requirements, legal requirements and these principles, and, periodically, to provide appropriate information to the

Board of Directors, shareholders, employees, the authorities and the public.

Business Charter for Sustainable Development, ICC Document No 210/356/A Copyright © International Chamber of Commerce (ICC). Published in its official English version by the International Chamber of Commerce, Paris.

POLICY EXTRACT – OVERALL POLICY

National Westminster Bank, UK

'National Westminster Bank is committed to achieving environmental best practice throughout its business activities, wherever this is practicable. We recognize that the pursuit of economic growth and a healthy environment must be closely linked and that ecological protection and sustainable development are collective responsibilities in which governments, businesses, individuals, and communities all have a role to play.

Our environmental responsibility programme is based upon continuous improvement, consistent with current knowledge. Environmental management continues to be a corporate priority, fully integrated into our business. We believe sound environmental practice is a key factor, demonstrating effective corporate management. We will seek to educate and train our staff to act in an environmentally responsible manner.

We will conduct internal environmental reviews and will publish the results. The reviews will measure our performance and ensure that we are meeting our policy goals as well as compliance requirements.

We will seek to develop suitable banking products and services which promote environmental protection, where there is a sound business rationale.

We will encourage our customers to consider fully the environmental implications of their business and the impact on them of environmental issues; we will share information with customers as appropriate.

We recognize that environmental risks should be part of the normal checklist of risk assessment and management. As part of our credit risk assessment, where appropriate, environmental impact assessments may be requested.

We will encourage our suppliers to pursue best practice. Our procurement policy will take account of this.

Through our community relations programmes, we will continue to support groups which help to protect the environment and inform wider audiences of the issues involved.'

Integrated system of environmental management

Sustainable development and environmental protection of the environment are now important issues for business. Management should thus recognize this as a key corporate priority and establish policies, programmes, and practices for conducting operations in an environmentally sound manner. These policies, programmes, and practices should be integrated fully into each business as an essential element of management in all its functions.

Integrated system of environmental management gained increasing acceptance when the 'Business Charter for Sustainable Development: Principles of Environmental Management' was issued by the International Chamber of Commerce at the World Industry Conference on Environmental Management (WICEM II) in April 1991, and it has been adopted as binding by many major companies. The Charter was therefore given at the end of the last chapter.

Integration means that the environment becomes an issue for consideration whenever any business decision is made, and systems and processes are developed to ensure that this happens. However, environmental management is not just another control procedure. It helps companies meet their ecological responsibilities while, at the same time, reducing risks and highlighting market opportunities. Numerous reports from companies tell of environmentally orientated management bringing about economical success and throughout the book you will find examples of this. At the end of this chapter, part of the integrated system of environmental management used at Winter & Sohn's, is described.

DEVELOPING AN INTEGRATED SYSTEM OF ENVIRONMENTAL MANAGEMENT

As environmental protection and sustainable development is now such a central and important issue, it is to be included in overall corporate goals and implemented in all areas and at all levels of company management.

In this chapter we will examine some of the motivation, roles and contributors to environmental management involved in business in the private sector (a note on its relevance to the public sector is included).

Motives for introducing sound environmental management

As mentioned earlier, there are three fundamental reasons for companies seeing the environment as an important issue in their commercial activities. These are:

■ acceptance of responsibilities
■ realizing the opportunities such a stance presents
■ avoiding risk or reducing it.

Acceptance of responsibilities

Whether a manager is motivated by altruistic goals or self-interest, the conservation of natural resources should now take high priority in all their business activities. This is because the alternative approach:

■ causes premature exhaustion of raw materials and energy that companies need for their ongoing activities
■ destroys the natural environment, which affects *everyone*, now and in the future
■ confirms the belief that a market economy is incompatible with nature conservation and this view then gains ground in public opinion and with politicians.

Realizing the opportunities presented

There is a tremendous untapped potential for instituting measures that protect the environment *and* reduce costs and increase income. Small- and medium-sized companies in particular are often unaware of such opportunities.

In production, reductions in energy, water, and raw materials used saves money and, at the same time, promotes sensible use of the environment's resources.

If the company also caters to the emerging environmental awareness of consumers, this opens up new market opportunities. The environment can be the trigger for new product development.

Finally, the company's pursuit of sound environmental goals will improve the motivation of its employees and assist in the recruitment of quality staff as people are attracted to companies with such an ethos.

Avoiding or reducing risk

Ignoring environmental issues can increase the risk of loss of business reputation, financial losses as a result of fines for transgressions, criminal proceedings, or even closure.

There is also the risk that environmentally harmful products or processes will be mentioned in the media and by ecological groups and the negative image of the company that this creates will impact business profits. Some companies are now using staff to act as an 'early warning system', in this regard. They help identify future environmental product risks at an early stage. The company can then develop product alternatives in good time.

Environmentally harmful activities may lead to the company or its owners and managers being held liable for the damage caused. Environmental policies and practices help to recognize the possibility of such risks and avoid them becoming a reality.

Roles and contributors

Having a policy regarding the protection of the environment is an issue that concerns senior management. Overall environmental responsibility should either be in the hands of a company director or be a priority task for heads of department or functions to ensure that it is implemented in all aspects of company activity.

An interdisciplinary environmental committee can also be set up, representing different areas of the company and its activities. This group can develop a flexible plan for environmental action and report regularly on how well the company is doing in attaining its goals.

In some countries, there are already legal provisions that require a person to be nominated by the company to be responsible for its measures to protect the environment. For example, under German law, companies in certain sectors of industry must appoint a person to be responsible for protecting the environment with regard to water, emissions, waste disposal, and so on.

This person's independence, within the company hierarchy and vis-à-vis line management, is ensured by requiring that they report directly to top management and that they are specially protected from being dismissed.

The environmental officer appointed to oversee an integrated system of environmental company management has a different role to this legally required person, however. This latter officer is voluntarily appointed by the company, and the person operates as an interdisciplinary coordinator and promoter of innovation. This officer's activities are much more comprehensive than those of the statutory officer, who mainly ensures that specific technical regulations are being adhered to. If possible, the environmental officer should be a senior management-level position and be independent of all line management.

This position is comparable to that of the personnel officer in terms of its scope. Thus, the environmental officer is concerned with environmental affairs in *all* departments and, though they cannot issue instructions directly, they have a major influence throughout the company on matters concerning the environment.

Contributors from a company's departments and groups

Various departments and groups can contribute to the development of an integrated system of environmental management. Each has expertise that they can focus on the issues and information that can be used to help predict risks and evaluate opportunities. Those best placed to do this within the company are:

- senior management, for overall policy decisions
- research and development, materials management, and production engineering, for production issues
- marketing and public relations, for assessing customers' perceptions and needs
- personnel and human resources, facilities managers, finance, and legal services, for other in-house issues.

We will examine briefly the contributions each of these groups can make. (See also Table 3.1, which is a guide as to which of the checklists later in the book will give the best idea as to what the various groups within the company can contribute).

Senior management   It is the role of a company's senior management to determine environmental policies and the ultimate plans. This involves:

- identifying the major ecological problems in the company's areas of activity (a form of 'key issue analysis') by analysing the opportunities and risks in the social environment and in the markets (legislation, level of

Table 3.1 Which checklists to refer to regarding the contributions particular groups can make to an integrated system of environmental management

Group	Checklist
Senior management	1–6
Research and development	7
Materials management	8, 11
Production engineering	9, 10
Marketing	13, 15
Public relations	14
Facilities management	12, 16, 18
Personnel and human resources	19–23
Finance and legal services	24, 25
	26–28

awareness of the general public and customers, environmentally relevant activities of competitors, scientific/technical developments).

It can then:

- specify the corporate goals in a manner that is in keeping with the part of the environment affected
- formulate both defensive and offensive ecologically orientated strategies
- define business field strategies, such as product innovation, variation or elimination.

Research and development (R & D) This is an area of company activity where long-term decisions are made regarding materials and production processes. R & D decisions that fail to take account of ecological trends in the market and in legislation, may threaten the very existence of the company.

The techniques used in R & D include *value analysis* and *product line analysis*. Conventional value analysis techniques are accepted and understood as ways of avoiding or cutting costs and/or increasing the revenue created by the company. The methods used can also be applied to take ecological considerations into account.

The newer technique of product line analysis addresses the essential economic, ecological and social impacts on a product, from the procurement of the raw materials required to make it the treatment of the resulting waste materials. It presents the consequences of various decisions in the form of a product line matrix, which serves, *inter alia*, for making comparisons between different options for a product.

Materials management   Materials management involves the ordering, storage, and distribution of the necessary inputs for the production of the company's product lines.

It is also concerned, increasingly, with the disposal of production-related residual materials and pollutants. Disposal is becoming a more expensive, more difficult process and, in some cases, even impossible. Consequently, recycling such waste is becoming more attractive, from the economic as well as ecological points of view.

It would also be the role of materials management to ensure a gradual changeover to more environment-friendly input materials. This significantly reduces the disposal or neutralization costs and, in addition, the risk of civil or criminal liability the company and its staff are exposed to.

Materials management also involves ensuring that materials are properly stored, depending on their potential danger to the environment, and that material flows are controlled to avoid wasting resources.

Materials management should prepare a report on the current environmental pollution created as a result of the company's activities and suggest targets to be attained to conserve materials and energy.

The term 'quality' should thus be extended beyond its normal bounds to include protection of the environment and materials management should conduct all purchasing negotiations with ecological issues in mind. As well as use, price, delivery lead time, and so on, it should take account of the impact on the environment of any purchase. This should, ultimately, lead to ever greater cooperation with suppliers regarding developing and supplying environmentally friendly products.

Materials management's contribution to reducing the environmental issues and impacts of the company can therefore be considerable.

Production engineering   Production engineering is generally the area that offers the most potential for reducing environmental pollution in manufacturing enterprises.

Considerable investment is often required for engineering 'end-of-the-pipe' solutions to overcome environmental problems or for re-engineering entire production processes to comply with environmental requirements (integrated solutions).

Increasing landfill and disposal costs are reducing pay-off periods. Stricter regulations may also mean that such an investment is essential, to avoid the risk of operations being closed down.

It is often possible to reduce material, water, and energy inputs by finding engineering based solutions. These, together with reductions in the quantity of waste material and effluent produced, help to reduce costs for the company. Examples are the use of thermostats, combustion promoting additives, water flow rate limiters, and computers to minimize waste material from cutting processes.

'Clean technologies' are profitable as input materials, such as optimal combustion systems, paint systems, and wet processes, are fully utilized. Assisting this trend is the designing and use of sophisticated measurement and control technology, such as automated control and metering of concentrations of process chemicals, and the recycling of materials and thermal energy.

The contribution this group can make is to highlight the potential together with the costs and benefits, of improved technology.

Marketing   Changes in the social and legal fields, tougher environmental laws, and the increased awareness of ecological matters on the part of consumers, open up new opportunities for the marketing of goods and services. Ecological marketing concepts are necessary, both to secure competitiveness and to meet the requirements for social responsibility.

The planning involved to take account of these factors may include:

- a product policy, to include recycling capability, the highlighting of environmentally friendly features, designing functional packaging using environmentally friendly materials, and ensuring that products are used in an environmentally friendly way, with a consultation service being offered to customers
- a communication policy, which makes full use of the increased environmental awareness of customers in advertising and public relations by presenting the benefits of the company's products in a truthful and verifiable manner
- a distribution policy, which selects environmentally friendly distribution channels and recycling systems, including establishing recycling centres
- a price and discount policy, which introduces ecologically orientated price differentiation and considers positive discrimination in favour of environmentally friendly products.

Public relations   A company must communicate about its efforts to protect the environment and other ecological issues fairly and openly and must have the means to do so. It should put forward its interests in constructive dialogue. The principles of truthfulness, clarity, and consistency between word and deed are important here. It is better to spend money on excellent *activities* than to spend it on excellent *reports* on *mediocre* activities.

Any policy and objectives statements to be made to the public or in-house should be subject to expert input and review.

Personnel and human resources   Environmental management is best promoted to employees by the adoption of a cooperative management style. Key issues concerning environmental plans involving staff are training, continuing motivation, and the provision of working conditions that match the company's message of caring for the environment.

Any environmental training plan must define:

■ internal target groups, to include the top management team, department managers, white-collar workers, blue-collar workers, and trainees/apprentices
■ the curriculum (including environmental economics, business ecology, specific company-related knowledge, and so on)
■ learning methods, such as excursions, group work, and 'learning by doing'.

To motivate staff, it is important to give each employee an opportunity to play their part in the plan. This can be achieved by introducing suggestions schemes, environmental quality circles or by creating incentives for getting involved in specifically environmental activities.

Facilities management   It is important that:

■ the principles of ecological buildings are incorporated systematically into the design of the company's premises
■ equipment and machinery used by staff is designed in an ergonomic manner to ensure the highest standards of industrial safety and hygiene
■ company transport vehicles are purchased and operated in an environmentally efficient manner
■ healthy food is provided in the company's canteen
■ if appropriate, counselling is provided for employees' households on environmental matters, such as how to economize on energy, water, and cleaning agents.

Those who are responsible for these functions can provide information on the impact on the environment of the company's facilities and the issues these raise. Environmental management can provide guidance and a means of monitoring the various functions.

Finance   This function is responsible for the control of the company's funds and advising on strategic long-term investment decisions.

Before any major investment is finalized, the finance department should verify that the most important issues regarding protection of the environment have been considered.

Pollution of the environment, especially pollution of the soil, which reduces the value of the company's real estate and, hence, its creditworthiness, may jeopardize the shareholders' investment and even result in the company ceasing trading. Ecological risk assessment of this type is, therefore, a vital area of responsibility for the finance department.

The finance department should also ensure that the company gains maximum benefit from any government subsidy programmes for measures it takes to protect the environment, such as special depreciation rates allowed for taxation purposes.

A company's financial accounts and reports are mainly concerned with economic matters. However, in the medium term, company accountants and others must develop data and systems for 'ecological accounting', a process that is currently in its development stage, but will become the key area for a complete company ecology information system in the future.

Accountants thus have much to contribute to the environmental key issue analysis that senior management will complete before deciding on what policies and objectives it wishes to set for the company.

Legal Services   More and more countries are introducing legislation that extends the responsibility for the violation of environmental protection laws beyond those directly responsible for the damage. Thus, not only the employees directly responsible for monitoring the plant, but the company's Board can now also be held liable for any accident or pollution. Indeed senior management are now considered to have overall responsibility for any such failures.

Thus, the Board increasingly has a real, personal interest in ensuring that environmental legislation, rules, and regulations are known and observed. For example, it must ensure that its ecological standards are included in contracts with suppliers and customers. These might specify that the supplier will be obliged to take back contaminated material or packaging that creates disposal problems for the company. A company's legal advisers can, therefore, highlight such issues and the consequences of doing nothing.

Other information and sources of cooperation

Senior management can also look outside the company for help in planning sound environmental management.

Business associations can play an important role in helping spread know-how on environmental management among their members. By promoting innovation towards environmentally sustainable industrial development, they can influence the behaviour of a large number of smaller companies. They can share costs or research and provide information on progress made within any region or industry.

Business associations at national level

At national level, chambers of industry and commerce, professional associations, regional and industrial associations, and voluntary professional associations can focus specifically on environmental management and sustainable industrial development. Indeed many have set up special committees to study environmental issues.

From the mid-1980s onwards, associations of companies have been established with the specific aim of assisting the implementation of environmental management by businesses.

The first organization of this kind was created in Germany in 1985—the German Environmental Management Association (BAUM). Since then, various comparable associations have been established in a number of other countries, including Austria, Brazil, Denmark, Israel, Japan, South Africa, Sweden, Switzerland, the UK, and the USA.

Other associations have been formed by particular industries to establish codes of conduct and share experiences. Examples of this kind of association are those found in the mining, oil and gas exploration, and chemical manufacturing industries.

Business associations at international level

Various international initiatives have been launched during the 1980s and 1990s with the objective of enhancing the role of business in the fulfilment of its social and ecological responsibilities.

In 1990, The International Chamber of Commerce worked with BAUM and the US organization Global Environmental Management Initiative (GEMI) to develop the 'Business Charter for Sustainable Development', to be used as an international code of practice for environmental management.

A number of international organizations and United Nations agencies have declared their support for this particular code of practice. Many have developed, or are currently developing, guidelines based on it to be used by their members to help them in the implementation of ecologically sustainable industrial development.

Just as companies have come together at national level to form independent associations to promote environmental management, the majority of these national associations have also come together at supra-national level to form the International Network for Environmental Management (INEM). This organization's aim is to promote environmental management and coordination between the national associations world-wide. The strength of the network lies in its regional base, its openness towards small- and medium-sized companies, and its focus on environ-mental management.

In education, institutions dedicated to the training of managers and company personnel, such as engineering colleges, universities, and business schools, are beginning to play their part in ensuring that the curriculum of traditional courses and industrial experience are expanded to include environmentally sustainable economic development. Examples of such moves are the COPERNICUS activities of the Conference of European Rectors (CER) and the activities of the Management Institute for Environ-ment and Business in Washington, D.C.

Thus, smaller companies have access to know-how and experience, locally and internationally. This body of knowledge can be drawn on to complement the inputs supplied by the departments and individuals within the company.

Government's role in environmental management   As the existence of mankind is increasingly threatened by overpopulation, the destruction of the environment, and the exhaustion of the planet's natural resources, there is a great need for nations and regions to be managed according to holistic environmental principles as well as individual companies within them. Thus, we also need to recognize the need for an 'integrated system of environmental government' that covers the public sector.

Governments, like companies, should aim for the goals of environmental protection and resource conservation in all areas and at all levels of activity within their control.

At company level, it has been demonstrated that increasing the efforts made to protect the environment does not stand in the way of business success, but, rather, it can actually increase its success. Similarly, an environmentally friendly orientation at public-sector level, need not obstruct a country's cultural and economic development.

There are fundamental differences between governing a country and managing a company. However, the chances of successfully implementing environmental policies are just as great for governments as they are for business. More and more countries are now politically mature enough to move in this direction, as we have seen.

THE WINTER MODEL: AN EXAMPLE OF AN INTEGRATED SYSTEM OF ENVIRONMENTAL MANAGEMENT

In 1972, on the 125th anniversary of the foundation of Winter & Sohn, manufacturers of Diamond Tools and Diamond Making, the company officially declared that protecting the environment is one of its corporate aims.

This concept has since become part of the firm's tradition, with the continued support of the joint owners, Ernst Michael Winter and Dr Georg Winter.

Over the years, the company has developed an integrated system of environmentalist business management, known as the Winter model. This incorporates all aspects of the company's activities, ranging from the training of apprentices to the selection of company cars. Much of the material included in the checklists in this book is based on the experiences of Winter & Son.

The motivation to start

The environmentally aware activities of Winter & Sohn are only part of the company's aims. The firm must still produce high-quality products and services and achieve its financial goals, which will place the company and the jobs it provides on a sound footing. However, the two aims of improving protection of the environment and conserving jobs do not need to be in conflict.

The company's commitment to the environmentalist's cause is not designed directly to boost sales. The company's customers are buyers of diamond-tipped cutting tools, from various industries, and synthetic diamonds, which Winter & Sohn produces. Most of them are more concerned about getting value for money from their purchases than with the ecological image of the supplier.

Winter & Sohn cannot reasonably be called a typical manufacturer of technology that protects the environment. However, the company was strongly motivated by the realization that the company, being a major consumer of natural resources, must have a strong sense of responsibility for conserving these resources.

In 1985, the company became the first holders of the environment prize, awarded by the Association of Young German Businessmen, while the Schleswig-Holstein Business Study and Promotion Association voted the company 'Environmentally Aware Company 1986' for its work on the environmentally aware approach to management.

The elements of Winter & Sohn's environmentally aware business management system

We have selected some of Winter & Sohn's in-house and external ecological activities to illustrate what one medium-sized company can achieve.

In-house activities

In the Winter model, business management acknowledges the importance of protecting the environment in all areas and at all levels of the company. This principle is binding on management, directors, and everyone else in the company.

Winter & Sohn have *two* environmental protection specialists with mutually complementary areas of responsibility.

The head of the environmental protection department is responsible for the operation, maintenance, and modernization of emission-relevant plant, for minimizing the consumption of chemicals, and for the preparation and implementation of operating instructions for handling hazardous materials. He reports directly to one of the two technical directors. He has an 'executive' role to play in line management, which is to implement the technical aspects of environmental management.

The company also has an environmental officer who reports directly to top management. His job is to ensure that the company complies with environmental legislation. He is not bound by management instructions, but only by his conscience and the relevant environmental legislation. His role is that of a 'controlling body', as it were, and he is the 'letter of the law' voluntarily taken into the company. He also works towards developing environmentally friendly processes and products, comments on emission-relevant processes and products, keeps the staff informed on environmentally relevant issues, and works towards integrating protection of the environment into the everyday running of the company.

Company staff are involved in the process via the suggestions scheme. Any suggestions for improvements that lead to savings in energy or water consumption qualify for a higher remuneration rate than other improvement suggestions (30 per cent instead of the usual 20 per cent of the annual savings for a two-year period). One such idea produced annual energy savings worth DM 60 000 for an outlay of just DM 24 000.

The suggestions scheme has been expanded considerably in the past few years. In 1991, for example, the net savings resulting from the scheme (that is savings minus remuneration payments) were more than half a million Deutschmarks. In 1989, Winter & Sohn's suggestion scheme was rated the best in the whole of Germany's metalworking industry by the highly regarded Management Institute DIB (Deutsches Institut fur Betriebs-wirtschaft.)

Staff training and awareness

To inform and motivate staff, the company organizes seminars about the environment and excursions for their trainees. Talks are given to workers on environmental issues and brochures from environmental agencies and the Ministry of Health are distributed to them.

The in-house newspaper has a section on the environment, and competitions are organized on themes that centre on nature.

A mobile shop selling organical goods was allowed to park regularly in front of the factory gates. This initiative proved unsuccessful, however. The range of products, the prices, and the approach needed to be improved, and it proved necessary to inform staff better of the benefits of these alternative foodstuffs.

Environmental counselling in employees' homes   The company under-took an 18-month pilot project, and employed five environmental counsel-lors to visit and offer advice to employees and other people in their homes.

These counsellors advised on how to:

- reduce water consumption
- make better use of electricity
- take the strain off the waste-disposal system by pre-sorting rubbish
- use fewer chemical products in the garden
- replace various eco unfriendly with officially approved alternative products.

Environmental counselling is organized periodically, for new staff and when new opportunities for environmentally sound practices and products occur.

The project was financed jointly by the company and the Federal Labour Agency's job creation scheme. The fact that Winter & Sohn produces no household articles itself, removed any suspicion that it might be trying to boost its own sales, using the counselling scheme as a front.

The Commission of the European Communities contracted an agency to extend this environmental counselling model project to the United Kingdom, France, and Spain. In the meantime, in many countries of the European Union there are now altogether several thousand counsellors for private householders and communities.

Environmentally aware product and process development   Developing environmentally acceptable products is already seen to be in the company's commercial interest.

Winter & Sohn produces diamond-tipped circular saw blades for stone cutting, the noise level of which is only half that of conventional diamond-tipped blades. As many customers have operations near residential areas, quiet blades are needed if they are to continue to operate in such locations.

Research and development work made it possible to eliminate the use of asbestos in all types of diamond-tipped wheel blades without any loss of performance and many years earlier than was required by legislation.

Until very recently, environmental acceptability was a barely noticeable byproduct of the design, but now, it is an important selling point, and, in the near future, it will be essential for the product to sell at all.

Winter & Sohn work hard on developing environmentally acceptable manufacturing processes. For example, new conveying equipment for powdered plastics has been installed that virtually eliminates dust.

Raw materials procurement   Buyers can exert influence on suppliers to switch to more environmentally acceptable processes or products.

Winter & Sohn commissioned a scientific institute to examine its material management policies and decide what changes could be economically advantageous or justified by virtue of their minimizing the impact on the environment. As a result, changes were made in buying policies for paper, office and cleaning suppliers, building materials, and motor vehicles.

Waste disposal   The company monitors the state-of-the-art technology in this area and performs beyond the requirements of legislation and regulations. In many parts of the plant, dust filters and waste gas scrubbers were installed long before they were prescribed by law, and subsidiaries in countries with less strict legislation are being brought up to the parent company's standards.

Every effort is made to recycle materials. The heavy metal oxides produced as a result of the neutralization of waste water that occurs during electroplating are processed, yielding cobalt and nickel. These, together, account for 10 to 12 per cent of the dry sludge produced. Considerable annual savings are made as a result of being able to reuse the metals recovered.

Industrial premises A high-quality working environment is a stimulus to good work and the well-being of employees.

Winter & Sohn built Europe's largest diamond grinding wheel production plant. It was designed by an architect, assisted by another whose background was in industrial design and the other of whom's specialism was in environmentally friendly buildings and design techniques. Ecological criteria were used for the overall design, technical equipment, lighting, and the selection of materials. During building work, a firm specializing in cybernetic techniques was used and they kept actual costs well below budgeted costs.

An insight that resulted from the construction of the building, was that it highlighted what building materials and technical equipment manufacturers should be concentrating on in the future. The quickest way to make the construction industry more ecologically minded, however, is to boost demand for environmentally acceptable products and services.

Plant location policy When relocating or setting up a new facility, management should take the opportunity to create good environmental conditions for itself and its staff.

Winter & Sohn were looking for a suitable location for a subsidiary in the USA. One interesting site that otherwise would have been perfectly suitable was ruled out because of the high level of atmospheric pollution caused by local industry there.

Intercompany and international cooperation activities

Working for the environment in professional associations Winter & Sohn is a medium-sized company and, thus, has only a limited potential to influence the aims and activities of the business associations it joins. However, the company, by using its membership of environmental issue committees has been able to persuade associations and Chambers of Commerce to represent their members and be the guardians of standards of environmental behaviour.

Using contacts to assist local residents initiatives On behalf of a local residents' group to reduce atmospheric pollution in Hamburg, Winter & Sohn conducted an international survey to find out what the state-of-the-art in flue gas cleaning technology was for removing gases from the flues of power stations. The original plan was to equip the newly built coal-fired power station with what was proven to be an obsolete desulphurization unit and consequently not built.

Partly as a result of this survey, the local authorities introduced relevant legislation. This, in its turn, influenced the national approach and attitudes towards the problem.

The cooperation involved between an industrial company and a local residents' group highlighted that:

■ there need be no basic conflict of interests between them on environmental matters
■ the company made grass roots contacts, and the residents' group received specialist back-up.

The company thus became a 'corporate citizen' and less anonymous to its neighbours, the public.

Environmental information and invention exchange   The company's environmental activities produced a number of contacts with inventors wanting to protect the environment. These contacts have highlighted the problems inventors have in marketing their new products or services.

Winter & Sohn sponsored an 'environmental invention exchange', at which innovators could present their ideas and discuss them with representatives from industry, the media, Chambers of Commerce, and public authorities.

Another aim of the scheme was to increase the pace of innovation. The barriers to innovation were found to be:

■ the protection of the market by established companies
■ restrictive standardization, safety and administrative provisions, which had not kept up with technical development.

The invention exchange programme was well received and aroused interest from European Community environment experts.

CODES OF GOOD PRACTICE – NUMBER 2

The German Environmental Management Association (BAUM): 'Codes of Practice for Environmental Management'

We understand Nature, society, the economy and each individual business unit as parts of a global ecological system, the equilibrium and bio-diversity of which is decisive for the continued existence of all life. As business enterprises, we affirm our particular co-responsibility for the conservation of the natural environment.

We are convinced that the sound, environmentally acceptable handling of the public assets of water, air, and soil, and of flora and fauna must be secured by means of market economy instruments, that this requires close collaboration between business and politics, and that joint efforts must be made to promote public awareness of environmental protection by means of information and education.

We see great entrepreneurial opportunities in an economic order that is environmentally oriented, freely constituted and guided by market forces, that provides sustainable prosperity not only for the present, but also for future generations. This order makes it possible to resolve the conflicts between business and the ecology.

With this in mind, we commit ourselves to the following code of business practice.

1 We understand environmental protection to be one of the priority corporate goals and include it in our business principles. We will work towards this goal as a continuous process.
2 We perceive environmental protection to be an important management task and will ensure that it is implemented in all company functions and at all levels in operationalized objectives and rules of behaviour.
3 We consider environmental protection to be an area of line responsibility. We will provide the expert competence by environmental protection officers or environmental committees, ensuring the availability of comprehensive information and its inclusion in the entire decision-making process.

4 We will integrate environmental protection as an autonomous criterion in our planning, control, and monitoring system, where possible in quantified form.

5 We will assess periodically, and in detail, the state of environmental protection within the company in order to identify weaknesses, to initiate any necessary corrective measures, and to document progress achieved.

6 We will provide our staff with detailed information on environmental matters, motivate them towards environmentally aware behaviour—including that in the private sphere—and attach particular importance to protecting the environment in our educational programmes.

7 We will intensify research and development for ongoing improvement of the environmental soundness of our products and processes. We will thereby use raw materials, energy, water, and other goods as economically as possible, taking account of the entire life cycle of the products, including waste disposal.

8 We will involve all our business partners in our efforts to improve protection of the environment. We will elaborate on environmental standards together with our suppliers, provide information and advice to the trade, and give our customers information on how to handle our products in such a way as to ensure that they are used and, ultimately, disposed of, in an environmentally acceptable way.

9 We are ready for constant dialogue with all groups within society. We will provide the media with information on environmentally relevant matters and work together with authorities, associations, and other institutions to protect the environment.

10 We regard the legal regulations as minimum requirements and will strive to achieve a higher level of environmental protection throughout our entire organization.

CODES OF GOOD PRACTICE – NUMBER 3

Good Management Practices, EEC Regulation No. 1836/93 Annex 1 D:
Another contribution to good environmental management comes from this European source—regarding the participation of companies in the industrial

sector in the Community's eco management and audit scheme. This leads us directly to the creation of environmental policies, which we will look at in Chapter 4.

The company's environmental policy shall be based on the principles of action set out below, and the activities of the company shall be checked regularly to see if they are consistent with these principles and that of continual improvement in environmental performance.

1 A sense of responsibility for the environment among employees shall be fostered at all levels.
2 The environmental impact of all new activities on the local environment shall be assessed in advance.
3 The impact of current activities on the local environment shall be assessed and monitored, and any significant impact of these activities on the environment in general shall be examined.
4 Measures necessary to prevent or eliminate pollution or, where this is not feasible, to reduce pollution emissions and waste generation to a minimum and to conserve resources to be put in place, taking account of possible clean technologies.
5 Measures necessary to prevent accidental emission of materials or energy shall be taken.
6 Monitoring procedures shall be established and applied to check compliance with environmental policy and, where these procedures require measurement and testing, to establish and update records of the results.
7 Procedures and action to be persued in the event of detection of non-compliance with its environmental policy, objectives or target shall be established and updated.
8 Cooperation with the public authorities shall be ensured to establish and update contingency procedures in order to minimize the impact of any accidental discharge into the environment that may occur.
9 Information necessary to understand the environmental impact of the company's activities shall be provided to the public and an open dialogue with the public should be persued.
10 Appropriate advice shall be provided to customers on the

relevant environmental aspects of the handling, use, and disposal of the products made by the company.

11 Provisions shall be taken to ensure that contractors working at the site on the company's behalf apply environmental standards that are equivalent to the company's own.

Using checklists

In this chapter, we will examine the checklist approach to planning and environmental strategy and some of the ways in which they can be used in the subsequent activities.

Checklist 1, the overview, can be used by senior management to identify the issues that environmental policies and practices should address and, together with Checklist 2, Setting priorities, decide where and how to start.

THE VALUE OF CHECKLISTS AND HOW TO USE THEM

A business enterprise is a complicated and sensitive structure, best compared with a living organism. To establish successful integrated environmental management, it is important to:

- include all levels and functions in the company in the process
- treat the functional areas as an interlinked system
- present new skills and know-how in a user-friendly manner
- tailor environmental activities to individual company requirements
- take employees seriously as individuals
- promote a positive corporate culture by establishing codes of practice
- constantly incorporate new ideas from theory and practice.

As we have seen, the first steps managers who decide to formally introduce environmental management into their organizations need to take are to decide:

- which activities or functions to address
- what is the most efficient approach to adopt for the task.

Experience already exists. Trade associations in oil and gas exploration, mining, chemical manufacturing, and travel have issued environmental guidance to their members, as have many Chambers of Commerce.

Other decisionmakers are also involved with environmental good practice. For example, politicians must review proposals for legislative changes or innovations regarding the environment. Government officials—both national and local—are required to evaluate and make decisions on environmental matters. All are potential checklist users.

Managers must also decide on what scale and to what schedule they want to introduce better environmental management. They can:

- initially undertake an environmental 'weak point' analysis
- be content with looking only for cost-reducing measures that help protect the environment
- focus only on one or two important areas
- undertake a complete environmental risks and opportunities analysis.

Checklists—types and approaches

A checklist is a catalogue of steps or items, in a logical order, that has been developed to assist people in relation to some defined purpose.

Some checklists are informal and used only once, such as the list you make before going shopping. Others are informal, but used often, an example being the business traveller's 'to remember' list, used before visiting another country. At the other end of the scale, authoritative checklists exist, created by bodies of experts. Codes of conduct are examples of checklists of this type. A series of such checklists can take the form of a guide or manual of good practice.

However, most managers develop their own checklists. They do this by either:

- adapting an established authoritative list to a particular purpose or activity or
- having created their own list, use an established list to check the completeness of the one they have created.

Checklists can be used:

- in brainstorming an issue, to help stimulate the creative or discovery process, so, in environmental work, say, the index of an authoritative book written on the subject would be used to this end;
- to identify key issues, by including all possible areas and then identifying those applicable to a particular issue;
- to formulate a policy statement; for example, the International Chamber of Commerce's sixteen principles for environmental management as given in the 'Business Charter for Sustainable Development' can act as a

checklist for businesses designing policy statements or wanting to monitor progress;

■ as a project control, to ensure completeness of any document, process, or procedure;

■ during field visits, inspections, and interviews, to keep the activity to the point and to ensure that all the main issues are covered (in this context, the checklist acts as an enquiry tool, taking the form of an open-ended questionnaire with phrases starting with the words, 'what', 'where', 'how', 'who', 'by whom', and 'when';

■ during audits and reviews, to confirm issues by questioning situations and performances, so then, the checklists take the form of closed questions, seeking for the answer 'yes' or 'no' and they tend to start with such words as 'do' or 'does', 'have' or 'has';

■ when developing a document or report—a checklist can help to establish its completeness, the order of the topic areas within it and define them as well as leading to a uniformity of presentations, which makes it easier to compare a number of reports.

The qualities of checklists

If they are properly designed and used, checklists have particular advantages over other approaches.

■ **They provide a holistic approach**

They show how environmental management can be achieved at all levels and in all functional areas. Figure 4.1 illustrates how this has been achieved with the checklists in this book. Checklist 1 gives an overview picture of the contents and the connections between the other checklists. Checklist 2 (Setting priorities) helps someone using it to not only decide which area, and, thus, which checklist, to start with, but to find the best sequence for a combination of checklists. Checklists 3 to 6 help complete the process of deciding on which issues the final policy will be based. Checklists 7 through to 28 consider qualitative issues in individual functional areas.

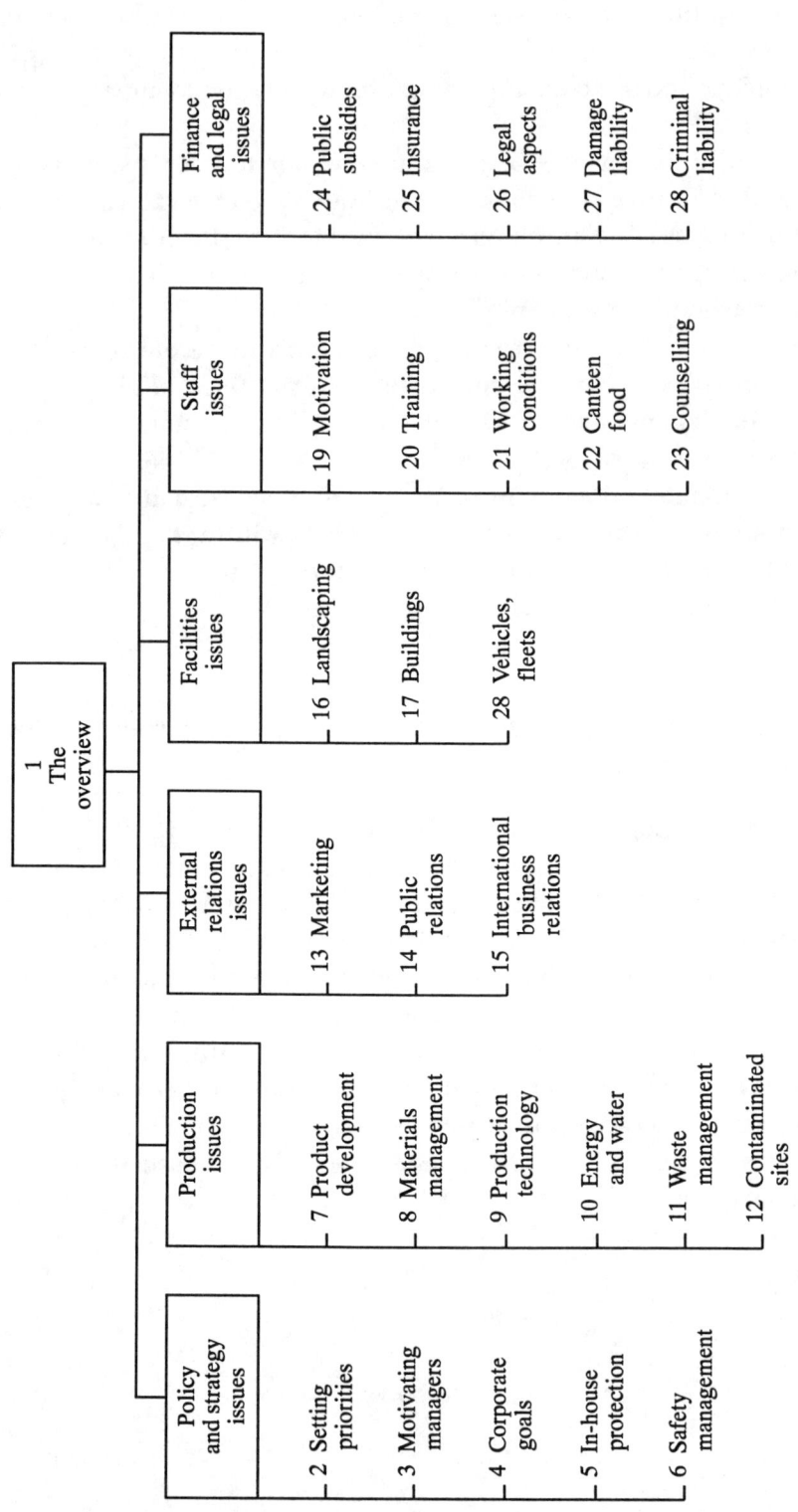

FIGURE 4.1   THE WINTER MODEL

■ **They can be interlinked**

The checklists can be interlinked by means of cross-references. Measures regarding protecting the environment simultaneously affect a number of areas (for example, materials management and production engineering), so cross-referencing enables management to promote desired synergistic effects and prevents undesired side-effects.

The interlinking of the checklists is a mirror image of the interlinked system of functional areas within a company. A thorough understanding of all the checklists and their cross-linkage enables management to act on the basis of a complete economic and ecological, financial and staffing, organizational and psychological view of the company. This also enhances the efficiency of the measures.

■ **They are easy to use**

Someone introducing an integrated system of environmental management into their company is in much the same position as the pilot of an aircraft as they, similarly, have very little time to collect and process the information they need, and, yet, they cannot afford to make a failed take-off or crash landing. Checklists give managers a readily available and easy-to-use tool.

Another advantage of checklists is that they are ideal for computerization as they are structured and contain the information in a form that makes it easy to transfer to a computerized expert system. Development work has already been done in this direction, but the limitations of using expert systems should not be overlooked.

■ **Checklists are flexible**

It is up to the individual company how far and how fast it introduces an integrated system of environmental management. The company may decide to:

- implement only those measures that are easy, fast, and inexpensive to introduce and, thus, improve the profitability of the company
- derive benefit from the application of individual checklists in isolation and use these to make an environmental weakness analysis of the company, using them to provide a starting point
- gradually expand its environmental activities, checklist by checklist.

The checklists offer a wide range of options, meeting the needs of very different situations. Points can be added at any time.

■ **They help in motivation**

Many of the checklists are concerned with psychological aspects. The checklists setting priorities, motivating managers, and staff motivation and staff training are concerned with people, who have their own unique personalities and sets of values. The mechanical application of a set of rules would be completely out of place in such instances. The checklists are not a psychological tool-kit; they are intended as a guide to help those who will bear responsibility for taking a right approach.

■ **They can be the basis for developing codes of conduct**

Some of the more important findings and decisions that result from the checklist reviews could be incorporated into codes of conduct. There are already many examples of companies that have made environmental thinking a part of their overall corporate ethics, corporate culture or identity, and some of these appear in this book.

Similarly, checklists for certain areas, such as 9, Production technology, may be more than simply procedures to be followed. They may take the character of codes of good practice, including moral principles, but have a status that is comparable to that of certain traditional professional ethical codes.

Some companies may use checklists as purely factual sets of rules. However, their impact will be strongest in those companies that incorporate the messages found in these and other checklists into the value system of the company, and communicate this clearly to staff and other stakeholders.

■ **Checklists are easy to update and add to**

There is rapid growth in successful and environmentally sound operating methods. Checklists need to be constantly updated and new issues added. Putting the checklists on computer, helps to make this easier to do.

Examples of how checklists can be used

The checklists in this book have been written with activity in mind to encourage responses along the lines of 'we have done this', 'we are considering this,' or 'we have not yet considered this'. Example 1 below illustrates this approach. The points on the checklist can, however, be turned round into questions. Such a format is appropriate for evaluations and audits. Questions can be framed so that the response is a 'yes' or 'no'. A comment or stipulating some sort of action might be expected when there is a 'no' answer. Indeed, Example 2 shows this kind of application for a checklist.

Example 3 illustrates how a checklist can be used as a progress monitor. Four stages of implementation have been illustrated:

- the evaluating process and policy decision made,
- developing an action plan,
- the implementation, and
- the review and monitoring.

Example 4 combines the use of authoritative principles (those of the International Chamber of Commerce) with another form of progress monitoring. Example 5 shows how cost-saving items can be identified using checklists and how they can often be introduced quite quickly. Example 6 illustrates the use of checklists to formulate policies.

Example 1: Using a checklist as a policy action aid

This example uses Checklist 11, Waste management.

The issue   To ensure that recyclable materials are monitored by integrating the recycling principle into materials management and storage.

Action   Set up a management system to coordinate all recycling activities.

Response   The alternatives: Done/Under consideration/Not considered/ Not applicable

Action   Organize the collection of and provide receptacles for waste.
Examples of action that can be taken:

- reduce volume by using compaction containers
- set up used oil collection points
- organize separate collection for paper, plastics, and aluminium
- collect solvents, solutions, acids, and dyes
- shred waste computer paper for use as packing material
- convert unsuccessful photocopies into note-pads.

Response   The alternatives: Done/Under consideration/Not considered/ Not applicable

Action   Request for product and safety information from suppliers and manufacturers.

Response   The Alternatives: Done/Under consideration/Not considered/ Not applicable

Action   Encourage employees to use collection points for materials they have for recycling.

Response   The alternatives: Done/Under consideration/Not considered/ Not applicable

Example 2: using a checklist as a questionnaire
This example uses Checklist 11, Waste management.

The issue   General terms of business

1 Have we a general purchasing conditions clause, making suppliers liable for the environmental acceptability of their products?
Yes/No
Comment or action

2 Do our purchasing agreements have clauses guaranteeing that products purchased can be disposed of without undue expense?
Yes/No
Comment or action

3 Do we have an agreement with suppliers that they will take back disposable containers?
Yes/No
Comment or action

4 Are all suppliers required to provide full information on materials and product characteristics?
Yes/No
Comment or action

5 Are exclusion clauses included ensuring that the purchasing firm is not liable if the supplier infringes legal obligations?
Yes/No
Comment or action

Example 3: using a checklist as an implementation guide
This example uses Checklist 21, Working conditions.

■ **Stage 1**
Evaluate current company practice against accepted standards and create a policy.
■ **Stage 2**
Develop action plans to implement policy.
■ **Stage 3**
Plan implemented and operating.
■ **Stage 4**
Management review system in place.

The issues Stress factor 7: Safety

	Stages			
	1	2	3	4
a) To ensure that all safety regulations are observed, including the wearing of personal protective equipment.	C	C	C	C
b) To install safety barriers so that staff do not enter danger areas around automatic machines and that stray objects thrown out by the machines do not endanger individual safety.	C	C	C	C
c) To provide anti-dazzle equipment and splatter protection.	C	C	C	C
d) To ensure that emergency shut-off equipment can be operated quickly, easily and safely, and operates automatically to preset limits.	C	C	P	P
e) To demarcate and clearly mark access routes.	C	C	P	O
f) To ensure that safety signs such as coloured symbols are always clearly visible.	C	C	P	O
g) To take additional precautions where safety equipment is not yet installed during commissioning or removed during maintenance.	C	C	P	O

Key

C = Completed; P = In progress; O = Not yet started

Example 4: using an authoritative checklist to create policies

Another use of the checklist approach is to adopt an authoritative set of environmental principles and develop policies and practices that match the principles. Using the 16 principles of The International Chamber of Commerce's 'Business Charter for Sustainable Development' it would be possible to:

■ decide on the company's needs for policies regarding each of the 16 points
■ formulate the policies and decide on strategies and plans to follow to achieve them
■ implement the strategies.

This approach could be used for the company overall *and* for each activity or site. The example that follows concerns safety and security. Checklist 6, Safety management, in Chapter 5, could be used to devise programmes and practices regarding this issue.

The issue   Security and safety

ICC principle	Policy adopted	Programmes or practices initiated
1 Corporate priority	+	+
2 Integrated management	+	+
3 Process of improvement	+	+
4 Employee education	+	o
5 Prior assessment	+	+
6 Products and services	+	o
7 Customer advice	+	o
8 Facilities and operations	+	o
9 Research	+	o
10 Precautionary approach	+	o
11 Contractors and suppliers	+	o
12 Emergency preparedness	+	+
13 Transfer of technology	n	n
14 Contributing to the common effort	+	o
15 Openness to concerns	+	+
16 Compliance and reporting	+	+

Key

+ = Fully implemented

o = In process of implementation

n = Not applicable or covered by another function

Example 5: Pinpointing cost-reducing measures

Some owners and managers may wish to use checklists to identify ways in which, as well as benefiting the environment, they will reduce their overheads and other costs. Others may wish to make an impact by taking immediate action. To highlight this aspect, examples of cost-saving measures have been marked with an asterisk in the checklists in this book. Examples of where these may be found are given below.

Checklist	Aspect	Checklist Point
3	Motivating managers	19
8	Materials management	4 and 18
9	Production technology	3, 8, 9, 10, and 16
10	Energy and water	7, 8, and 9
11	Waste management	9
17	Buildings	15, 17, 18 and, 20
18	Vehicles, fleets	3, 4, 6, 7, 9, 10, 12, 13, 18 to 32, and 34

Example 6: Using checklists to formulate an environmental policy

A policy is a general guideline for action, used when implementing any strategy or plan. When published, a policy becomes a public declaration of an organization's intent.

Policies rarely specify quantified targets or a time frame for their achievement. Instead, these are included when strategies are formulated and goals and short- and long-term objectives are designated to phases of implementation of the policies.

The format of a policy

An environmental policy statement is intention captured in word. It will contain phrases such as 'The company'

■ recognizes the priority of . . .
■ intends to work towards . . .
■ will reduce the impact of . . .
■ anticipate environmental issues when . . .
■ operate plant and facilities with . . .
■ establish management systems for . . .
■ comply with . . .
■ share with . . .
■ conserve resources by . . .
■ educate and train staff to . . .
■ support and encourage ventures that . . .
■ report and communicate to . . .

Two actual examples of this format, taken from 'Responsible Carer: A public commitment' issued by the Chemical Manufacturers Association, are:

■ To recognize and respond to community concerns about chemicals and our operations.

■ To develop and produce chemicals that can be manufactured, transported, used, and disposed of safely.

The issues covered

The matters addressed within a policy statement relate to the environmental
issues raised by the business' operations and the impacts it has on the
environment that it has discovered during the environmental impact review.
For a primary producer, such as one involved in mining, the emphasis will be
on the health and safety of its employees and site stewardship. For a retail
company, however, likely issues would be cooperation with suppliers,
packaging policy, recycling, and so on.

A typical environmental policy might therefore contain:

■ the overall set of principles the company wishes to abide by, such as those
concerning sustainable development, protection of the environment, use
of resources, operations, and health and safety goals.

An example of this approach can be seen in Philips' environmental policy
statement, which reads:

Environmental care is an integral part of the industrial and product policy of
Philips. The four basic principles are:

■ sustainable development
■ prevention is better than cure
■ the total effect on the environment counts
■ open contact with the authorities.

Such statements are followed by the specific action the company intends to
take to achieve these ends, such as commitments to:

■ following recognized codes of behaviour
■ integrating environmental management into overall management
■ improving standards
■ reducing risks
■ carrying out research and development on products and processes
■ cooperating with suppliers and customers
■ reducing waste and increasing recycling
■ reducing energy and water requirements
■ cultivating community relations
■ improving staff motivation and training
■ meeting and exceeding regulatory requirements

■ monitoring and evaluating performance
■ communicating policies, action, and achievements.

At the end of the following chapters extracts from the environmental policies of companies in different industries and from different parts of the world are included so you can see how other companies have tackled this issue.

Charters of environmental good practice and codes of conduct issued by authoritative bodies have also been included as these can also be used as guides to policy and strategy development.

CHECKLIST 1: THE OVERVIEW

This checklist highlights the areas covered by a typical integrated system of environmental management and introduces a step-by-step approach to the checklists for the individual areas. It is a 'tick off' list for senior management, to be used to decide which areas are to be considered and what action is to initiated. The individual checklists give detail of the issues.

The order of the items on this checklist is only one of many possible sequences that could be used for this practical introduction to the system. For example, the 'Marketing checklist' may be the first functional priority, as it will be from this source that the motivation to produce or retail environmentally friendly products will come. The categories used therefore are not intended to indicate priorities, but, rather, simply to make the system easier to follow.

The integrated system can be introduced into a company regardless of its organizational structure. For example, it does not change the application, if research and development and materials management are separate departments or if they are part of another department. Nor does it affect the issue if waste disposal comes under technical services or materials management.

Issues to be identified for which policies are required
See also Chapter 5.

1 Decide in which areas and at which levels improved environmental performance and management can be achieved.
2 Specify a time sequence for the introduction of environmental management, adapting it to the specific circumstances of the company (see Checklist 2, Setting priorities).
3 Familiarize the management team with perceiving things, thinking about

things, and acting in an environmentally aware way (see Checklist 3, Motivating managers).

4 Introduce measures to protect the environment into overall corporate goals and strategies (see Checklist 4, Corporate goals).

5 Create in-house groups to work to protect the environment and appoint suitable members of the staff to manage them (see Checklist 5, In-house protection).

6 Identify the overall risks to the environment that are to be addressed (see Checklist 6, Safety management).

Address functional areas for which policies and objectives need to be written
See also Chapter 6.

7 Develop ecological products through initiatives in the marketing department or by motivating the marketing department (see Checklist 7, Product development).

8 Focus on the environment-friendliness aspect of materials to be purchased, transported, and stored (see Checklist 8, Materials management).

9 Introduce advanced production technology to reduce environmental pollution and waste disposal costs (see Checklist 9, Production technology).

10 Achieve a major reduction in costs and help the environment, by making economies in energy and water consumption (see Checklist 10, Energy and water).

11 Reduce pollution and material costs by recycling, and ensure that waste is disposed of properly (see Checklist 11, Waste management).

12 Clean up contaminated sites and take precautions to avoid acquiring contaminated sites (see Checklist 12, Contaminated sites).

Marketing and external relations
See also Chapter 7.

13 Make use of the opportunities and eliminate the risks arising from 'green trends' in the market (see Checklist 13, Marketing).

14 Ensure publicity for environmental projects—including pilot projects—with a view to attracting imitators, but make sure the publicity is accurate (see Checklist 14, Public relations).

15 Extend environmental management to exports, imports and foreign subsidiaries (see Checklist 15, International business relations).

Facilities
See also Chapter 8.

16 Ensure natural landscaping of company sites with trees and plants, as a sign of the company's awareness of the environment (see Checklist 16, Landscaping).
17 Ensure that construction and maintenance of office and factory buildings is based on ecological principles (see Checklist 17, Buildings).
18 Select and equip company vehicles bearing environmental aspects in mind (see Checklist 18, Vehicles, fleets).

Staff issues
See also Chapter 9.

19 & 20 Promote a balanced approach to environment and quality issues in staff motivation and training (see Checklist 19, Motivation, and 20, Training).
21 Improve working conditions on the shop floor, in the office and other workplaces (see Checklist 21, Working conditions).
22 Provide healthy canteen food, including organically produced food (see Checklist 22, Canteen food).
23 Promote environment-friendly behaviour and the health of staff by offering environmental counselling in their own homes (see Checklist 23, Environmental counselling).

Finance and Legal Issues
See also Chapter 10.

24 Check the availability of government grants and subsidies before embarking on investment in measures to protect the environment (see Checklist 24, Public subsidies).
25 Insure against unavoidable and incalculable risks, making use of innovative insurance schemes (see Checklist 25, Insurance).
26 Ensure compliance with environmental legislation and government regulations, and remember environmental aspects when negotiating contracts (see Checklist 26, Legal aspects).
27 Minimize liability risks by having organizational control procedures and

by the careful appointment and training of staff (see Checklist 27, Damage liability).

28 Take precautions to avoid cases of criminal responsibility (see Checklist 28, Criminal liability).

To act as illustrations of how this overview checklist approach and selection of priority areas works, there now follows an extract from EEC Regulation No. 1836/93 (July 1993), and two company's environmental policy statements, from Digital, the American manufacturer of computers, and PowerGen, the producer of electrical power in the UK.

All three make useful checklists for managers during the development and writing of environmental policies.

EEC Regulation No. 1836/93 (July 1993), 'Voluntary participation by companies in the industrial sector in Community eco management and audit scheme. Annex 1 C'

The following issues shall be addressed within the framework of the environmental policy and programmes and of environmental audits.

1 Assessment, control, and reduction of the impact of the activity concerned on the various sectors of the environment.

2 Energy management, saving, and choice.

3 Raw materials management, savings, choice, and transport; water management and savings.

4 Waste avoidance, recycling, reuse, transportation, and disposal.

5 Evaluation, control, and reduction of noise within and outside the site.

6 Selection of new production processes and changes to production processes.

7 Product planning (design, packaging transportation use, and disposal).

8 Environmental performance and practices of contractors, subcontractors.

9 Prevention and limitation of environmental accidents.

10 Contingency procedures in cases of environmental accidents.

11 Staff information and training on environmental issues.

12 External information on environmental issues.

POLICY EXTRACTS

Digital's 'Earth Vision'

'Digital has a long tradition of achievement in environmental health and safety. Today, as the world faces growing environmental problems, we have a unique opportunity to provide strong leadership in achieving national and world progress in this area.

Accordingly, we are reaffirming our commitment to:

- provide our employees with a safe and healthful workplace
- protect the environment and the community
- conserve natural resources
- design, produce, and distribute products in a safe and environmentally protective manner
- communicate known hazards, along with necessary safety precautions, to our employees, customers, and the community
- evaluate potential hazards associated with our products and operations
- consider full compliance with the law as being the minimum acceptable standard.

Business managers are responsible for adherence to these policies. Of equal importance, each Digital employee has responsibility for maintaining a safe and healthful work environment.

Finally, as a corporation, we will seek exemplary solutions to global environmental problems through our products and information technology.'

Powergen's Environmental Policy Statement

'Electricity is a socially and environmentally beneficial product.

PowerGen recognizes the interaction between electricity generation and the environment, and aims to achieve and maintain a high standard of environmental care.

PowerGen will assess the environmental implications of its activities as an integral part of its decision making.

PowerGen will:

- promote the development of more efficient and cleaner ways of producing electricity
- promote the efficient use of electricity and other forms of energy
- handle raw materials and byproducts safely
- develop ways of improving the environmental impact of existing and proposed activities
- manage land with sensitivity and promote conservation creatively
- maintain close liaison with the appropriate regulators, authorities, and environmental organizations
- promote research into the environmental effects of its activities
- promote environmental awareness in the community.

PowerGen will implement this policy, consistent with its objective of being the country's lowest cost electricity producer.

PowerGen will maintain internal procedures to support this policy and its effectiveness in the light of changes in knowledge and understanding.'

Checklists for policy and strategy issues

Policy
and strategy
issues

2
Setting priorities

3
Motivating managers

4
Corporate goals

5
In-house protection

6
Safety management

FIGURE 5.1   POLICY AND STRATEGY ISSUES IN THE WINTER MODEL

CHECKLIST 2: SETTING PRIORITIES

This checklist is designed to help in the setting of priorities and deciding on time scales for action. Systematic environmentally aware management is not something that can be introduced in a short period; it needs several years of planning, good timing, and stamina.

Clearly, it is important to start at the optimum point, decide on the best sequence of operations, and then stick to a realistic schedule. Given the wide range of company types, this checklist cannot give specific guidance that will cover each individual case. Nor provide a complete alternative to you using your own knowledge, tact, experience, and intuition to reach appropriate decisions. However, what it can do is to set out rankings of importance. If these rankings are used, it is possible to reach the right decision more easily. Using them also helps you to become acquainted with certain principles, so the danger of making wrong or hurried decisions is lessened.

Four areas in which decisions need to be made about priorities are covered by the checklist:

- business priorities
- ecological and technical priorities
- personnel and organizational priorities
- psychological priorities.

Respect business priorities

1 Adopt the environmental protection measures that are required by law. (See also Checklists 3, Motivating managers, and 26, Legal aspects.)
2 Adopt environmental protection measures that will be of benefit to the company. (See all the points marked with an asterisk in the various checklists, especially in Checklist 3, Motivating managers.)
3 Adopt measures to protect the environment that will have a neutral effect on the company. (See also Checklist 3.)
4 Then, and only then, if the conditions are right, adopt measures to protect the environment that will not be a burden on the company. (See also Checklist 3.)

Respect ecological and technical priorities

5 Avert serious health hazards. Introduce stringent safety procedures, for example, ensuring that concentrations of noxious substances at the workplace are below the threshold limit value, rather than place workers' lives and health at risk. (See also Checklist 21, Working conditions.)
6 Save energy, water and raw materials. Reduce energy, water, and raw material consumption by using more sophisticated regulating technology, mechanical cleaning processes and design improvements, rather than having to meet the environmental and financial consequences of overuse. (See also Checklists 10, Energy and water, Checklist 9, Checklist 7, Checklist 8 and Checklist 11.)
7 Use ecologically sound materials. Use only materials (manufacturing inputs, raw materials, ancillary inputs, and consumables) that can be manufactured, used, and disposed of without any major detriment to the

environment. This is preferable to having the practical or moral dilemma of disposal.

8 Prevent the creation or development of environmentally detrimental substances. Residual, converted, and noxious substances can be avoided by switching to 'integrated techniques' (such as fluidized solids technology) rather than having to resort to 'end-of-pipe' techniques (such as gas scrubbers and de-dusters).

9 Reuse heat and environmentally detrimental materials. Reuse heat and recycle residual, converted, and noxious substances in the production process, rather than try to dispose of them and harm the environment.

10 Suppress environmentally detrimental substances, including noise, where they arise. Suppress residual, converted, or noxious substances and noise at source. Use emission abatement techniques, such as enclosing noisy machinery, which deals with noise before it has a chance to cause any negative effects.

11 Reduce environmentally detrimental substances to a 'manageable' state. Reduce residual, converted, and noxious substances to a degree of purity that will avoid their becoming part of noxious 'cocktails'. If their noxious potential is minimized, the company will have to meet the cost of expensive conversion or separation processes.

12 Reduce the need for individual protection. Eliminate the effects of noise, heat, and noxious substances by technical means, such as noise barriers, fans, or extractors, rather than creating the need for additional protective clothing to be worn by those exposed. Experience has shown that ear protectors, respirators, or protective clothing are often not used or maintained.

Respect personnel and organizational priorities

13 Start with the 'right' members of staff. Begin introducing measures to protect the environment in sectors, departments, and workplaces with supportive staff, instead of having to introduce and preach the gospel first.

14 Recruit the 'right' people. While examining job applicants' academic and technical qualifications, consider also their knowledge of and attitudes to the environment. This will save time, money, and effort on persuading and training staff later.

15 Give responsibilities to the 'right' member of staff. Try to appoint an environmental manager who is equally well qualified in ecology, economics, and psychology. This is preferable to having to spend valuable time and money on training to make up for imbalances and shortcomings in someone less qualified.

16 Create the 'right' organizational units. In large companies, use the idea of 'profit centres' as a model for setting up several autonomous, self-regulating 'ecology centres'. These centres may be more flexible than would a single, centralized group considering environmental matter.

17 Offer the 'right' training courses. As part of the programme of conventional apprentice and adult training and that in environmental issues, encourage initiative and self-regulation, rather than having to issue dozens of instructions and make provision for monitoring work later on.

Respect psychological priorities

18 Give priority to the more personal measures implemented to protect the environment. Start with these. A simple example of such a measure would be, where maintenance funds are limited, to paint the inside walls at a workplace with biological paint, rather than starting with the outside walls.

19 Give priority to habit-forming measures for protecting the environment. Then, move on to measures that do not depend directly on workers and, thus, have a less obvious pedagogical effect. As everything cannot be done at once, start small by, for example, replacing conventional toilet paper with recycled paper, fitting out waste-paper baskets with waste separators, and equip vehicles with start-stop devices. Once these measures are in place, *then* go on to grow ivy up unsightly factory walls or whatever.

20 Give priority to environmental measures that have a tone-setting effect. To create a good impression, start by equipping the directors' cars with catalytic converters and ensuring that directors' stationery is made of recycled paper, rather than starting with one of the specialist departments.

21 Give priority to environmental measures that have eye-catching effects. Adopt measures that have a surprise effect, are refreshingly original, appeal to the heart or tend to promote solidarity, rather than starting with unspectacular routine measures.

22 Give priority to environmental measures that are 'instantaneously' successful economically. These produce an immediate positive response. Later, you can move on to measures that are more likely to pay for themselves in the long term and are, thus, less suitable as 'motivating openers'. For example, introduce the simple energy-saving measures before making major investments in energy-saving technology that has a

protracted pay-off period. (See the points marked with an asterisk in all the checklists, but especially those in Checklist 10, Energy and water.)

23 Introduce environmental measures that are likely to receive general approval. For example, measures that are required by law and those that are of economic benefit, such as dust filters and thermostats. These are normally uncontroversial. Only then move on to economically neutral measures, such as putting green information on staff noticeboards, for which there might be psychological resistance. Only after this should measures be attempted that are economically disadvantageous in the short term (such as seminars on the environment for trainees). These measures will only be generally accepted if key management staff are given sufficient time to develop genuine environmental awareness.

24 Leave controversial environmental protection measures until later, and then work towards general approval for them. For instance, do not try to counter the hazards of passive smoking by imposing a general ban on smoking. Allow some time to elapse, then seek a consensus, otherwise smokers may be provoked into closing ranks and forming a kind of in-house 'anti the environment' movement. However, the compromise must not be achieved at the cost of the health of non-smokers. Management obviously has a simpler task in countries or states where smoking in offices is prevented by law! To take another example, do not attempt to introduce a general low-meat or organic diet in the works canteen. Instead, allow some time to elapse, then ensure that alternative meals are available. People's eating habits are often perceived as a quasi-religious matter and the company should not get itself involved in any such a conflict.

CHECKLIST 3: MOTIVATING MANAGERS

The environmentally aware approach to business can only be introduced with the agreement and enthusiasm of senior management and, in a public company, motivation has to start with the Board of Directors and the shareholders.

This checklist will be of most value to senior executives as it is they who have to convince and motivate their managers. It looks at:

■ the personal skills required
■ the overall strategy to be used to convince and guide managers.

The asterisks by the points in the checklist indicate measures that can usually be introduced easily and quickly to prevent or reduce costs.

Personal skills—self analysis

1 Ask yourself 'Do I have enough respect and understanding for my colleagues, and do I treat them with, at least, the sense of responsibility I apply to my natural environment (flora and fauna)?

2 Ask yourself 'Am I really concerned about the environment or is what I am doing intended to give myself a better image or boost my ego?

3 Ask yourself (in all honesty) 'Am I already acting in an exemplary environmentally aware fashion or do my *deeds* detract from what I *say*?'

Empathize with the beliefs and feelings managers express during this self-analysis.

4 Promote the company's environmental management policy to heads of departments. Use examples that are relevant to their own departments, so for:

- the head of personnel, talk in terms of human relations
- the head of sales, talk in terms of publicity, the company's image, and advertising
- the head of a technical department, talk in terms of fresh motivation for the employee's suggestions scheme
- the head of the materials management department, talk in terms of reducing waste disposal problems by introducing an ecological purchasing policy
- the head of finance, talk in terms of saving costs.

5 Use issues that motivate the departmental heads personally, such as:

- where there is an obvious need for safety to be stepped up by implementing more rigorous environmental liability provisions, there is a greater likelihood of serious problems occurring if these are neglected stringent penalties being imposed as a result
- where there is an obvious need for a corporate spirit, focus the ideal of care for the environment on society, the workforce, and the family
- where there is a pressing need to do genuine pioneering work in the area, focus on those points where economics and ecology meet
- where there is a nagging reluctance to identify with 'alternative ideas', show what a positive experience it has been for other companies.

6 Avoid using insincere or manipulatory motivation techniques—these run counter to the principle of human respect. Further, these techniques are easily seen through and have the opposite effect to that which is sought.

7 Prepare for decisions to be taken on in-house environmental protection

measures well in advance, by providing information in good time and motivating members of the management team to consider them carefully.

8 Before taking a decision on measures that could be controversial, wait for an opportune moment, such as after the announcement of a successful year's trading, a special anniversary or a major order.

9 Continue to encourage members of the management team who did not vote or agree with an issue concerning the protection of the environment rather than treat them as defeated opponents.

10 Publicize in-house positive decisions on environmental measures. This ensures that the management team is seen to be acting in unison and serves to bind individuals more strongly to the collective decision.

11 Where there is a positive response to a collective decision about measures to protect the environment, stress the involvement of all concerned, both within the company and in the media, where appropriate.

12 Where there is a negative response to a collective decision made about implementing a measure to protect the environment (such as complaints about the quality of recycled paper), stand by those members of the management team who are under fire and thus strengthen team spirit.

13 Take every opportunity to thank and praise members of the management team for their environmentally aware attitudes. This will help with motivation regarding future measures.

Develop an overall strategy to convince and guide managers

Prepare a medium-term strategy (initially for your own use only) as to how and when in-house environmental activities should be placed on the agenda for decision making by the management team.

Remember that the nature, extent, and timing of the proposed activities should be in line with a slowly emerging environmental awareness in the management team.

Ensure that the sequence of actions is adhered to and covers a number of meetings—not all of the actions should be proposed at once. A suggested sequence could be:

■ Phase 1: measures required by law
■ Phase 2: measures that will be of benefit to the company
■ Phase 3: measures that will have a neutral effect on the company
■ Phase 4: measures that will impose a burden on the company.

Phase 1 : measures for protecting the environment laid down by law

14 Draw up and present a programme for management to discuss and agree on, aimed at implementing mandatory measures to protect the environment. For example:

- acquire or construct a waste water treatment plant to comply with the legal requirements
- construct a low-noise factory building or reduce ambient noise to (and below) the legally permissible level.

15 Gain the agreement of the management team by emphasizing that:

- contravention of the environmental protection laws is now an important matter
- companies acting illegally are liable to need to meet compensation claims or even to close down the business
- in the event of any criminal proceedings, members of the management team can be personally liable to fines and even prison sentences.

16 When it is time for a decision to be taken by the management team, ensure that all concerned are fully aware that protecting the environment:

- is now an issue that cannot be avoided
- must be on the agenda for management meetings at the highest level
- has the possibility of consensus.

17 When it comes to making the decision, seek to strengthen the feeling of corporate responsibility for the environment under the banner: 'We are loyal to the law of the land. As far as protection of the environment goes, we will not compromise.'

18 Encourage the situation where mandatory measures to protect the environment become voluntary measures. Launch Phase 2 (below) immediately after, or even with, Phase 1.

Phase 2: measures for protecting the environment that will benefit the company

19 Draw up and present a programme of 'selfish' measures to protect the environment to be decided on. Examples might be:

- *■ reducing energy costs by installing control units in the heating system
- *■ reduce waste disposal costs by using compaction containers instead of open domestic refuse containers
- *■ reducing water costs by installing water-saving devices for the cisterns of the company's WCs
- *■ reducing the costs of raw materials, transportation, and disposal by recycling heavy metals from electroplating sludge

*■ reducing the risk of legal liability by replacing leaky or potentially leaky oil tanks

*■ boosting turnover and improving profits by developing and marketing alternative products, which result in less pollution being produced.

20 Seek a unanimous vote in favour of at least some of the proposed measures, on the grounds that:

■ the planned measures for protecting the environment will pay for themselves more quickly than other investment projects

■ such measures can avert more serious risks than can similar risk-reduction measures

■ an environmental marketing measure promises better turnover and profit growth than similar marketing measures.

21 Give a boost to the corporate sense of responsibility for the environment under the banner: 'We are doing something for the environment and if it benefits the company, all the better!'

22 Give the positive psychological influence of Phase 2 several months to work. Support the effort with success stories (such as water, energy, and raw materials savings) before moving on to the psychologically more demanding third phase.

Phase 3: decide on measures for protecting the environment that have a neutral effect on the company

23 Draw up a programme of neutral measures for protecting the environment, such as measures that neither benefit nor burden the company. Examples are:

■ installing special noticeboards for such information alongside the official noticeboards for management and works council announcements

■ replacing environmentally detrimental cleansers with alternative biological ones.

■ extending the canteen menu to include organically produced dishes at similar prices to existing dishes

■ allow environmental counsellors and consumer organizations to hold information meetings.

24 Again, do not place this entire programme on one agenda. Spread the various points over several meetings. Gain agreement and decisions on activities that are easily implemented, such as noticeboards, and then move on to activities requiring more organization or that may be

controversial at later meetings, such as environmental counselling in the canteen.

25 Aim to obtain a unanimous vote in favour of the measures from the management team, on the basis that:

- the measures will place virtually no burden on the company
- by enhancing staff motivation, the company will itself derive benefit
- planned environmental awareness of the staff will result, in the medium and long terms at least, in a reduction in the risks associated with *not* being environmentally aware and in an enhancement of business opportunities. The net result will be a quantifiable benefit for the company
- It is important to point out that, although this set of measures may be of only neutral benefit to the company, it will derive material benefit from such measures at earlier stages, such as the energy-saving measures agreed to in the second phase.

26 Devote special attention to convincing doubting members of the management team. Some may take the view that any activity not geared strictly to producing maximum profits could be a dangerous diversion.

27 If it becomes evident that it is not possible to obtain a unanimous vote in favour, consider withdrawing the proposal. Reintroduce it when increased environmental awareness suggests that the measure will be passed.

28 Realize that a unanimous vote in favour of a particular measure at a later stage is often more useful in terms of spreading the environmental gospel in the company than an earlier decision in favour that was hard won, perhaps with a slender majority.

29 Give the management team several months to get used to the idea of benefit-neutral ways of protecting the environment before moving on to the fourth, and psychologically most difficult, phase.

Phase 4: decide on measures for protecting the environment that will place a burden on the company

In proposing these measures, the critical stage of environmentally aware management has been reached.

In the short-term, the objectives for protecting the environment will be in conflict with the profit motive, the company's lifeline. Therefore, any further steps must be dictated not just by concern for the environment, but also by a sense of responsibility for the company and the people working for it.

30 Draw up a provisional list of measures that will be of ecological benefit,

but will place a burden on the company in, at least, the short term. Examples are:

- systematic training for trainees in how to protect the environment
- applying the same high domestic standards for protecting the environment in production facilities of subsidiaries abroad, despite lower standards in those countries
- applying environmentally benign building principles for the next new building project or even
- subsidizing a farm that can provide staff with cheap, organically grown products.

31 Consider carefully whether the measures are viable for the organization:

- take a detailed look at the company's financial situation to see if it can cope with even a very restricted and short-lived fall in profits
- make sure that there is an effective financial early warning system
- ensure that the management team includes people who are guided purely by the profit motive, who can be relied on to advocate a strictly profit-orientated policy, and who will be prepared to call a halt if necessary
- ensure that the person appointed as environmental manager is as much aware of cost-control principles as they are of the need to protect the environment
- in the absence of any of the above preconditions, restrict decision making to issues in Phases 1 to 3 until all the requirements are fulfilled
- work constantly on improving the company's profitability, for example by making special efforts in marketing and rationalization to release resources to finance environmental activities.

32 Again, ensure that the psychological requirements are fulfilled so that the management team will vote in favour of any Phase 4 measures. Once all the necessary conditions have been met, aim for a unanimous vote in favour of the proposed measures, on the following grounds:

- the cost-increasing environmental measures on one side of the balance sheet are counterbalanced by successful energy- and water-saving measures on the other
- the general position of the company is such that it can afford to take on a more public responsibility for the environment
- in the medium and long terms, what may be seen initially as a financial sacrifice will probably turn out to be a useful investment.

33 Take the opportunity to prepare the ground for subsequent decisions by thanking all concerned for their sense of responsibility and creating a corporate ecological spirit under the banner: 'Protecting the environment is worth a few sacrifices'.

CHECKLIST 4: CORPORATE GOALS

If companies are to act in an ecologically acceptable manner, they must:

- analyse their philosophy critically
- formulate objectives that take environmental questions into account
- develop appropriate strategies.

An objective analysis of the situation (where do we stand?) must be the starting point. This will determine the company's goals (what do we want to achieve?) and help management decide on medium-term policy (what steps should be taken now?)

Identify key ecological issues in the company's areas of activity—key issue analysis

1 Analyse opportunities and risks within the company's operating environment and in the market-place (the external factors). These can be:

- legislation (such as the laws on emission limits and waste disposal)
- public awareness (such as press reports, demonstrations)
- consumers' awareness (such as changes in attitude and behaviour)
- competitors' activities (such as the introduction of products that minimize ecological damage)
- scientific and research developments (such as catalyst technology).

2 Analyse the company's strengths and weaknesses (the internal factors), such as:

- finance available for environmental questions (such as development)
- open-minded and flexible management attitudes
- the company's range of products and its relevance to markets in the field of environmental protection.

3 Draw up a consistent ecological strategy for the company, by:

- undertaking a detailed analysis of its strengths, weaknesses, opportunities and threats (SWOT analysis)
- identifying and assessing the 'critical' factors in the strategic balance,

such as the application of existing know-how to environmental markets or the lack of adequate finance for the necessary investments involved.

Determine the company's objectives on ecological and environmental matters

4 Formulate models and principles for the company's strategy to:

■ show that the market economy and free enterprise system can be compatible with ecological constraints

■ safeguard the company's existence by recognizing general trends at an early stage and plan accordingly

■ seek competitive advantages by minimizing damage to the environment

■ adopt a dynamic approach to ecological challenges in all areas of the company's activity and help find solutions

■ cooperate with business and academic partners to speed up knowledge in the environmental sector.

5 Lay down long-term environmental objectives for the whole company such as to:

■ capitalize on the goodwill of staff, the public, and government, which will result from a commitment to the environment

■ take advantage of the lower costs that result from saving energy, the economical use of resources, and other progress in environment-related technology

■ minimize risks arising from management or product liability, changes in statutory limits or surges in demand for products that are environmentally sound

■ cooperate with trade associations, the media, and government to generate further knowledge

■ influence legislation by lobbying at the pre-legislative stage.

6 Assess the relationship between the company's environmental and economic objectives by:

■ assessing how environmental objectives will affect turnover, costs, and profits

■ Identifying major areas of conflict between these objectives, such as short-term higher costs, lower turnover, or cash-flow problems

■ setting out long-term priorities based on objectives.

7 Clarify the ecological dimension to all departmental objectives. For example, regarding:

- the labour market, make the company more attractive to workers concerned about ecology, reinforcing staff loyalty
- procurement, adopt an environmentally aware bias when purchasing raw materials, ancillary inputs, and consumables
- production, cut costs by saving energy, raw materials, and water
- marketing, take environmental considerations into account when considering logistics, such as transporting materials or products by rail, not road.

Formulate ecologically sound strategies

8 Determine basic strategies:

- decide on whether or not to adopt a defensive stance or take the initiative
- whether or not to take action on a narrow or a wide front (seek to concentrate efforts on the specific areas in which the company is competent, but engage a specialist to solve a particular environmental problem if necessary.)

9 Plan environmental strategies for the company's various activities:

- Define areas of activity in product, market, and technological terms, describe product values, market segmentation, and technologies with reference to environmental considerations, and determine the priorities for work in specific market segments
- determine the company's basic attitude to others in the market-place, such as competitors, distributive trades, and customers, and consider the scope for demarcation of functions or cooperation
- establish strategies for product ranges, such as improving the environmental acceptability of some products, introducing new products and changing or replacing the existing ones
- establish ecology portfolios and ensure that they are suitably balanced.

10 Formulate environmental strategies for each department.

CHECKLIST 5: IN-HOUSE PROTECTION

The function of in-house arrangements to protect the environment is to ensure that environmental attitudes are introduced, fostered, and reinforced in a coordinated and regular manner throughout the company.

The provisions described in this checklist are intended to supplement those already existing. In particular, the voluntarily appointed environmental manager, as mentioned earlier, has much wider scope than does a statutory environmental officer, whose presence is required by certain national laws. Some firms only require that their environmental officers look after the technical aspects of water and air pollution and waste disposal, whereas this would be just a small part of an environmental manager's responsibilities.

Appoint or nominate an environmental manager

1 Issue a formal company job profile and list of duties for an environmental manager. These should include:

- assisting in bringing about conversion to more environmentally acceptable products and coordinating this when it takes effect
- monitoring developments in environmental policy and establishing an early warning system with the help of in-house and external experts
- liaising with work councils or staff associations on all environmental matters
- participating in environment committees and groups inside and outside the company
- monitoring new developments and products as part of a comprehensive environmentally aware procurement policy
- providing superior public presentations of the company's environment-related activities to complement those of other departments
- arranging for precautionary pollution measurements to be taken and then suggesting consultants to investigate ways of saving energy and water
- investigating the feasibility of allowing other companies to use environmentally related spare capacity in the company's plant, such as waste disposal or recycling plant, on a remunerative basis
- participating in all environmentally related training activities.

2 Establish the environmental manager's position at senior management level. This task should be entrusted to a particularly energetic and environmentally conscious member of the executive Board.

- Provide comprehensive information within the company on the duties, purpose, and objectives of the new post

- Draw up an organizational chart clearly showing the positions, responsibilities, and functions
- Provide the environmental manager with active support
- Ensure adequate liaison and discussion between departmental managers/directors/members of the executive Board and the environmental manager.

3 Discuss and resolve any conflicts between environmental and other key departmental objectives without delay.

4 Draw up a budget for supporting external environmental activities, such as those of associations for protecting the environment.

5 Plan separate investment for environmental purposes within the overall investment programme and carry out a post-activity assessment to see if the objectives were met.

6 Give the environmental manager the opportunity to highlight environmental issues and possible solutions during meetings with the workforce and in-house information visits.

Plan environmental activities

7 Make a study of the environmental issues and weaknesses in all departments, including subsidiaries and associated companies. Draw up a plan of action of what is to be done, by whom and by when. To identify shortcomings, a systematic audit may be required of all known and predictable environmental problems affecting the company and an assessment made of their relative importance. More particularly, a systematic analysis will be needed of the likelihood and repercussions of incidents so that preventive arrangements can be made.

8 Wherever possible, incorporate specific objectives in the action plan. Examples might be:

- eliminate any unreasonable risks arising from the storage and handling of hazardous substance within six months
- switch to materials which are less detrimental to the environment within 12 months
- aim for a 20 per cent reduction in water consumption in electroplating operations by the end of the year.

9 Draw up contingency plans. All staff concerned with implementing measures to protect the environment within the company should be involved in contingency planning. This would enable them to act calmly, quickly, and purposefully and avoid the kind of panic that could easily lead to ill-considered action.

10 Ensure that the materials management department draws up a list of key materials containing the following information:

- inventory number and name
- annual consumption
- supplier
- chemical designation
- any dangerous reactions and toxicity
- any ecological hazards
- transport code
- any technical precautions required
- disposal
- alternatives
- unit price.

11 Draw up an internal balance sheet setting out, and quantifying as far as possible, the advantages and disadvantages, if any, of environmental activities.

Set up an environmental technical committee

12 This committee should deal with all environmental problems or questions affecting the company such as those concerning materials, energy supplies, water supplies, disposal of special-category wastes, scope for recycling, environmental problems in the production process, and compliance with statutory limits for pollution, noise, dust.

13 The committee's structure and activities should include:

- terms of reference
- meetings at regular intervals with formal minutes being taken and distributed
- the chairman of the committee assessing its performance
- ensuring that the environmental manager is represented on this committee.

Form an environmental interdisciplinary advisory group

14 In addition to the technical committee, an interdisciplinary committee, with representatives from all company departments and the environmental manager, can be useful. This committee could deal mainly with wider, non-technical questions relating to the environment and should assist the environmental manager in certain duties.

15 As in the case of the technical committee, lay down the terms of

reference and frequency of meetings, ensure that minutes are kept and that the chairman assesses its performance.

CHECKLIST 6: SAFETY MANAGEMENT

Security and safety issues are not confined to facilities and equipment; they are applicable to *all* aspects of the production process and the company's products. Security is the consequence of the concern of the company to cope with its responsibility and liability as employer and neighbour.

The benefits to any company and its employees of an integrated security policy are not only felt in human terms they have economic, ecological, and legal dimensions. For example, the staff are less likely to suffer injury as a result of accidents at work and so the risk and expense of liability claims and criminal proceedings can be considerably reduced. Equally, minimizing the chances of exposing the environment to risk of damage as a result of a fire, spillage or other accidents should become an integral part of the security and safety management of any company.

International, national, and local accident prevention and safety regulations exist that set minimum performance requirements. Every company should aim to improve things beyond these, to secure an optimum level of corporate security and thus minimize risks to the environment.

The concept of security management is one of recognizing and evaluating risks. Monitoring and controlling risks can be managed by staff following the appropriate, agreed procedures. The stages in this process are covered in this checklist.

Analysing a company's strengths and weaknesses
1 Promote in the staff a readiness and willingness to seriously confront risks to corporate security.
2 Undertake a comprehensive and thorough analysis of potential dangers. This analysis should not be confined to examining only the technical aspects of security, but include all possibilities of human error. These should include areas that are liable to cause sudden accidents such as:

- those peculiar to the production site itself
- plant and equipment
- raw materials
- products and production methods
- storage of dangerous substances
- logistics of distribution.

Using external assistance and expertise

3 Recognize that routine involvement with company practices and operations can often lead to a type of corporate blindness, so:

■ use the services and know-how of qualified experts, such as chemists, geologists, lawyers, and economists

■ in start-up situations, consult professional institutes and similar organizations, having dealt with many similar situations in the past, their experts usually have a 'good eye' for the typical risks facing a company like yours.

Cooperate with appropriate authorities

4 Develop a climate of trust and good relations with local health and safety authorities. Have open discussions and invite them to visit the company premises.

5 Involve representatives of the relevant authorities in decisions relating to the environment and its security.

Eliminate obvious weaknesses

An analysis of a company's strengths and weaknesses will highlight the particular issues that affect the organization and need to be accounted for in future plans. The first step is to address areas of current risk.

6 Eliminate promptly weaknesses discovered and any acute source of danger.

7 Take preventive measures to reduce risks by:

■ increasing environmental and safety awareness

■ promoting appropriate training

■ creating organizational charts that illustrate all aspects of environmental issues and risks

■ developing management guidelines that include codes for responsible environmental behaviour

■ providing regular information on changing laws and regulations

■ providing updated information on the technical issues that relate to environmental matters

■ holding regular training meetings on safety at work and protecting the environment.

Senior management should attend specialist seminars to familiarize themselves with techniques, keep up to date, and to compare their company's progress with that of other organizations.

Establish a public relations profile

8 Establish a relationship of trust with the local and national media and appoint a senior manager to liaise with them. Topics would include specific company actions taken to improve the environment or changes within the industry generally.

9 Develop a public relations plan to use in the event of a sudden accident. This should be aimed at preventing or limiting damage to the company's reputation. This plan should help avoid the spread of false, incomplete information or even rumour.

10 Involve employees' representatives and keep them informed about relevant issues and decisions.

EXAMPLES OF GOOD PRACTICE

Following each of the six chapters of checklists, real-life examples of good practice in environmental management are included. These highlight different strategies and practices being utilized by businesses and organizations in their efforts to progress towards better environmental management. These examples can only illustrate one or two features of what a particular organization has achieved. Much more is being done by all of them.

In our selections, we have tended to give examples from the early stages of the implementation of companies' environmental management within the organization. Many readers, particularly those from medium-sized and smaller business, will be at this point of their environmental management planning.

The examples have been collected by BAUM in Germany from various sources in the UK and other countries. Good practice, of course, is not limited to any one country or group. Environmental magazines and journals often have a section of case studies and examples of good practice, and so environmental managers should be encouraged to keep press cuttings or jot such examples down in a notebook for future reference. They should also contribute to this inventory of experience by virtue of their own actions.

The total integration of environmental management

IBM UK the manufacturer of computers, introduced an extensive programme of environmental management that include an environmental assessment of all company activities. An environmental master plan for its manufacturing and development facilities was prepared. Waste disposal contracts are audited and new sites are subject to an environmental impact assessment.

Hertie Waren-und kaufhaus GmbH practised environmental protection according to the slogan 'Environmental responsibility: our concern'. Following company principles, Hertie implements measures to protect the environment as a comprehensive policy, not only as a supplier of goods but also by:

- shipping the majority of its goods by rail
- training selected employees as environmental advisers
- emphasizing recycling and energy-saving within the company
- purchasing ecologically sound, lightly packaged materials
- in its customer relations and community initiatives.

BASF, a German manufacturing company, has established a 'constitution' that includes the following clause: 'economic considerations do not have priority over environmental and worker protection'.

The company has an extensive programme of seminars aimed at emphasizing the importance of this message to management.

Using outsiders

Elida-Gibbs GmbH in Germany made protecting the environment central to company policy with an environmental management plan that brought ecological thinking to all areas of the company's operations. Awareness at management level has been heightened through dialogue with critics, scientists, the media, trading partners, and consumer organizations. The environmental management team collating and evaluating the information ensures that it is used in practice.

Verband der Chemischen Industrie in Frankfurt set up its own consultancy for chemical and environment-related issues. Its aim is to give advice on such areas as protecting the environment and people's health, occupational safety and technical safety to smaller firms. The professional advisers involved give their services voluntarily.

Focusing on roles and responsibilities

The Body Shop International, the UK based company, has a management structure the aim of which is to improve accountability for environmental activities, including the appointment of environmental advisers in each department.

Job descriptions include environmental responsibilities and the requirement to keep up-to-date with changes in technologies and legislation.

Eco-desks as centres of excellence

The young fashion company, **Esprit de Corp GmbH**, based in Dusseldorf, took its first ecological steps in the late 1980s with office and canteen supplies, production and packaging materials. Esprit companies worldwide introduced 'eco-desks' (advice centres) to assist companies wanting to use more ecologically sound methods and materials in production, architecture, presentation of the products, packaging design, and advertising. In some areas, this has resulted in a radical, favourable alteration of a company's image.

Environmental evaluation and reporting

British Petroleum, the multinational oil company, has a group environmental policy statement. It also has specific environmental objectives, which ensure that protecting the environment is treated as an integral part of any project. It carries out a variety of types of audit, such as compliance, site activity, corporate, and issue audits. To ensure that its environmental objectives are met, it issues a publicly available environmental report on what has been achieved.

Planning in partnership

Staati, Mineralbrunnen Gmbh in Bad Bruckenau, is pursuing a comprehensive, ecological programme that covers all activities engaged in by the company. All the newest and best ecological developments—from waste water management to noise control—have been incorporated in the construction of the first ecologically sound bottling factory. With the support of the Staatsbad spa and Bad Bruckenau's city council, the programme now covers the entire spa. Further, widespread public interest has led to a 20–30 per cent increase in annual turnover. An ecology balance sheet shows what has been achieved.

IBM, Deutschland, GmbH appointed an environmental protection officer and two environmental and chemistry coordinators who, together, coordinate the company's key aims in this field. Large projects are subjected to an environmental impact assessment and must be approved by the environmental protection agent at the planning stage with respect to air and water pollution, waste disposal, noise control, and saving energy.

Involving other managers

Schulke & Mayr GmbH launched a two-pronged approach to protecting the environment. The head of the Occupational Safety and Environmental Protection department took control of ecological issues and a working group (appropriately called 'Ecology') was set up, its members being drawn from all sectors within the company. All company projects are thus now subjected to thorough ecological scrutiny.

Sony, Deutschland, GmbH has established an environmental working group—which is in keeping with the policy of the parent company and other

European subsidiaries—under the watchful eye of a full-time project manager. Activities that are proposed for evaluation include the recycling of electronic waste and using recyclable packaging.

MIGROS, the Swiss trading group, realized that its environmental approaches would not work without the commitment of management and staff. Four hundred of its managers attended seminars on the world environment crises and other staff members attended video films on the same theme during working hours.

CODES OF GOOD PRACTICE – NUMBER 4

The following is another authoritative set of guidelines—this time from a specific manufacturing association. These are adhered to and published by the leading companies in this industry. Again, the list makes an excellent guide when forming an environmental policy for a manufacturing company.

Member companies of the Chemical Manufacturers Association's 'Guiding Principles for Responsible Care'

Specifically the Guiding Principles to the Responsible Care initiative, a statement of the philosophy and commitment by each member company regarding environmental health and safety responsibilities in the management of chemicals.

1 To recognize and respond to community concerns about chemicals and our operations.
2 To develop and produce chemicals that can be manufactured, transported, used, and disposed of safely.
3 To make health, safety, and environmental considerations a priority in our planning for all existing and new products and processes.
4 To report promptly to officials, employees, customers and the public information on chemical-related health or environmental hazards and to recommend protective measures.
5 To counsel customers on the safe use, transportation, and disposal of chemical products.
6 To operate our plants and facilities in a manner that protects the environment and the health and safety of our employees and the public.
7 To extend knowledge by conducting or supporting research on the

health, safety, and environmental effects of our products, processes, and waste materials.

8 To work with others to resolve problems created by past handling and disposal of hazardous substances.

9 To participate with Government and others in creating responsible laws, regulations, and standards to safeguard the community, workplace, and environment.

10 To promote the principles and practices of responsible care by sharing experiences and offering assistance to others who produce, handle, use, transport, or dispose of chemicals.

POLICY EXTRACTS—Strategy issues

Noranda Minerals Inc., Canada

'Noranda Minerals' operations strive to be exemplary leaders in environmental management, by minimizing the environmental impact on the public, employees, customers, and property, limited only by technological and economic viability.'

ESKOM—South Africa

'To practice and foster the sustainable use of renewable natural resources and the responsible use of non-renewable resources in the conduct of all aspects of our business.

To practice and promote integrated environmental management to achieve sound business performance and stewardship of the country's heritage and assets.

ESKOM will pursue this commitment to sound environmental management for the benefit of our customers, employees, authorities, and suppliers as well as the communities we serve, to achieve our goal of excellence in environmental management and performance.'

Rhône-Poulenc, France

'Environmental stewardship lies at the very heart of Rhône-Poulenc's strategic priorities, alongside the enhanced safety of people and installations. This is a moral issue of responsibility to our employees, to the communities in which we work and live, and to the future generations.

Each of our business units is committed to incorporating

environmental considerations into its fundamental mission and values, its strategy, its research programmes, and action plans.

Rhône-Poulenc's policy of protecting the environment defines the basic principles that guide actions taken in each of the groups business segments worldwide to achieve a sustainable compromise between industrial efficiency and environmental stewardship.'

Union Carbide, USA

'We are recognized as the leader in providing quality corporate health, safety, and environmental direction for a large, international corporation that manufactures and markets numerous products, some of which are potentially hazardous. This recognition spans Union Carbide management levels, government legislative bodies and regulatory agencies, industry and professional associations, customers and suppliers, communities in which we operate, and public interest groups.'

Checklists for production issues

FIGURE 6.1   PRODUCTION ISSUES IN THE WINTER MODEL

The diagram lists:

- 7 Product development
- 8 Materials management
- 9 Production technology
- 10 Energy and water
- 11 Waste management
- 12 Contaminated sites

CHECKLIST 7: PRODUCT DEVELOPMENT

The purpose of any product development process is to adapt a company's range of goods and services to the needs of the market. These needs correspond, in many cases, with those of the environment. Some of these products already have an impact on the environment and, therefore, are subject to regulations.

Even for products where the potential for pollution is less obvious, development should take environmental aspects into account. This is the vital stage at which decisions are made regarding the materials and processes to be used.

This checklist highlights both ecological and economic aspects that should be considered during the product development process.

Apply value analysis for ecological as well as economic purposes

1 Check whether or not the manufacturing process involves excessive consumption of non-renewable raw materials, such as water and air.

2 Determine what amounts of energy are required to manufacture the product:

- per working hour
- per product unit.

3 Check whether or not the consumption, use, and maintenance of the plant causes a high level of air, water, or soil pollution.

4 Check whether or not the materials used for a product can be easily reintegrated into the ecological and raw material cycles. Carefully consider the:

- potential for reactivating destroyed product
- energy required for reactivation
- usable wastes
- energy required for waste disposal.

5 Check whether or not the materials and components lend themselves to recycling. For example:

- askarel transformers containing PCBs can only be disposed of only at special tips
- fluorescent and discharge lamps containing pollutants such as heavy metals should be collected and returned undamaged to the manufacturer.

Consider the ecological consequences of the design, material composition, use, and disposal of a product

6 Avoid using substances that are detrimental to the environment and find substitutes for hazardous substances. Some technical examples of this process are to replace the following with less hazardous alternatives:

- cyanide electrolysis
- antimony oxide, used to make textiles and plastics flame-retardant

- antimony sulphite in brake linings
- arsenic oxide, used as a refining agent for glass
- lead in friction bearings
- lead used for soldering
- cadmium, used for coating with zinc and aluminium.

7 Aim for standardization to reduce the number of parts used:

- use DIN plugs and other standardized parts
- increase the number of multipurpose parts.

8 Take ecological aspects into account when selecting equipment.

9 Consider legal requirements and regulations in early development work. Two examples are that:

- screws to be exported to Sweden must not contain cadmium
- particleboard may contain only small quantities of formaldehyde.

10 Design products to minimize the overall quantity of materials needed to make them:

- reduce the thicknesses of walls and plates, but without increasing risks to safety as a result
- reduce waste in cutting processes by, say, making more use of rectangular rather than round shapes
- reduce waste by the flush positioning of blanks.

11 In chemical engineering, select the process with the greatest ecological advantages:

- sulphuric acid can be obtained from gypsum, kainite, hydrogen sulphide, or sulphide ores
- cellulose can be manufactured by the calcium bisulphite process (high level of SO_2 emission) or the magnesium bisulphite process (low level of SO_2, emission, MgO emission).

12 Exploit energy-efficient designs, bearing in mind all the preliminary production stages and the energy required for disposal of waste:

- dimensions: small is better than large
- exploit the material content
  - less weight saves energy
  - ceramic elements improve heat insulation
  - sintered ceramic elements reduce the fuel required.

13 Design products that can be disposed of easily so that the environment is less likely to be used as a waste dump:

■ minimize packaging:
   – for large-diameter grinding wheels, use hexagonal packing cases, which require 15 per cent less wood than do square cases
   – Use standardized packaging in order to make the best use of space in transport vehicles and shops.
   – select packaging materials that require low energy levels to produce them.
   – design packaging that can be used in more than one way
   – design packaging for multiple use.
■ develop long-life products:
   – increase the functional and stylistic life of products
   – increase their life by using quality materials
   – design products to make repairs and service easier.

CHECKLIST 8: MATERIALS MANAGEMENT

From an environmental point of view, the purchasing of materials can be either harmful, neutral or beneficial to the environment.

The responsibility for materials may be in the hands of one or several departments. However, for the purposes of this checklist we will assume that there is a materials management department responsible for the purchasing, storage, and delivery of materials and products.

It will ensure that the firm can produce and deliver its products economically, and will cover all stages from purchasing of raw materials to the delivery of the finished goods.

The department may also be responsible for the process of buying major capital goods, such as vehicles. Its activity can often account for upwards of 40 per cent of a firm's overall costs.

This checklist follows the various stages of the process:

■ determining the current status of materials management and the environment
■ formulating an ecologically-orientated buying strategy
■ researching the market for more ecologically sound products
■ selecting suitable suppliers, and
■ providing environmentally sound storage and handling facilities.

Those points with asterisks by them are measures that help protect the environment and can usually be introduced quickly to prevent or reduce costs.

Determining the current status of materials management and the environment

1 Prepare a 'balance sheet' of materials and energy:

- record the form, quantity, composition and operational data of the materials used for production, and the transformations they go through during the production process
- record the effects on the ecology by:

  - observing emissions and their ecological impact on site
  - identifying the effects on the area concerned by logging their movement and dispersal patterns—their persistence (time required for biological degradation), accumulation (transport and concentration in the food chain), and possible transformation processes.

2 Consider environmental parameters for materials management:

- establish environmental elasticities, giving the percentage increase in 'environment take' (for example, of emissions of dangerous substances from the factory, the amount of special-category waste, and so on) caused by a 1 per cent increase in a specific purchasing volume
- establish the recycling rate as a quotient of the proportion of recycled material and total material consumption.

Formulating an ecology-oriented purchasing strategy

3 Plan to replace environmentally hazardous materials in the production process (see also Checklists 7, Product development, and 9, Production technology). For example:

- replace asbestos in brake and coupling linings, in seals, in floor coverings, roofing, and chemical products used in building
- replace cadmium, used in electroplating (to protect the surface) with low-cadmium high-purity zinc, galvanic aluminizing, or aluminium vapour treatment
- replace chlorinated hydrocarbons in cold cleaning solvent with substances that do not pollute the waste water
- replace transformers containing PCBs with air-core or silicon-filled types.

4 Plan to use more eco-friendly materials for general purposes, such as:

- wallpaper made from recycled paper
- low-pollutant paints
- low-lead and low-chromate anticorrosion coatings
- salt-free substances for dispensing ice on roads and paths in winter
- environmentally safe drain-cleaners
- products made from recycled plastics (such as plant pots, garden furniture, signpost bases, floor coverings, building sheeting)
- * paper towels and paper cleaning tissues
- * recycled paper for stationery (forms, letter paper, envelopes, folders)
- returnable bottles in canteens
- reusable crates for foodstuffs in canteens
- * water-saving cisterns and shower fittings (see also Checklist 10, Energy and water)
- * replace conventional fluorescent lamps with energy-saving lamps (such as three-band fluorescent lamps, compact fluorescent lamps, single-socket fluorescent lamps, halide lamps, high-pressure sodium lamps).

5 Replace ecologically unsound office materials (in particular filing and organizational aids made from synthetic materials) with articles made of natural materials, such as

- cardboard or wooden filing trays
- folders made of cardboard
- files made of cardboard (without plastic lamination), with removable covers and lever mechanism
- wooden card file boxes
- wastepaper baskets (made of wood, woven cane, or recycled paper) with separate compartments to enable waste paper to be sorted at source as required for recycling
- rulers made of beech with metal inserts
- wooden or metal stamps, stamp pads, and stamp holders
- pens with refills, refillable ink pens, fountain pens, untreated pencils
- solvent-free glues, pastes, and glue sticks
- water-based correction fluid.

Researching the market for more ecologically sound products

6 Specify product requirements and collect information on products:

- list any products purchased by the company and note any possible ecological problems (such as particleboard containing formaldehyde, used for the tops of washing machines, dishwashers, and so on)

■ note product components and their characteristics (such as the eco-toxic effect of PCBs in transformers)

■ identify special characteristics of products (for example, their shelf life and any problems involved in storing or transporting them).

7 Collect information from suppliers, particularly details of production processes (such as short-bath or long-bath process in the textile industry, economical rinsing process in electroplating, magnesium bisulphide process instead of calcium bisulphide process in the manufacturing of paper).

8 Collect information on alternative products from suppliers and industries:

■ consult information sources on alternative products

■ employ institutes active in environmental protection for market research

■ analyse ecologically orientated specialized literature and journals.

9 Consult the in-house R & D and engineering departments about using alternative materials.

Selecting suitable suppliers

10 Decide on suitable firms to make enquiries of:

■ define the status of a required item using an ecological ABC analysis

■ decide how many national and international suppliers to consult based on the item's ABC status, for example, A items: 10 suppliers, of which 5 abroad; B items: 6 suppliers, of which 3 abroad; C items: 3 suppliers, of which 1 abroad.

11 Decide which form the enquiries should take, then base them on the following:

■ the production process
■ means of protecting the environment from pollutants
■ location of production facilities
■ measuring instruments to meet legal requirements
■ legal provisions, consumer protection, and test requirements in the various countries
■ use recycled paper for the enquiry forms.

12 Evaluate the replies received, bearing in mind both ecological and economic considerations:

- check that the details supplied are complete
- check price, technical data, quantity, and delivery conditions
- note details of energy consumption and any pollutants produced during use, including the volume and emission levels of these
- find information sources that classify their pollution level
- identify those materials for which disposal might have an adverse effect on the environment
- note any safety limits exceeded and name the pollution factors
- compare resource consumption with a competing product with similar performance and range of use, noting any potential for reducing consumption
- determine how waste from production and recycled materials might be reused in production
- record details of product life, model changes, and any savings of raw materials and labour
- note disposal details, such as household waste or special-category waste.

13 Classify suppliers' offers in terms of the environmental benefits using them would bring:

- decide on a scale of assessment
- fix criteria weightings for the issues involved, deciding on what associated conditions ('if, ... then ...') apply and establishing where on the scale the rejection point is.

14 Discuss and decide with suppliers:

- whether or not they are prepared to reveal environmental information about their products
- what type of packaging will be used
- whether or not they are prepared to reuse returnable packaging
- what delivery method will be used
- whether or not they will supply clearance certificates for the products
- whether or not they will contribute towards disposal costs (see also Checklist 26, Legal aspects)
- whether or not they will cooperate with trade and specialist associations.

Providing environmentally sound storage and handling facilities

15 Lock up dangerous chemicals and substances.

16 Apply ecological principles in storage areas, such as using low-exhaust fork-lift trucks and reusable transport cases.

17 Select the packaging best suited to the production process.

18 Recycle packaging materials that cannot be reused:

- collect paper and cardboard for recycling
- * reuse packaging received from suppliers for your own purposes
- send plastic packaging for recycling.

CHECKLIST 9: PRODUCTION TECHNOLOGY

In all manufacturing processes, the technology used in production plays an important role in the nature and volume of any emissions produced by it.

Ecology-orientated innovations help reduce pollution, but they can also have economic benefits. They can lead to a reduction in the consumption of raw materials, water, and energy and lower the disposal costs of waste and sewage.

Such technology may also improve product quality and so enhance the overall image of the organization, which will be further enhanced by the fact that it will be seen to be environmentally aware.

The four main areas involved in production are:

- materials and processes
- technologies
- recovery of materials and heat
- post-production emissions.

Those points with asterisks by them are measures that help protect the environment and can usually be introduced quickly to prevent or reduce costs.

Use ecologically sound materials and processes

1 Do not use raw materials or processes that are known to be hazardous. Either eliminate such processes or replace them with ones that cause less pollution. For example:

- instead of using the solvent trichloroethylene (a notorious hazard to health), use trichlorethane or perchlorethylene, which are less hazardous

■ replace cadmium or chrome coatings with zinc ones
■ replace conventional paints with low-solvent paints (water-based) high-solid systems or powder coatings
■ use energy sources with low emissions, such as low-sulphur fuels or light heating oil, or gas instead of heavy heating oil.

*2 For wet processes, reduce the temperature or switch to low-temperature processes, such as cold cleaning solvents and cold bleaching and dyeing processes

*3 Avoid dry processes and the cooling of workpieces. Avoid having to store them at an intermediate stage by switching from a non-continuous to a continuous manufacturing process.

 4 Prepare fuels so that full combustion is achieved. For example in heating, break down heavy oil into finer particles.

 5 Use additives that improve the yield from raw materials and/or reduce emissions. For example, use:

■ combustion-promoting additives, that act as catalysts to maximize and accelerate combustion processes
■ steel converters that are oxygen-blown rather than air blown.

 6 Interrupt or change production as little as possible, if this means that the plant has to be cleaned or heated.

Use clean technologies

 7 Prevent emissions from dust-producing substances during delivery, storage, crushing, and mixing by using hermetically sealed storage, transport, and production facilities.

 8 Use technologies that achieve an improved input–output ratio. Good examples of these are:

■ conversion combustion equipment, as used in fluidized-bed combustion in energy production, or back-pressure furnaces, used in the production of iron
■ using modern paint systems to reduce splashes and improve efficiency (these can bring about improvements in efficiency of from 50 per cent, for the normal air spray, to up to 95 per cent for dipping, rolling, or flow coating)
*■ in wet processes, reducing the input of chemicals by using a weaker concentration and/or a smaller bath volume.

 9 Use modern measurement and control technology for the following:

- *■ automatic monitoring and measuring of the concentration of treatment or process chemicals, which can help reduce material inputs, protection costs, waste and plant downtime
- *■ automatic injection of clean water for rinsing and washing processes (due to the conductivity of the water, this not only reduces the amount of clean water required, but also increases the level of useful substances remaining in the waste water, which assists in the recycling of them)
- *■ in drying processes, automatically controlled production speed and exhaust air humidity saves energy and improves machine utilization and quality of the product
- *■ optimizing combustion processes reduces emissions and improves combustion efficiency in energy production.

10 Increase the lifetime of treatment baths by

- ■ using ultra-filtrations or other techniques
- *■ pre-rinsing workpieces, for example with hot water.

11 Reduce leakages and faults that cause harmful emissions by:

- ■ carrying out regular safety checks
- ■ using sealing materials
- ■ frequent maintenance of equipment, pipes, connections, pumps, and shut off devices.

12 Remove water from workpieces mechanically by squeezing.

13 Increase energy efficiency by insulating, sealing or covering equipment that has a high working temperature.

Recover useful materials and heat.

See also Checklist 11, Waste management.

14 Avoid mixing effluents containing different substances as this makes it more difficult to recycle or recover any useful ingredients in them.

15 In order to facilitate recycling, isolate noxious effluent by concentrating them. In the case of air emissions, seal the equipment. In the case of wet processes, this can be achieved by cutting down on rinsing and cleaning water used.

16 Recycle useful substances contained in effluents, either in future production or convert them into other useful products. Examples of this include:

*■ recovering heavy metals, acids and so on from effluents by means of decentralized ion exchanges, reverse osmosis, ultra-filtration and vaporizing plate techniques

*■ recovering acids and organic solvents from the exhaust air by using absorbers

*■ using slightly soiled water for pre-rinsing or recirculating water several times over.

17 Recover heat by:

■ using heat exchangers to exploit heat resulting from production and the heat that accumulates under factory roofs and in certain rooms

■ circulating hot exhaust air back into the production or combustion process.

Adopt measures to avoid harmful emissions being produced

18 Keep equipment enclosed to avoid the release of pollutants into the environment.

19 Use more effective environmental equipment. For example, in metal surface treatment, the application of water-saving measures gives scope for replacing the extremely unreliable flow-through plants with safe, efficient charge plants.

20 Use equipment to protect the environment that produces little waste. For example, desulphurization equipment produces reusable substances, such as sulphur, sulphur dioxide, sulphur acid or gypsum, instead of sludge, and thus creates a smaller amount of waste.

21 Ensure that equipment used to treat pollutants is working properly by putting in place a regular maintenance programme and monitoring and warning systems.

22 Reduce the effects of any leaks or faults in waste water treatment plants by, for example:

■ having an automatic emergency production shutdown facility in the event of a fault

■ connecting all drains to the waste water treatment system.

23 Recycle or process wastes by sending:

■ used acid to metal processing plants for ore extraction

■ concentrates containing heavy metals to central processing plants

■ metal or metal-bearing wastes to secondary processing plants

■ waste paper and glass to collection points for recycling

■ sewage sludge to farmers to be used as manure.

CHECKLIST 10: ENERGY AND WATER

In the energy-intensive sectors of industry, the cost of power is one of the key factors affecting competitiveness. Even in those companies where energy consumption is lower, savings and rationalization of use can be achieved. This also applies to water, which is an energy 'carrier' for many heating and cooling systems, a processing agent in many plants, and important in the movement of sanitary waste.

The process of reviewing energy and water consumption in a company can generate new ideas for optimizing the manufacturing process itself. If energy and water are consistently well managed, there are bound to be savings in raw materials and other costs as well.

Those points with asterisks by them are measures that help the environment and can usually be introduced quickly to prevent or reduce costs.

Plan energy- and water-saving measures

1 Undertake an energy and water review to determine where the company consumes most electricity, heat, and water. List these areas and the quantities consumed.
2 Calculate the total cost of bought in energy from outside and/or water consumed. Calculate the cost of the water and energy used by each operating unit.
3 Create a project group to train staff to manage energy and water consumption and monitor performance.

Set measurable goals for economizing on energy and water consumed

4 Appoint people to be responsible for energy and water in each work area or department.
5 Create links between those appointed to do this, the project group and, if necessary, an energy adviser, to set goals for each area or department.
6 Discuss what savings are possible and the effects and impacts of these proposals.

Devise methods for economizing on energy and water consumed

7 Examples of measures that require low levels of investment and have an immediate impact include:

*■ installing flow restrictors on taps

* ■ installing automatic shut-off valves on showers
* ■ checking for leaking pipes and discharge points and having these repaired immediately there is a problem
* ■ using temperature regulators on rinsing baths
* ■ installing adequate insulation for hot water pipes
* ■ cleaning the surfaces of heat exchangers frequently to obtain maximum efficiency
* ■ installing manometers, thermometers, flow meters, expansion valves, and flow restrictors wherever economically viable (these will also assist monitoring)
* ■ having water and cooling water pumps operate as a function of the flow rate.

8 Examples of longer-term investments would be:

* ■ installing recooling plants instead of using the public water supply
* ■ using individual water heaters whenever there is the potential for large amounts of heat to be lost due to storage or long pipelines
* ■ dividing water supplies according to quality and quantity (drinking, service, and industrial water)
* ■ using direct cooling with outside air or closed coolant circuits instead of once-through cooling methods
* ■ in wash- and shower-rooms, installing automatic cut-off thermostat valves for mixing hot and cold water
* ■ installing water treatment plants to recycle washing, service, and rinsing water.

Introduce energy- and water-saving maintenance arrangements
9 For example:

* ■ check washing facilities, showers, and toilets regularly to ensure that there are no leaks
* ■ turn off water points that are not needed
* ■ repair leaking taps immediately
* ■ ensure that hot water leaves the heating plant or distributor at a temperature below 50°C (hot water should be available at a temperature no higher than 45°C
* ■ use minimal amounts of cooling water as the less water used, the higher the outlet temperature
* ■ reduce the fresh water requirements of cooling towers to a minimum, and turn off cooling water circuits when they are not required

*■ turn off service hot water circuits if they are not going to be used within a determined period of about four hours

*■ turn off circulation pumps for service water outside operating hours

*■ if possible, produce separate internal costings for town water, in-house water, well water, and circulatory water (calculate appropriate cost allocations

*■ adjust the water quantities needed for WCs, showers, and rinsing baths to the minimum acceptable levels.

Constantly monitor and improve

10 Make all improvement measures the responsibility of one department or individual and monitor progress periodically.

11 Compare goals and targets set with actual achievement and communicate these to those responsible via short reports.

12 Communicate achievements in saving energy to other interested groups, both within and outside the department. Never be totally satisfied with what has been achieved, though—keep looking for improvements that can be made.

CHECKLIST 11: WASTE MANAGEMENT

The problems of disposing of waste, the shortage of waste sites, and the difficulties involved in developing new ones are becoming more critical every year. Thus, finding environmentally acceptable methods of disposal of waste and extending the possibilities of recycling methods have become important factors in the decision-making process of businesses and local authorities.

Many firms already consider these aspects at the product development stage, when selecting manufacturing processes and purchasing materials.

This checklist sets out which aspects firms should consider when making decisions on how to deal with their waste in ways that protect the environment.

Again points with asterisks are measures that help protect the environment and can usually be introduced quickly to prevent or reduce costs.

Plan recycling measures and how to dispose of waste

1 Draw up a 'materials and energy balance sheet' to identify and analyse waste materials produced. This should:

■ name, describe, and identify residues:

- specify individual types of material (such as wood, textiles, paper, leather, asbestos)
- in the case of compounds, list their origins (say, from a production process, the manufacturing of the company's main product)
- Give details of their main characteristics (for example, their composition, dimensions, and physical, chemical, and biological characteristics)
- list their visual characteristics (such as their colour and appearance)
- list their medical characteristics (such as their acute toxicity, long-term toxicity, and so on)
- list their production characteristics (such as the manufacturing process that produced them, the degree of processing involved in their production).
■ Classify residues (such as degree of aggregation, size, origin, use, and disposal possibilities)
■ Use a residue key for classification purposes.

2 Check the possibility of avoiding waste by eliminating harmful residues during production.

3 Check the possibility of reducing waste by reducing the creation of harmful residues during production.

4 Check the possibility of using physical and chemical processes to transform waste into harmless substances and energies. For example, if a mixture of methyl alcohol, formic acid, acetic acid and ether is heated to $900-1000°C$, it forms carbon dioxide and water.

5 Check the potential for recycling waste and pollutants within your own or external production processes.

6 Check how well wastes are dispersed by:

■ testing the dilution effect (say, for emissions from fires, whether or not they are sufficiently diluted to avoid polluting the surrounding air)
■ testing the concentration.

7 Check the potential for recycling the waste in your own and other companies:

■ ascertain how flexible the organization of the production system and process set-ups are to see whether or not they could cope with recycling requirements
■ estimate the effects of recycling on income and expenditure

- ascertain the potential for recycling in terms of the company's range of products and services:
  - consider and analyse quantitative changes
  - analyse structural changes
  - study the effects of design and packaging and do not use alloys that are unsuitable for recycling, reduce the proportions of non-ferrous metals used, use corrosion-resistant metals, and ensure that the various components can be separated easily
  - bear in mind the varying nature of raw materials
  - consider the possibility of changing production processes
- notify waste disposal companies of any substances that cannot be recycled in your own production processes
- play an active part in managing a recycling programme.

Monitor recyclable materials

8 Set up a system to manage residues and coordinate all recycling activities.

9 Organize collection of waste to be recycled and provide suitable receptacles:

- reduce the volume of waste by using compaction containers
- set up used oil collection points
- organize separate collections of paper, plastics, and aluminium at source by supplying compartmentalized bins in the workplace
- collect solvents, solutions, acids, and dyes
- shred waste computer paper and reuse it as packing material
- *■ convert unsuccessful photocopies into notepads.

10 Ask suppliers and manufacturers for product and safety information sheets.

11 Allow employees to use collection points for any materials they might have for recycling.

Where necessary, change the terms on which you do business

See also Checklists 8, Materials management, and 26, Legal aspects.

12 Add to your general purchasing conditions clause, making suppliers liable for the environmental acceptability of their products.

13 Add clauses that require suppliers to guarantee that their products can be disposed of without undue expense.

14 Obtain agreement with suppliers that they will take back disposable containers.

15 Add a clause requiring suppliers to provide full information on materials and product characteristics.

16 Add an exclusion clause ensuring that the purchasing firm is not liable if the supplier infringes their legal obligations.

Evaluate and monitor waste disposal companies

17 Check that the intentions and actions of disposal companies are honest and eco-friendly.

18 Check that disposal companies are legally bound to insure themselves and that your own firm will not be liable in the case of improper disposal of waste (see 'Checklist 25, Insurance).

19 Ask to see waste disposal firms' permits.

20 Ask disposal firms what conditions the authorities have imposed on them and make spot checks to ensure that these are being met.

21 Keep internal records that correspond with the documents accompanying loads for waste disposal.

CHECKLIST 12: CONTAMINATED SITES

Environmental management includes identifying and cleaning up any contamination that may be present on company sites. It is essential to eliminate such problems early to avoid both environmental risks and financial costs.

Site contamination may originate from:

■ the previous use of the site, especially if it was a dump for municipal and trade waste

■ it being an unauthorized dump, tip, or landfill site, containing environmentally hazardous production residues, such as reclaimed material and building waste

■ previous industrial activities that have taken place on the site

■ corroded pipes, defective sewers, improper storage of hazardous substances and so on, all of which contaminate water or soil.

Emissions from contaminated sites are a hazard to water, air, flora and fauna, and, of course, to human beings.

Furthermore, unless it is discovered and cleaned up, existing contamination on a company's site may lead to the company being prosecuted. There have even been cases where liability of this kind has driven the company into bankruptcy.

Under strict liability law, a company will be held responsible for the contamination even if there has been no negligence or intent on its part. This will normally be the case, for example, if the company has just acquired the site without knowing that it has been contaminated by the seller or a previous owner.

Before acquiring land, therefore, it is essential to check whether or not there is any contamination on the site. This is a part of the management's duty to exercise due care and attention. It is also a duty of the lawyer involved in the transaction to warn the purchaser of any risk of contamination.

A warranty from the seller that the site is not contaminated is often of little value to the buyer. If the site is later found to be contaminated and the buyer is held liable, it will often be fruitless to take the seller to court. The seller may be unable to reimburse the high clean-up costs involved anyway.

The situation in the case of bank loans made with the property as security is similar. Before granting such a loan, the bank may examine the site to see whether or not it is contaminated. If it is, this will often reduce the amount of any loan secured in this way.

If a company discovers that it is sitting on a contaminated site, whether it has been caused by the company itself or not, there is a great temptation to 'let sleeping dogs lie'. However, this policy is not only *morally* questionable, it is likely to be unwise economically, too. It is often possible, for example, to prevent really serious damage being caused by stopping the contamination process as early as possible. Also, deliberately failing to take action to stop the contamination process could render the managing director liable to criminal prosecution.

The following checklist is designed to help reduce the risks of contamination at an industrial site. For certain aspects, technical skills and equipment are needed.

Investigate the site's history

Gather as many facts and as much information about the site as possible from written documents and interviews. Collect old documents concerning the site from the Chamber of Commerce, local authority, or previous owners. Talk to employees, former employees, neighbours, fire brigade, and so on about production methods, materials used, and any accidents that have occurred.

1 Obtain copies of or inspect old maps and aerial photos.

- look for any obvious changes in the site, such as former ditches, excavations, or old basements

- evaluate aerial photos—in Europe, for example, look for bomb craters, which were often used afterwards as waste dumps.

2 Collect information on former users/manufacturers, including their:

- line of business (dates and circumstances)
- size of business (for example, production figures)
- processes they used, such as electroplate jobbing with chloro-carbon degreasing
- materials they used, particularly noxious ones, such as cyanides, fluorides, chlorocarbons, and pickling acids.

3 Identify the positions of any former production facilities:

- obtain plans showing their positions on the site and note particularly any places where noxious materials were used, such as in a pickling shop
- obtain information on the storage of noxious substances and safety measures employed during production and storage.

4 Find out about contamination on neighbouring sites:

- obtain information on cases of contamination in the area known to local authorities.
- if any records of contamination are found, investigate their nature and extent and the legal situation concerning them.

Undertake a field survey

5 Find out about the geological and hydrological features of the site:

- check the geographical features of the site, such as if it is positioned on a slope or in a valley
- conduct a site survey with geologists
- study geological and ground water maps and details of the geological substructure and hydrogeological conditions
- obtain information about any surfacing (find out, for example, when an asphalt surfacing was laid)

Evaluate the data and information gathered

6 Decide whether or not to pursue your investigations further:

- if, for example the site was used only for offices, and it is obvious that there is no risk of contamination from them you do not need to investigate further

- if there is any doubt, however, undertake a preliminary survey to assess the level of any risk.

7 Draw up guidelines for complementary surveys. It is worth considering three types, one for each possible form of contamination:

- a water survey, to identify contamination that may have found its way into the ground water via precipitation
- a soil survey to identify problems that may have been caused by drift, eluviation, or direct contact with pollutants
- a soil air survey to discover if there are any gases that may have been caused by anaerobic degradation of organic substances or volatile chlorinated carbons.

8 Check the position of the site—in particular, if it is in a water protection zone or close to a residential area?

9 Check whether any environmentally hazardous substances have been used or stored on the site, identifying the water hazard class or waste class.

Conduct water and soil surveys

Analyse all information, concerning water on the site, such as the positions of any wells, water levels, springs, rivers, and lakes.

10 Obtain all geological and hydrogeological data for the site.

11 Use this information to determine drilling points for ground water test stations.

12 Examine ground water near the surface for:

- its hydrogeological situation (for example, the direction in which it flows, the depth of the ground water table, and the geological soil profile)
- chemical contamination.

13 Identify where to place ground water test stations upstream and downstream from the site.

14 Specify the positions of the measuring points, depending on the size of the site, ensuring that there are at least three measuring points in order to determine the ground water contour (hydrological triangle).

15 When setting up the ground water measuring points, include separate measuring points for the individual ground water levels.

16 Where aquifers are found in loose rock, record the data relating to the complete thickness.

17 In the case of split aquifers, work together with the competent regional geological authorities.

18 Prepare a list for parameters for the ground water investigation, dependent on the type, age, position, and size of the site. If information is available on the substances and concentrations used there, specify parameters for investigating these substances. If it is not, proceed step by step:

■ first, determine aggregate parameters in the laboratory and make measurements on site (such as PH value, conductivity, temperature, redox potential, oxygen, colour, odour, appearance, water level, flow rate)

■ second, specify individual parameters (such as for heavy metals, chlorinated carbons, aromatics).

19 Evaluate the investigation's findings and decide whether or not investigations of soil or soil air are needed.

20 Before beginning a soil survey, select the methods of survey to use, such as trial drillings, exploratory operations, core drilling. Drilling points should be on the sites of former or current production, and locations upstream or downstream chosen for investigating former storage sites. At these points, soil samples will need to be taken (for example mix samples and horizon samples should be taken from obviously contaminated sites). The maximum depth of drillings required will depend on where the ground water is, the position of sealing clay layers, and on the specific task.

21 Draw up a list of parameters for the soil survey, similar to that produced for the water survey. Investigate:

■ the original substance

■ the elute (aqueous extract).

22 If volatile components are expected to be present in the soil or the ground water, investigate the soil air by taking individual samples or perform continuous sampling to ascertain gas levels. In order to specify the sampling points, use either of the following methods:

■ grid

■ site them at well-known critical production points (such as electro-plating, degreasing, storage, filling or transfer stations, transport routes).

23 Prepare a list of parameters for the soil air investigation.

24 Assess the survey's findings for water, soil, and soil air, and evaluate the risks posed by any hazards.

25 Work out proposals for cleaning up the contamination.

EXAMPLES OF GOOD PRACTICE—Production issues

Manufacturing and the related industries have been subject to environmental laws and regulations for some time. They further reinforce the need to examine processes and products as it is necessary for them to at least meet the minimum standards set. Many businesses, however, have gone beyond meeting just the minimum standards and have found that good environmental practice can mean a more profitable business.

The examples that follow have been grouped into the categories of product development and production technology, packaging of products, materials management, including purchasing policies, waste management and economies made in energy and water. Many of the companies, although entered in just one category here, have achieved cost savings or increased revenues in all the others. Further these companies have not stopped there, but have gone forward to do even better.

Product development and production technology

Industrial Chemical Industries (ICI) has developed a way to make ammonia that uses little energy and reduces the levels of air pollution usually created by making it. The 'LCA Process' reduces nitrogen oxide emissions by 87 per cent, sulphur dioxide by 95 per cent, and carbon dioxide by 60 per cent. It also reduces the ammonia content of the liquid effluent produced by 75 per cent. If all the world's ammonia producers used this process it would be equivalent, in terms of the reduction in nitrogen oxide produced, to taking five million cars off the road.

Neumarketer Lammsbrau has been producing 'eco beer' since 1984. The malting and brewing processes are carried out according to environmental criteria, and both departments are equipped with extensive energy-recovery devices. This 'eco beer' is sold exclusively in kegs or in returnable bottles and cases. Further, neither artificial fertilizers nor chemical pesticides are used in the growing of the hops and barley.

The essential raw materials needed to produce the beer are organically grown. An agricultural engineer has been employed to find grain growers prepared to be long-term suppliers and to aid them in acquiring the basic know-how of organic farming. All of the hops used and 25 per cent of the grain are now organically grown.

In 1989, **Procter & Gamble GmbH** began to replace the chlorine-bleached sulphate cellulose used in its disposable nappies with oxidation-bleached material, thus avoiding a lot of water pollution. In addition, the cellulose content has been cut by approximately 30 per cent and the weight reduced by 17 per cent, and, as a result, considerable less packaging is required. This had a knock-on effect, producing savings in transportation costs and storage requirements. In fact raw materials and energy requirements for packaging and transportation dropped by 50 per cent.

Ganter Schuhfabrik GmbH is increasingly replacing glue and paint containing solvents with those manufactured by a dispersion technique. Contaminated solvents are distilled and the solvents recovered for re-use, cutting solvent consumption by 75 per cent. Also, the company no longer throws its yarn bobbins away, but returns them to the supplier for refilling instead. In addition, the change to electronic data exchange between management and production saves the company the cost of 300 kg of paper, annually.

Schulke & Mayr GmbH sent a questionnaire to its main suppliers about the ecological soundness of their products. The responses were collated into a 'positive/negative catalogue', being viewed as such depending on the ecological soundness or otherwise of the raw materials used to make them. This listing is used as a guide for future product development.

Bergmann GmbH is one of the largest suppliers of solid wood furniture and it has developed a comprehensive environmental programme. Wood waste is used in the company's own heating plant, while other waste material is separated and disposed of appropriately. The furniture—made exclusively of wood from Scandinavian forests that are managed for permanent production—is treated with natural oils and waxes.

Wella AG has employed the British company, Imperial Chemical Industries PLC, to produce biodegradable shampoo bottles. The basic material, Biopol, is manufactured from micro-organisms that are fed on ordinary sugar, thus conserving the fossil fuels traditionally used to produce plastics. In addition, the process provides a market for agricultural surpluses.

BASF AG Ludwigschafen has an environmental monitoring team. The central desk for the collection of environmental data is manned 24 hours a day. The team's task is to collate and analyse the up-to-the-minute data that is produced by the company's monitoring of the air, waste water, water, and noise produced by its plants. Levels of sulphur dioxide, nitrogen monoxide, ozone, dust, and dissolved organic carbon, as well as the strength and direction of the wind, are all continuously recorded.

At the **PWA Papierwerke Waldhof-Aschaffenburg AG** devising and using innovative production processes to protect the environment and decrease waste are central aspects of the company's policy. In 1989, the company won a prize for its efforts to protect the environment, being the first cellulose tissue factory in the world to use a completely chlorine-free bleaching process. In the entire production plant, PWA manufactures around 500 000 tonnes of non-chlorine-bleached cellulose. The company is also Central Europe's largest user of old paper, absorbing over 700 000 tonnes annually.

RWE-DEA AG uses environmentally friendly methods to extract crude oil from the Baltic and North Seas. The oil platform Schwedeneck-See, offshore from the Baltic bathing resort of Damp, is so constructed that not a single drop of liquid can run out of it into the sea. Even rainwater is collected and pumped ashore for disposal. This high level of attention to protecting the environment by preventing pollution of the sea is observed even in the drilling phase. At the Mittelplate field off Friederichskoog, too, strict measures are enforced to ensure that there is as little visual and noise disturbance as possible. Further the Mittelplate Consortium transports the crude oil to Brunsbuttel in its own double-hulled lighters, specially built to ensure safe working in this zone of mud-flats.

Packaging of products

The chocolate and confectionery manufacturer, **Wissoll Wilh. Schmitz-Scholl** has its own answer to the growing number of problems involved in the packaging of products—edible packaging for chocolates, which it developed in cooperation with a manufacturer of waffles. Despite this, it has a team working full time on the development of healthier, more natural, and environmentally sound products and packaging.

The products of the Swiss retailer **Migros** demonstrate a combination of purpose, economy, and ecology. Extra packaging—such as cardboard boxes around tubes of toothpaste—have been done away with and refills are available for many products, such as shampoo and instant coffee. Necessary items, such as glass jars or foil tops for yogurt, have been made thinner and lighter to cut down consumption. Further, its outlets do not sell canned drinks and spray cans containing propellants with CFCs have not been seen on their shelves since 1988.

Packaging manufacturer **Bischoff & Klein GmbH & Co.** has regulated its packaging machines so that the settings are more precise, as well as using thinner foil and a new-style glue. These measures have cut the company's material requirements by 30 per cent.

The Swiss foodstuffs company **Frisco-Findus** has been able to save 6 tonnes of packaging material annually by using injection rather than suction-moulded plastic packaging for its frozen products. Also, by partially replacing its insulating materials with, for example, newspaper, it has created an annual saving of 1.3 tonnes of cardboard and 250 cu.m. of polystyrene.

Materials management and purchasing

Bischoff & Klein Gmbh & Co. has drawn up purchasing lists asking suppliers for details of the composition of their products. Components containing harmful materials have been replaced with environmentally acceptable substitutes and, as a direct result, the company has been able to avoid having to install another expensive purification plant.

B&Q, a UK retailer of DIY products, sends an environmental question-naire to all its suppliers. The questionnaire asks for details of suppliers' policies and practices with regard to energy conservation, waste manage-ment, and emissions. Suppliers failing to meet B & Q's standards are not dropped immediately, rather, the company works in partnership with such suppliers and environmental consultants to help them improve.

Jordans, a food products company, makes, among other products, biscuits, muesli and wholegrain flour. It has established a half-way standard between conventional and organic foods—'Conservation Grade Food Produc-tion'. This has encouraged its suppliers to look at alternative ways of producing food to meet the market's demand for 'natural' products.

Elida Gibbs GmbH has introduced changes in the policies the material purchasing department operates by that aimed at reducing environmental pollution. As a result, bactericides in deodorants, and PVC packaging are no longer acquired. Environmental considerations influence the purchasing of raw materials and have led to changes in the aerosol propellant used. Health, safety, and environmental factors are discussed with suppliers to minimize any potential risk and to raise standards. An interesting example of the effect of this is the changeover to potassium sorbate, a synthesized form of a natural food preservative.

Waste management

The leading fast food chain, **McDonald's Deutschland Inc.** has invested over DM 2 million in Germany in research into making the company more environmentally friendly. The aim was that no McDonald's waste should end up in rubbish dumps or in incinerators. A first step towards this was the replacement of all polystyrene foam packaging with cardboard made of at least 72 per cent recycled material. Further, beer and mineral water will be served on tap or in returnable bottles rather than cans and recycled paper is used for almost all brochures and paper tableware in the restaurants. Throughout Germany, McDonald's restaurants recycle cardboard, polyethylene foil and used cooking oil, as well as composting some food scraps.

3M runs a waste-reduction programme they call 'Pollution Prevention Pays' (3P). The programme includes: reformulating products so that they use raw materials and processes that cause as little pollution as possible, modifying manufacturing processes to save energy and reduce waste, and redesigning equipment and recycling materials. As a result the 3P programme has produced worldwide savings of more than $500 million. Not content with this, 3M has introduced a tougher programme, called 3P+.

Freeman's mail order warehouse generates 30 tonnes of combustible waste a week, mainly plastics and cardboard. An incinerator and boiler were installed to use the waste to generate heat and hot water for the warehouse. The system paid for itself in four years.

On the grounds that they want to protect the environment, **Staatl Mineralbrunnen Siemens Erben OHG** will fill only reusable containers. In 1989, the company changed to containers standardized by the Cooperative of German Spas, thus cutting sorting costs for the trade. Further, the inks used to print the bottle labels are free of heavy metals and the use of cleaning and disinfecting solutions is kept to the minimum, steam having replaced chemicals for sterilizing bottles. An automatic regulation and monitoring system prevents the spring being overexploited.

Sonderabfall GmbH which disposes of special waste from hospitals, has developed hermetic containers that ensure that no one comes into direct contact with the waste. The specialized containers are transported in a refrigerated truck to a special waste incinerating plant.

Britannia Recycling, scrap processors, recycles about 1000 tonnes of polypropylene car battery cases a year. The cases used to be thrown away. The plastic is bought by the building and horticultural trades. It took just two years for Britannia to pay back its investment in the necessary equipment.

Two major manufacturers of recycled tyres, **Gummi-Mayer KG** and **Vergolst GmbH** achieve considerable savings in resources by remoulding and, simultaneously, they dramatically reduce waste. One new tyre requires 35 litres of crude oil and a sophisticated structured weave of a cord-like material or very thin steel. A 'recycled' tyre requires only 5.5 litres of crude oil. In addition, the company relieves dumps and incinerators of over 130 000 tonnes of used tyres annually—about a third of Germany's total.

Iceland Frozen Foods, a retailer of frozen foods and electrical appliances, collects old fridges and freezers when it delivers replacements. The CFC refrigerants these old units contain are removed and returned to ICI, the chemical company, for recycling. Iceland has also developed a portable system that enables engineers to repair fridges in the home. The costs have been small, but the environmental benefits of these developments are great.

National Power, the UK generator of electricity, produces 7.3 million tonnes of ash a year in its coal-fired power stations. It has found a market for nearly half of the ash: it is used to make building blocks and as an infilling aggregate by construction companies.

Green Land, a company making farm waste-handling systems, has developed a waste-digesting system that turns farm wastes, such as manure, into gas and fertilizers. The gas can be used to supplement a farm's energy needs and the residue used, or sold, as liquid fertilizer and a peat substitute.

AEG Hausegerate AG demonstrates its ecological orientation at manufacturing level. The amount of waste produced has been reduced by the introduction of plastic injection-moulding techniques using hot runner moulds. As deep-draw components are coated using special equipment, there is no need for solvents. The packaging used for the appliances is also environmentally sound.

Economies made in energy and water consumption
Demmel Schilderfabrik GmbH & Co. has reduced its water consumption by about 20 per cent by installing separate water meters for the different electrostatic precipitation baths. In addition, existing techniques are being honed to become more efficient and eco-friendly.

The Digital Equipment Corporation has introduced 'Visonetic Energy' monitoring to aid energy- and water-saving programmes in its Kaufbeuren plant. The company was able to cut its consumption of electricity in one year by almost 1.5 million KWh. The saving for water reached 12 400 cu. m, while gas and heating costs were reduced by 10 per cent.

Ganter Schuhfabrik GmbH has undertaken a number of energy-saving measures in its production sector. A combination of an insulated factory roof and the warm air supplied by the machines has cut its heating costs by 30 per cent. Further by replacing its two reciprocating compressors with a screw compressor, the company has reduced its energy consumption by 40 per cent. To minimize electricity demand at peak times, so-called 'power watchers' switch off certain sets of machines to prevent them overloading the system.

KEG, Krankenhausentsorgungsgesellschaft GmbH uses recovered energy in the form of steam from a neighbouring household waste incinerator exclusively to disinfect hospital waste. Heat released through condensation is then used to heat water required in other areas.

The Austrian firm, **Zellstoff und Papierfabrik Frantschach AG** has developed a cleaning process and water circulation system to cut the water requirements of one of its plants from 150 litres per kilo of paper, to 25 litres.

Kronos Titan GmbH began operating weak acid preparation plants in Nordenham in 1987 and in Duisburg in 1989, in a joint venture with the firm Sachtleben Chemie GmbH. These factories produce a high concentration sulphuric acid, reducing the need for manufactured acid. A byproduct is ferric sulphate, which is used to purify waste water. Weak acid from the factory is now no longer disposed of in the North Sea, as the dumping of waste acid in the ocean became illegal on 31 December 1989 as a result of EC regulations.

In 1991, **Volkswagen AG** brought a new paint shop into operation in its Wolfsburg factory at a cost of DM 1 billion. Most of the work in the new plant can be carried out without the use of solvents—with water being used instead. The new plant uses less than 50 per cent of the permitted level of organic solvent, whereas the limits were previously breached by 6 per cent.

CODES OF GOOD PRACTICE – NUMBER 5

An authoritative statement of particular significance for production is the following from the Coalition for Environmentally Responsible Economics (September 1989), a statement known as the ' Valdez Principles'.

This followed the worldwide concern at the oil spillage caused by the tanker Exxon Valdez, which polluted a valuable part of the coast of Alaska.

VALDEZ PRINCIPLES

By adopting these principles, we publicly affirm our belief that corporations and their shareholders have a direct responsibility for the environment. We believe that corporations must conduct their business as responsible stewards of the environment and seek profits only in a manner that leaves the Earth healthy and safe. We believe that corporations must not compromise the ability of future generations to sustain their needs.

We recognize this to be a long-term commitment to update our practices continually in light of advances in technology and new understandings in health and environmental science. We intend to make consistent, measurable progress in implementing these principles and to apply them wherever we operate throughout the world.

1   **Protection of the biosphere**
    We will minimize and strive to eliminate the release of any pollutant that may cause environmental damage to the air, water, or earth or its inhabitants. We will safeguard habitats in rivers, lakes, wetlands, coastal zones, and oceans and will minimize contributing to the greenhouse effect, depletion of the ozone layer, acid rain, or smog.

2   **Sustainable use of natural resources**
    We will make sustainable use of renewable natural resources, such as water, soils, and forests. We will conserve non-renewable natural resources through efficient use and careful planning. We will protect wildlife habitats, open spaces, and wilderness.

3   **Reduction and disposal of waste**
    We will minimize the creation of waste, especially hazardous waste, and, wherever possible, recycle materials. We will dispose of all wastes through safe and responsible methods.

4   **Wise use of energy**
    We will make every effort to use environmentally safe and sustainable energy sources to meet our needs. We will invest in improved energy efficiency and conservation in our operations. We will maximize the energy efficiency of products we produce or sell.

5   Risk reduction

We will minimize the environmental, health, and safety risks to our employees and the communities in which we operate by employing safe technologies and operating procedures and by being constantly prepared for emergencies.

6   Marketing of safe products and services

We will sell products or services that minimize adverse environmental impacts and that are safe as consumers commonly use them. We will inform consumers of the environmental impacts of our products or services.

7   Damage compensation

We will take responsibility for any harm we cause to the environment by making every effort to fully restore the environment and to compensate those persons who are adversely affected.

8   Disclosure

We will disclose to our employees and to the public incidents relating to our operations that cause environmental harm or pose health or safety hazards. We will disclose potential environmental, health, or safety hazards posed by our operations, and we will not take any action against employees who report any condition that creates a danger to the environment or poses health and safety hazards.

9   At least one member of the Board of Directors will be a person qualified to represent environmental interests. We will commit management resources to implementing these principles, including the funding of an office of vice-president for environmental affairs or an equivalent executive position, reporting directly to the CEO, to monitor and report upon our implementation efforts.

10   Assessment and annual audit

We will conduct and make public an annual self-evaluation of our progress in implementing these principles and in complying with all applicable laws and regulations throughout our worldwide operations. We will work toward the timely creation of independent environmental audit procedures, which we will complete annually and make available to the public.

POLICY EXTRACTS—Production issues

ICI, UK

Under its environmental policy, ICI will do the following.

'Encourage and facilitate the interchange of environmental technology throughout ICI and its subsidiary and related companies so as to promote best practice and sustain continuous improvement in environmental performance.
Provide information and assistance to ensure that ICI's products may be used, stored, and disposed of in an environmentally responsible manner.'

IBM, USA

Its corporate policy objectives are as follows.

'Develop, manufacture and market products that are safe for their intended use, efficient in their use of energy, protective of the environment, and that can be recycled or disposed of safely.

Use development and manufacturing processes that do not adversely affect the environment, including developing and improving operations and technologies to minimize waste, prevent air, water, and other pollution, minimize health and safety risks, and dispose of waste safely and responsibly.

Ensure the responsible use of energy throughout our business, including conserving energy, improving energy efficiency, looking for safer energy sources, and giving preference to renewable over non-renewable energy sources when feasible.'

Kraft General Foods, USA

The following are Kraft's principles for food packaging.

'In our efforts to limit the impact of food packaging on the environment, Kraft General Foods is committed to:

1 using the minimum amount of material consistent with food safety and protection standards
2 evaluating packaging materials based on their environmental impact
3 promoting recyclability by labelling packages with generally recognized symbols and codes

4 maximizing the use of recycling materials, consistent with food safety and protection standards
5 supporting research and technology that offers solutions to the municipal solid waste issue
6 continuing our internal search for ways to reduce municipal solid waste from our offices and manufacturing operations
7 working with communities and governmental bodies to reduce solid waste.

By working together with consumers, public officials and other organizations for uniform, national food packaging standards, we can reduce solid waste and maintain the wide array of food products and packages preferred by our customers.'

Noranda Minerals, Inc., Canada

'Noranda Minerals' operations will implement a product steward-ship programme which protects our employees, customers, the public and the environment, by providing risk management information for the safe use, transportation and disposal of our products, our recyclable materials, and our wastes.'

Philips, Netherlands

'Philips encourages the collection and qualified recycling of products at the end of their useful life by third parties. In this respect Philips will provide the necessary information concerning its products.'

Checklists for external relations issues

7

```
┌──────────────┐
│  External    │
│  relations   │
│  issues      │
└──────────────┘
  │
  ├─ 13
  │  Marketing
  │
  ├─ 14
  │  Public relations
  │
  └─ 15
     International business
     relations
```

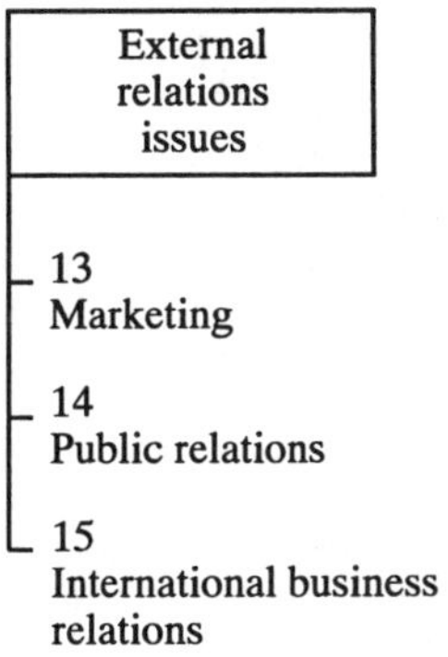

FIGURE 7.1   EXTERNAL RELATIONS ISSUES IN THE WINTER MODEL

In this chapter, we will be looking at the environmental issue and opportunities that arise in relation to external business relationships.

Three issues are covered: marketing, public relations, and international business relations. However, bear in mind how marketing interacts with production, as does international business. Also, staff training and working conditions, considered later in Chapter 9, are just as important when producing or selling in another country as they are in the home country. The interlinking nature of the aspects covered in the checklists is important and so most cannot be used in isolation.

Certain environmental interest bodies focus part of their efforts towards international business. One such is the Keidanren, the Confederation of Japanese Business. In 1991, they issued guidelines to assist organizations operating abroad. These are given at the end of this chapter and they make a useful basis on which to develop your own policies and monitor performance.

CHECKLIST 13: MARKETING

All marketing strategies are aimed at meeting customers' needs, while achieving the company's own long-term prosperity and objectives.

Ecological factors have become an important element in the success of market-orientated management as a result of more stringent environmental legislation and customers' increased ecological awareness.

Ecologically acceptable marketing concepts therefore need to be developed, not only in order for companies to be socially responsible, but also to ensure that the company remains competitive.

This checklist sets out the three main areas to be considered when developing or reviewing an environmental marketing strategy. First, the environmental marketing objectives themselves, then how to integrate them into current marketing activities, and, finally, the adjustment of current policies to meet the new environmental strategies.

Establish ecological marketing objectives

1 Ensure that this type of marketing fits into the company's overall philosophy and future objectives.

2 Formulate marketing objectives so that performance can be measured and monitored, both:

■ in economic terms (for example, secure a set percentage of specified new environment-related markets within a specified period) and

■ in terms of the company profile (that is, ensure that the company has a reputation for addressing environmental problems).

3 Prioritize the objectives by:

■ product or product category

■ customer category

■ region.

Integrate marketing activities

4 Draw up a product policy, to include such objectives as the following:

- manufacture or sell products that contain a minimum of scarce raw materials and use materials that can be recycled
- label products to draw attention to their environmentally positive features
- use packaging made from environmentally acceptable materials and packaging that can be reused
- provide after-sales and advisory services that include instructions explaining how the product can be used in an environmentally acceptable manner.

5 Draw up a communications and public relations policy, to include items such as the following:

- recognize the increasing concern consumers have about the environment and respond with appropriate advertising and public relations activities
- enhance the image, reputation, and expertise of the company on environmental issues by exposing groups or selected customers to ecological arguments and publicity, ensure that any claims are true and can be substantiated
- allay public distrust of the business world's attitude to environmental matters by taking part in broadly based activities, in particular with trade associations.

6 Draw up a distribution policy, containing such objectives as the following:

- develop agreements and methods with manufacturers and distributors to create recycling systems
- establish centres for recycling and provide advice at the point of sale or distribution to encourage consumers to use these centres
- use transport systems that limit energy consumption and pollution to the minimum.

7 Draw up a price and discount policy, to include such objectives as the following:

- where higher prices cannot be avoided as a result of introducing ecologically sound manufacturing processes, make it clear to distributors and consumers how these costs were calculated—consumers may well be willing to pay a premium price if they feel it is for a good reason
- calculate whether or not the additional cost of ecologically acceptable

products can be spread over the costs of other products made by joint costing.

8 Check that all individual measures and actions form part of an integrated whole that makes a definite environmental impact. Make adjustments to these where necessary.

Adjust marketing policies and organization to the agreed environmental strategy

9 Ensure that all levels of marketing management are sensitive to ecological issues:

- improve awareness by providing information and training
- foster an *esprit de corps* and pride in setting an example on environmental matters.

10 Ensure that the company's organization can implement the strategies by:

- adapting departmental structures where necessary
- appointing a person at senior-management level to be responsible for all environmental questions concerned with marketing.

11 Develop incentive and monitoring systems:

- provide incentives for achieving or exceeding the environmental targets by means of bonuses and other schemes
- develop control and monitoring systems to check whether or not environmental objectives are, in fact, being met.

CHECKLIST 14: PUBLIC RELATIONS

The purpose of public relations—or, more commonly referred to simply as PR—is to create permanent links between the company and the public in order to build up and maintain confidence and understanding.

Information should be provided by the company on the action it is taking, or plans to take, to protect people's health and the environment. Such information also promotes protection of the environment because it increases the public's awareness of the issues and encourages others to follow the company's good example.

Aspects of PR noted in this checklist are intended to provide guidance on how to conduct the PR function in an environmentally aware way.

Be truthful, be clear, and ensure actions are consistent with words

1 Make PR statements on environmental activities only if they are true and can be verified. A company's claim to a strong positive stance on the environment may bring about closer public examination of its activities and make the company's own staff more critical. Thus, statements that cannot be substantiated may turn out to be counterproductive.

2 Concentrate on specific activities. Do not talk only in general terms about the company's pro-environmental attitude. Grounding statements with actual examples makes them easier to understand and more plausible. 'Flowery' talk about the company's dedication to protecting the environment, often leads the public to believe that the company prefers words to action.

3 Report on what the company has done, as well as on what it plans to do. The image of the company created by any PR statement must match the current situation. 'Noble intentions' for the future are not acceptable to the public and may even be seen as hiding a depressing reality.

Do good work rather than produce good reports on mediocre work

4 Take advantage of the fact that the media like reporting on new ideas and attitudes about protecting the environment:

- involve PR staff in planning environmental activities
- take action that has a good public image and stretch it over a long period to ensure that it is repeatedly reported in the media
- check whether or not material planned for ecology-related PR advertisements or spots can be converted into specific ecological activities as the benefits or innovative character of these could be featured in the press or on TV, providing more publicity for the company.

5 Involve the public in the planning and implementation of environmental activities. For example:

- allow company waste collection facilities to be used by local people as well wherever possible
- help maintain and extend wildlife habitats near company premises—apprentices or trainees could be involved in the upkeep of these areas
- join local ecological groups as a company or encourage members of the staff to join, unless the group's aims are incompatible with those of the company
- extend the environmental counselling scheme for employees' house-holds to local people

- encourage other companies to give voluntary support for ecological management and, by joining forces, enhance the effects of PR work
- cooperate with other companies, authorities, public and scientific bodies, for a greater combined effort and impress the public
- remember that ecological actions carried out primarily for the cause itself usually have a better PR effect than those solely engaged in to promote the company.

Focus on all key target groups and activities

6 Issue PR statements on the company's internal and external ecological activities, such as:

- progress in the disposal or recycling of waste materials, effluents and exhaust air, the use of waste heat, and the reduction of noise levels
- improvements in working conditions, enhanced safety, and healthier canteen food
- success in safety research and technology and the ecological compatibility of production processes, plant, and waste disposal equipment
- success in persuading other companies, with their own ecological associations, to set ecological targets.

7 Choose, draft, and disseminate PR statements to ensure that they reach the following groups:

- the company's staff and people living in the immediate vicinity of the factory or workplace
- the company's customers
- environmental experts of official bodies, associations, institutes, or other firms
- interested non-experts, such as working people and pensioners, students, and school-children (children should not be excluded as they are deeply interested in the environment and can influence their parents)
- people of all views—those with a positive attitude, the sceptics and members of critical citizens' groups.

CHECKLIST 15: INTERNATIONAL BUSINESS RELATIONS

Environmental management does not stop at national borders. The lives and health of people in other countries are no less important than in those in the home country. Indeed, any environmental damage caused elsewhere will often have an impact on the home country. Environmental management should cover exports, foreign production, and imports from other countries.

To emphasize the importance of having high standards, since 1993, the European Community has been one market. With the Single European Act, the Council of Ministers can adopt decisions on standards for the environmental aspects of product on a qualified majority. If there are enough member states with low environmental standards, therefore, this can influence the level of the standards that will be applied to all the others.

This market can operate smoothly only if member states reach acceptable agreement on what the general requirements and environmental standards for the characteristics of products manufactured in the Community are to be.

Environmental issues to consider when exporting

1 Ensure that goods intended for export meet the same quality standards as those for the domestic market, unless, of course, requirements are more stringent in the importing country.
2 Provide clear information and, if necessary, technical training for purchasers and users to enable them to use, transport, and store the goods without endangering the environment or human health, and to dispose of goods safely after use. This training could include information regarding the handling and use of the products, health risks, emergency measures in the event of an accident, transport, storage, and waste disposal.
3 Restrict or discontinue exports if the environment or human health is threatened in the importing country.
4 Provide literature on any risks associated with the products that is written in the local language. This information could include safety data sheets, labelling, and customer leaflets.
5 If, for some reason, products have to be recalled, the manufacturer should inform all customers and users of any risks and the precautions to be taken.
6 Exporters should keep records of all exported products that carry potential risks to the environment. This information would include the type of product, the quantity, and the destination.

Production in foreign countries

7 Ensure that the production facilities of foreign subsidiaries work to the same standards as those of the parent company. These should include:

- plant safety
- thresholds for pollution emission
- other factors affecting the environment.

8 If necessary, restrict or discontinue the manufacture of products that are a danger to the environment or the health of the inhabitants of that country.

9 Raise the level of the environmental technology of all companies within an international group to that of its most advanced member.

10 Ensure that the products made by foreign subsidiaries meet the same standards as products produced for the parent company's domestic market.

Environmental issues to consider when importing

11 Be fully conversant with the nature of the environmental standards of any foreign producer, particularly their emission standards or the quality of their agricultural products. A company's buyer should use their purchasing power to influence the supplier to make improvements and, if necessary, switch to a more environmentally orientated supplier.

EXAMPLES OF GOOD PRACTICE—External relations issues

Many businesses use their environmental achievements to promote their products directly or promote the company's image as an aware or caring neighbour.

The examples of successful practice included here fall into three categories—product promotion, public relations, and environmental good practice on the part of organizations aimed at international activities.

Product promotion

Brauns-Heitmann's customers are able to refill their laundry liquid containers at a 'filling station'. This favours the environment as well as the pocket.

Aachen hairdresser, **Alexander Pietschmann**, brings ecology to his clients. In his salon, hair is coloured with henna and other plant extracts, such as walnut or rhubarb root, rather than synthetic dyes. Also, sprays and shampoos containing dioxane are avoided.

Members of the **German association of paint manufacturers** found that sales rose after they introduced environmentally sound products. Water-based paints, solvent-free powder paint and dispersion paints for external use, all environmentally friendly, showed marked increases in the quantities sold.

The **NAZA** retail group of Stuttgart promotes its environmental image by stocking items such as:

- loose fruit, vegetables, meat, sausages, and cheese
- toilet and writing paper made from recycled and chlorine-free bleached paper
- environmentally sound household cleaners and washing powders
- dairy products and drinks sold in returnable containers
- the choice of using paper and linen instead of plastic carrier bags.

TSB Unit Trusts Limited, Unit Trust Management Company, has launched a unit trust that invests solely in companies that can demonstrate a commitment to improving their environmental performance or offer products or services that help protect the environment. Environmental factors are generally taken into account in making investment decisions for all other funds as well.

Public relations

AMAG, the Swiss importer of Audi–Voltwagen, ran a series of newspaper advertisements offering half-price rail season tickets to anyone ordering a new car. The aim of the promotion, ironically, was to encourage rail use and reduce the number of cars on Swiss roads.

Yamanouchi Ireland Co. Limited, part of a Japanese pharmaceutical group, has made protecting the environment and openness part of its key policies. The majority of its environmental monitoring is done by independent bodies and it encourages the public to visit the plant and discuss environmental issues. Many hundreds have taken up the invitation.

Deutsche Bank AG has formed an 'environmental databank' in conjunction with several other independent partners and within the framework of the 'Deutsche Bank environmental protection service'. The databank stores information about sources of environmentally orientated services, products, and technology. The two-way service enables suppliers to bring their company's services to the attention of potential clients and gives users, such as borough councils, chambers of commerce, private firms, and advisory services, an overview of what, and who, is available to help solve their particular environmental problem.

An Austrian electrical wholesaler **Electro Netto Hadwiger Hardt Handelsgesellschaft** began collecting and disposing of old electrical appliances on request. The service was free and people were not obliged to purchase new appliances. The wholesaler combined a public environmental need successfully with a public relations objective.

Pro-carton, introduced a pilot project in mid-1991, recycling cardboard boxes as a way of supporting the waste disposal scheme implemented by the city of Hamburg. With the backing of the used paper trade and 100 Co-op supermarkets, the citizens of Hamburg were invited to put cardboard boxes out for collection together with the paper they usually put out. Supermarkets advertised the project and distributed shopping bags made of 100 per cent recycled paper. Cartoons showed the cardboard boxes' route from the supermarket to being put out for collection and from there to the recycling centre. The aim was to show the consumer how to reduce the quantity of household waste and contribute to environmentally sound waste disposal.

To mark its 100th anniversary, **Allianz AG** set up a foundation with a sum of DM 100 million. One of its main aims is to promote pilot schemes for the preservation of nature and the countryside. Projects include the rehabilitation of riverbanks and conservation of nature reserves.

Ciba-Geigy AG distributed plastic bags to householders near its factory in Basel. These were used to collect odour samples for examination by their scientists. It is hoped that this will help to identify any shortcomings in the air filters or the production process.

Deutsche Lufthansa AG whose planes bear a crane symbol, has become active in the sponsorship of groups working to protect the environment. It has declared support for the German Bird Protection Society in the funding of a project to protect cranes.

Hewlett-Packard GmbH has established a chair in environmental analysis at Karlsruhe University. The company donates DM 700 000 annually in sponsorship for the chair.

As part of its secondment programme, **IBM Deutschland GmbH** puts managers at the disposal of charitable organizations for periods of two to three years to work on projects to protect the environment. The computer firm covers the cost of salaries and expenses for this period.

International marketing

A group of consultants in the UK designed a water current turbine to assist with irrigation in the Sudan. The turbine, which can be built in the Sudan using a limited number of machine tools, has the output of 70 per cent of a 3-

inch diesel pump manufactured by its main competitor. However, it uses no fossil fuels and is adapted to local conditions, operator skills, and available materials. It uses simple technology that can be produced, maintained, and operated by the local population.

The Lorrach company, **Bomin Solar GmbH & Co. KG** developed a new method for storing solar energy similar to the process of photosynthesis in plants. During the day, sunlight is used to separate magnesium hydrate into magnesium and water, while, at night, the chemical reaction produced releases energy as heat. The process is well suited to the decentralized energy supply required for villages in developing countries. India, the Sudan, and Tunisia have already expressed interest.

The furniture manufacturer, **Flototto Einrichtungssysteme**, ran a market survey to test how well it would accept the use of rubberwood in place of ramin wood. It received a positive response, so the company will be producing its decorative mouldings, the firm's greatest source of turnover, in environmentally sound rubberwood within 6–12 months. In anticipation of this, WWF, Germany, has already agreed to co-operate with Flototto-Einrichtungssysteme in vouching for the environmental acceptability of the concept. In the long term, the company will thus not only achieve the ecologically essential move away from ramin, but will also safeguard 500 jobs in Indonesia and increase foreign earnings by processing the raw material in the country of origin.

The Frankfurt company **Lurghi GmbH** was involved in the construction in California of one of the first cow-dung-fired power plants. In it, 800 tonnes of dung will be burned daily, saving 50 000 tonnes of crude oil per annum.

CODES OF GOOD PRACTICE – NUMBER 6

Keidanren's—The Confederation of Japanese Business—'Global Environmental Charter'

The basic philosophy

A company's existence is closely bound up with the global environment as well as with the community in which it is based. In carrying on its activities, each company must maintain respect for human dignity and strive towards a future society where the global environment is protected.

We must aim to construct a society whose members

cooperate together on environmental problems, a society where sustainable development on a global scale is possible, where companies enjoy a relationship of mutual trust with local citizens and consumers, and where they vigorously and freely develop their operations while preserving the environment. Each company must aim at being a good global corporate citizen, recognizing that grappling with environmental problems is essential to its own existence and its activities.

Guidelines for corporate action

Companies must carry on their business activities to contribute to the establishment of a new economic social system for realizing an environmentally protective society, leading to sustainable development.

1 General management policies

Companies should always consult the guidelines below when carrying on their activities. They must work to:

- protect the global environment and improve the local living environment
- take care to protect ecosystems and conserve resources
- ensure the environmental soundness of products
- protect the health and safety of employees and citizens.

2 Corporate organization

Companies shall establish an internal system to handle environmental issues by appointing an executive and creating an organization in charge of environmental problems.

Environmental regulations shall be established for company activities, and these shall be observed. Such internal regulations shall include goals for reducing the load on the environment. An internal inspection to determine how well the environmental regulations are being adhered to shall be carried out at least once a year.

3 Concern for the environment

All company activities, beginning with the siting of production facilities, shall be scientifically evaluated for their impact on the environment, and any necessary countermeasures shall be implemented.

Care shall be taken in the research, design, and development stages of making a product to lessen the possible burden on the environment at each level of its production, distribution, appropriate use, and disposal.

Companies shall strictly observe all national and local laws and regulations for protecting the environment and, where necessary, they shall set additional standards of their own.

When procuring materials, including materials for production, companies shall endeavour to purchase those that are superior from such viewpoints as conserving resources, preserving the environment, and enhancing recycling.

Companies shall employ technologies that allow efficient use of energy and preservation of the environment in their production and other activities. Companies shall endeavour to use resources efficiently and reduce waste products through recycling, and shall appropriately deal with pollutants and waste products.

4 Technological development

In order to help solve global environmental problems, companies shall endeavour to develop and supply innovative technologies, products, and services that allow conservation of energy and other resources together with preservation of the environment.

5 Technology transfers

Companies shall seek appropriate means for the domestic and overseas transfer of their technologies, know-how, and expertise for dealing with environmental problems and conserving energy and other resources.

In participating in official development assistance projects, companies shall carefully consider environmental and anti-pollution measures.

6 Emergency measures

If environmental problems ever occur as a result of an accident in the course of company activities or deficiency in a product, companies shall adequately explain the situation to all concerned parties and take appropriate measures, using their technologies and human and other resources to minimize the impact on the environment.

Even when a major disaster or environmental accident occurs outside of a company's responsibility, it shall still actively provide technological and other appropriate assistance.

7 Public relations and education

Companies shall actively publicize information and carry out educational activities concerning their measures for protecting the environment, maintaining ecosystems, and ensuring health and safety in their activities.

The employees shall be educated to understand the importance of daily close management to ensure the prevention of pollution and the conservation of energy and other resources.

Companies shall provide users with information on the appropriate use and disposal, including recycling of their products.

8 Community relations

As community members, companies shall actively participate in activities to preserve the community environment and support employees who engage in such activities on their own initiative.

Companies shall promote dialogue with people in all segments of society over operational issues and problems, seeking to achieve mutual understanding and strengthen cooperative relations.

9 Overseas operations

Companies developing operations overseas shall observe the 'Ten Points Environmental Guidelines for the Japanese Enterprises Operating Abroad' in the Keidanren's 'Basic Views of the Global Environmental Problems'. [*Author's note*: These guidelines follow next.]

10 Contribution to public policies

Companies shall work to provide information gained from their experience to administrative authorities, international organizations, and other bodies formulating environmental policies, as well as participate in dialogue with such bodies in order that more rational and effective policies can be formulated.

Companies shall draw on their experience to propose rational systems to administrative authorities and international organizations concerning the formulation of environmental policies and to offer sensible advice to consumers on lifestyles.

11 Response to global problems

Companies shall cooperate in scientific research on the causes and effects of such problems as global warming and they shall also cooperate in the economic analysis of possible countermeasures.

Companies shall actively work to implement effective and rational measures to conserve energy and other resources even when such environmental problems have not been fully elucidated by science.

Companies shall play an active role when the private sector's help is sought to implement international environmental measures, including work to solve the problems of poverty and overpopulation in developing countries.

'Ten Points Environmental Guidelines for the Japanese Enterprises Operating Abroad'

The following guidelines were issued in 1991 by the Keidanren—the Confederation of Japanese Business—to assist Japanese organizations operating abroad.

1 Establish a constructive attitude towards protecting the environment and try to raise complete awareness of the issues among those concerned.

2 Make protecting the environment a priority at overseas sites and, as a minimum requirement, abide by the environmental standards of the host country. Apply Japanese standards concerning the management of harmful substances.

3 Conduct a full environmental assessment before starting overseas business operations. After the start of activities, try to collect data, and, if necessary, conduct an assessment.

4 Confer fully with the parties concerned at the operational site and cooperate with them in the transfer and local application of environment-related Japanese technologies and know-how.

5 Establish an environmental management system, including the appointment of staff responsible for environmental control. Also, try to improve qualifications for the necessary personnel.

6 Provide the local community with information on environmental measures on a regular basis.

7 Be sure that when environment-related issues arise, efforts are made to prevent them from developing into social and

cultural frictions. Deal with them through scientific and rational discussions.

8 Cooperate in the promotion of the host country's scientific and rational environmental measures.

9 Actively publicize, both at home and abroad, the activities of overseas businesses that reflect our activities on the environmental consideration

10 Ensure that the home offices of the corporation operating overseas understand the importance of the measures for dealing with environmental issues as they effect their overseas affiliates. The head offices must try to establish a support system that can, for instance, send specialists abroad whenever the need arises.

CODES OF GOOD PRACTICE – NUMBER 7

The United Nations Centre on Transnational Corporations: 'Criteria for Sustainable Development Management'

First Corporate Steps

1 Establish and publish a transnational corporate sustainable development policy statement emphasizing sustainable growth, protecting the environment, resource use, worker safety, and accident prevention. Translate the policy statement into all the working languages of affiliate enterprises.

2 Review strategic planning, resource acquisition plans, and operating procedures so as to align them with the sustainable development policy. Announce significant efforts to reduce the use of natural resources and minimize the generation of wastes.

3 Review and modify corporate structure, lines of responsibility, and internal reporting mechanisms to reflect the sustainable development policy. Encourage overseas affiliates to modify procedures in order to reflect local ecological and social realities.

4 Educate staff on the ways in which sustainable development affects their firm and how they can utilize these criteria in their specific tasks. Reward employees who discover and

report environmental problems or who recommend new, environmentally sound products and processes.

5 Prepare sustainable development assessments for all major upcoming investment and operating decisions. Distribute them to affiliate offices as models for their own sustainable development assessments.

6 Perform an environmental audit of ongoing activities, particularly those in developing countries, to verify that the criteria have been adequately considered. Establish a comparative scale for identifying affiliates with strong and weak environmental track records.

7 Report publicly on the enterprise's most hazardous products, processes, and toxic emissions. Distribute widely information on the methods in place to reduce these potential hazards and to cope with unanticipated emergencies.

8 Institute research and development work on the reduction and/or elimination of industrial products and processes that generate greenhouse gases. Arrange for environmentally safer technologies to be available to affiliates in developing countries without extra internal charges.

9 Inform joint venture partners and subcontractors about the corporate sustainable development policy. Establish ground rules for discontinuing business relationships with associate firms that operate with a disregard for basic health and environmental concerns.

10 Disseminate these criteria to other firms in relevant trade associations, local areas, or affiliate companies. Share the experiences with these criteria with local governments, national authorities, and the United Nations.

POLICY EXTRACTS—External relations issues

Philips, Netherlands

'Philips will strive to inform the customer in such a way that he will be able to take the respective environmental consequences into account in his decision to buy, provided an assessment of the total environmental impact of its products has been made.'

Rohm & Haas Company Europe

'We will communicate, listen, and be responsive to our employees, customers, neighbours and governments, and we will share information concerning potential hazards resulting from our operations or our products.'

American Express, USA

The Environmental Protection Committee's objectives.

'Communicate environmental policies to employees, clients, and customers, through:

- periodic reports in employee publications
- interviews with senior executives on environmental programmes
- dialogue with consumer groups on issues of concern
- information and mailing for customers.'

ICI, UK

ICI's environmental policy.

'Provide information to enable ICI's processes, when used under licence, to be operated with acceptable environmental impacts.'

Checklists for facilities issues

```
┌─────────────┐
│  Facilities │
│    issues   │
└─────────────┘
   │
   ├─ 16
   │  Landscaping
   │
   ├─ 17
   │  Buildings
   │
   └─ 18
      Vehicles, fleets
```

FIGURE 8.1 FACILITIES ISSUES IN THE WINTER MODEL

In this chapter we will be examining the environmental issues concerning the land, buildings, and certain of the facilities used in business. As machinery and equipment have already been considered in Chapter 6 in Checklist 9, Production technology, however, these aspects will not be covered here in order to avoid repetition.

CHECKLIST 16: LANDSCAPING

In the industrialized nations, more and more of the ground is being covered by buildings and paved surfaces. In Germany, for example, 10 per cent of the total ground surface is already covered in this way. This obviously has detrimental effects on ground and surface water, air, the climate, flora and fauna and on the self-regulatory processes in the environment. It also affects the health of human beings.

Urgent consideration should be given to ideas about how the land is used and the need to minimize any resulting environmental problems.

A company's site, with its buildings and free spaces, is a showcase for its image and attitudes. Sound ecological landscaping is an opportunity for a company to demonstrate its awareness of the ecology to the outside world.

It is true that employees and visitors traditionally expect the site to look neat and tidy. Fashions in landscape design are often not environmentally friendly. Thankfully, however, there are clear signs that ideas are changing.

Natural surfaces are more attractive than close-cropped lawns and asphalted courtyards, and they are often a lot cheaper to maintain.

Ecology is a complicated science and to be able to protect nature requires expert knowledge. Therefore, seek advice from experts before implementing any of the ideas given in this checklist as they may not be right for your particular location.

Protect the soil and groundwater

1 Minimize paving. Give the soil a chance to breathe. Make sure that there is as much vegetation as possible on the site. Let the rainwater seep away on the site, feeding the groundwater. Therefore:

- use as little paving as possible
- choose the 'mildest' form of soil compaction possible, such as gravel beds, lattice bricks or pebbles (natural stones) rather than slabs with sealed joints. Avoid asphalt and concrete
- check whether areas that have already been paved over, can be restored to a more natural surface.

2 Protect topsoil against erosion:

- protect flower beds, shrub beds, and the soil area around tree roots by covering them with organic mulches, such as bark, straw, or grass clippings
- areas out of public view can be left in a wild state, where local wild plant species can grow.

3 Avoid mineral fertilizers. Fertilizer salts are damaging to the soil and their production is harmful to the environment. Instead:

- use compost or commercially available organic products as fertilizers
- do not use peat, which should be left in its native wetlands to assist nature conservation.

4 Do not discharge rainwater into the sewage system:

- create a seepage pond
- discharge rainwater into a seepage well
- collect rainwater and use it for household purposes.

Promote lavish plant life

Vegetation produces oxygen, it cools and humidifies the air, gives shade, binds dust, and provides habitats for wildlife.

5 Plenty of greenery and plant life provides employees with a healthy and pleasant working environment.

6 Plant dense groups of bushes and free-growing hedges, select trees that have vigorous growth, and let grass grow long.

7 Train climbing plants up walls, fences, pergolas, car ports, and façades. If plants are chosen wisely, and the brickwork is intact, this greenery will protect the walls.

8 Plant grass on rooves. Many flat or shallow-angled roofs are suitable for growing grass. This is easy and inexpensive, and a grass roof can help to insulate the building and save heating costs. It can also ease the pressure on sewers as it absorbs some of the rainwater that would otherwise run off the surface. If the strength of the structure does not permit a covering of grass growing on a 15-cm deep layer of soil, it is worth considering growing grass on a 5-cm deep layer of soil, which may also still be a good base on which to grow rare and attractive plants. Properly qualified roof contractors and landscape architects should be employed to organize this work.

Choose appropriate plants

9 Consider soil quality, sunshine, and other microclimatic factors when selecting plant species. Healthier plants need less care and possibly do not need to be treated with pesticides.

10 Give preference to native shrubs and trees. Local wildlife has adapted to local vegetation gradually, during the very slow process of evolution, so plants from other areas or countries tend to support only a small proportion of the local wildlife.

11 Highly sophisticated and exotic ornamental shrubs should be replaced with hardier species. Tried and tested hardy shrubs of the kind found in country or monastic gardens are attractive to a great many insects and are no less beautiful than modern plant varieties. This also applies to roses.

Give wildlife a chance

12 Create a habitat for birds. Mount nesting boxes/ledges and shelters on buildings and trees and, if possible, provide access to attics or partitioned-off parts of attics and sheds. Whether the company site is located in a natural setting on the edge of a small town, an industrial estate close to a woodland or a garden suburb of a large city, provide habitats for various types of wildlife, such as kestrels, owls, swifts, swallows and house martins, redstarts, spotted and pied flycatchers, bats, and insects. Consult bird protection experts when selecting and mounting nesting boxes and ledges.

13 Avoid setting unintentional traps for wildlife:

- fit wire netting over vertical ventilator shafts, water butts, drainpipes, and basement shafts to keep wildlife out (these structures are often traps for amphibians, birds, and small mammals and, if they fall in, they are likely to die of hunger or thirst)
- fill spaces between insulating panels and outer walls with sand or gravel
- mark windowpanes with visual warnings, to prevent birds crashing into them
- before burning old woodpiles, move the timber around as there may be nests or young animals inside.

14 Convert any unused lawned areas into wildflower lawns (the choice of plants—lean, dry, or wet type of meadow—will depend on the nature of the land).

15 Create a natural pond habitat. A natural-style pond can become a habitat for aquatic plants, salamanders, frogs, toads, and dragonflies. It is best not to put fish in the pond as then there tend to be problems with algae build-up and turbid water, and they silt up very quickly. If there is no room for a pond, provide a bird bath and, perhaps, a mud puddle where swallows can find nesting material. If a bird bath is placed at ground level, ensure that there is clear visibility for several metres in every direction so that the birds will be able to see predators in time.

16 Create small natural refuges (heaps of stones or twigs, dead tree trunks) on south-facing sunny slopes on sandy/loamy soil.

Do not make things too tidy

17 Allow shrubs that have finished flowering to remain untouched in autumn and winter. Their hollow stems and the remains of leaves and flowers provide winter quarters for insects. They also provide natural winter food for birds.

18 Leave fallen fruit on the ground for a time. Fermenting fruit is a good source of food for certain types of wildlife, such as hedgehogs and butterflies.

19 Rake autumn leaves together into heaps under bushes and pile up twigs cut from bushes, trees, and shrubs. These provide a habitat for a host of tiny creatures.

Use natural materials

20 If the site is large enough, separate off a compost area for the organic waste collected on the site or in the cafeteria, instead of disposing of this waste in the usual way. If the compost heap is properly made, it will not create odours or attract vermin.

21 Make sure that the outside furniture fits in with the surroundings. If possible, choose natural materials, such as wood or stone. Protect these with environmentally acceptable products.

22 Consider using furniture made from recycled materials.

CHECKLIST 17: BUILDINGS

One major investment most companies make is the acquisition of buildings. Regardless of its size, every structure impinges on nature in the broadest sense. A building also has to meet the requirements dictated by the use to which it is to be put. It should, at the same time, present the firm's image and status positively and help boost employees' morale. Firms should thus consider both the economic and environmental aspects when planning new buildings.

The following checklist shows that the economic aspects are not incompatible with the environmental ones.

Those points with asterisks by them are measures that help protect the environment and can easily be introduced quickly to prevent or reduce costs.

Planning a new building

1 Consult a specialist (an architect specializing in environmentally benign buildings) from the outset.

2 Check the proposed site for negative features and use only suitable sites. For example:

■ establish whether or not there is already any pollution (of the water, soil, air, climate) by inspecting the site and consulting whatever environmental data is provided by authorities or health departments and have experts take measurements

■ have sites surveyed for any geopathogenic zones (fault zones) by a qualified geobiologist (diviner) or radiesthelist.

Use environmentally aware building concepts

3 Plan the building so that it harmonizes with the landscape and with existing local building styles.

4 When deciding on the form, position of the building, and arrangement of rooms, take account of the topography, climatic conditions, and direction in which it will face. Try to make passive use of solar energy, for example, in the Northern hemisphere putting windows in south-facing walls and having closed façades for north-facing ones.

5 Consider the results of the geobiological survey when planning the layout of the building:

■ do not position workplaces above hidden fault zones

■ position roads, storage areas, toilets, and so on above fault zones instead.

6 Plan internal organization and working procedures so that:

■ one workplace does not adversely affect another (for example noise, dust, fumes being produced near the cafeteria)

■ a waste disposal and recycling policy is practicable.

7 Incorporate variety into the design of façades.

8 Provide for green areas within the buildings.

9 Train climbing plants up façades and plant 'green' roofs to replace any vegetation which has to be destroyed.

Use building materials that produce the minimum pollution

10 Observe the following points regarding pollution and health hazards when selecting building materials. Avoid materials that are hazardous:

■ during their production, such as those that waste resources, consume high levels of energy, cause toxic emissions or byproducts

■ during use, for example paints that expose workers to solvent vapours

■ in the subsequent use of the buildings, such as respiratory diseases caused by formaldehyde fumes from certain building materials

■ to remove, the most notable example of this kind of hazard being the asbestosis caused by asbestos fibres being breathed in and air pollution caused by burning plastics.

11 Where possible, use attractive, natural materials, such as wood, clay, bricks, and natural stone.

12 If the use of less ecologically sound materials is unavoidable, use them only for specific purposes. For example, use steel and reinforced concrete only for load-bearing walls, and not for all walls.

13 Ensure optimum heat insulation in all cases.

Use ecologically sound fittings and installations

14 Formulate alternative plans for all major installations, taking into account local factors and using cost–benefit and environmental impact assessment methods.

15 Regarding lighting, give priority to health aspects (see Checklist 21, Working conditions):

- *■ ensure that all workplaces have daylight
- ■ use glass windows, which let ultraviolet rays through
- ■ ensure that natural lighting is available for corridors and stairways
- *■ if additional lighting is needed in the workplace, use artificial light that match the spectrum of natural daylight.

16 Avoid electrical installations that create hazards:

- ■ restrict electrical installations to the minimum necessary
- ■ use star, rather than ring, circuits
- ■ use sheathed cables.

17 Plan heating, air-conditioning, and ventilation systems to save energy and protect employees' health (see also Checklist 10, Energy and water)

- ■ ensure that all windows at workplaces can be opened
- *■ restrict air-conditioning to the strict minimum
- *■ use low-temperature heating systems only
- ■ give preference to radiant heat (such as hot air in underfloor cavity blocks) rather than fan heaters
- *■ exploit all heat recovery and heat-power combination possibilities.

18 Plan plumbing installations to economize on drinking water (see also Checklist 10, Energy and water):

- ■ avoid using drinking water (ground water) for production—use river water, sea water, rainwater, or treated waste water instead
- ■ reduce drinking water consumption by using 'grey' water (for example, the waste water from showers to flush toilets)

- separate rainwater and dirty water
- use rainwater for washing and cleaning
- use rainwater to water gardens and grounds
- channel rainwater through a pond
- separate and reprocess industrial sewage water
- *equip toilet cisterns, showers, washbasins, and so on with water-saving devices.

19 Give priority to reducing the volume of waste (see also Checklist 11, Waste management):

- introduce a sensible and practical system that separates collections of different types of waste at source
- eliminate hazards caused by special-category wastes
- send waste to processors for raw materials to be recovered
- compost and make use of organic wastes.

Create natural surroundings for buildings

20 The surroundings of buildings are often as important to the environment as the buildings themselves, so:

- *store excavated topsoil carefully and use it for landscaping later
- keep surfaced areas (roads, parking spaces, yards) to the minimum necessary
- do not seal surfaces by using concrete, asphalt or similar, but use interlocking set paving or compacted gravel instead
- use indigenous plants, which will be best suited to the site
- reduce heat requirement for buildings by planting hedges and trees as windbreaks
- avoid excessive heat exposure to the heat of the sun by planting deciduous trees to the south of the building
- use large pieces of surrounding land to create habitats for local wildlife
- do not use chemical substances to kill plant pests.

CHECKLIST 18: VEHICLES, FLEETS

Company vehicles should provide safe and reliable means of transport for its personnel and products.

In most developed countries, more pollutants enter the air from vehicle exhaust pipes than from smokestacks. The effects on human health and the environment are well known. These include lung diseases, damage to the respiratory organs, blood, and circulatory disorders. Forests also suffer from vehicle pollution.

Reducing fuel consumption, exhaust fumes, and noise caused by vehicles, would considerably benefit human beings and the environment.

The following measures will help reduce pollution. They are considered in relation to four issues, buying new vehicles, maintenance of the current fleet of vehicles, driving habits, and the planning of journeys.

Those points with asterisks by them are measures that help protect the environment and can usually be introduced quickly to prevent or reduce costs.

Buy low-pollution vehicles

1 Buy vehicles with efficient three-way catalytic converters. Numerous tests have shown that cars with catalytic converters generate some 90 per cent less noxious emissions like carbon monoxide, hydrocarbons, and nitrogen oxides. Until soot filters are available, diesel vehicles cannot be recommended as an alternative to cars equipped with catalytic converters. Although diesel vehicles consume less fuel, they do emit carcinogenic hydrocarbon compounds. Whether these compounds alone do actually cause cancer is still a matter for discussion, but preventive measures to protect the environment should err on the safe side. The fact remains, however, that a diesel car is still preferable to a petrol car without a catalytic converter.

2 Make exhaust and noise emission levels part of the company's purchasing criteria:

   ■ compare exhaust levels as there may be considerable differences between vehicles
   ■ obtain recommendations and guidance from the Department of Transport.

*3 Do not specify metallic paintwork. Aromatic hydrocarbons released during spraying make metallic paints a health hazard and pollute the air with solvent vapours.

*4 During long journeys, use the fifth gear whenever possible.

5 Fit vehicles with low-noise and long-lifetime exhaust systems. Systems are available that keep noise below specific limits and are usually guaranteed to be service-free for two years or 75 000 km.

*6 Use approved-quality remoulded tyres.

Maintaining vehicles to protect the environment

*7 Fit petrol vehicles with transistorized ignition systems. Conventional contact-breakers wear quickly, reduce the performance of the engine, and increase petrol consumption.

8 Use brake and clutch linings that do not contain asbestos.

*9 Fit a device that cuts off fuel supply when the driver takes their foot off the accelerator pedal. This can save up to 20 per cent in fuel consumption.

*10 Similarly a device that cuts off the fuel supply while waiting at traffic lights, will reduce fuel consumption and also reduce air pollution in a built up area.

*11 Have all vehicles serviced regularly.

*12 Check tyre pressures at regular intervals. A 0.5 bar difference from the prescribed figure can increase fuel consumption by 5 per cent.

*13 Change spark plugs in petrol vehicles regularly and, if possible, use broad-band plugs. Spark plugs play a major role in achieving maximum combustion of the fuel–air mixture.

14 Replace the air filter regularly. This can reduce fuel consumption by up to 10 per cent.

15 Ensure that the carburettor is properly adjusted. A badly adjusted carburettor can increase fuel consumption by up to 20 per cent, with a corresponding increase in exhaust fumes.

16 Wash car engines only at garages or filling stations where the run off is collected and not allowed to pollute soil or fresh water.17 Dispose of used oil properly.

*18 Use unleaded petrol if the car's engines are adapted for this.

Adopt and encourage environmentally aware driving

*19 Do not drive aggressively or at high revs. Driving at high speed consumes 25 per cent more fuel than a restrained driving style and produces twice as much carbon monoxide. The engine noise produced is also greater.

*20 Drive smoothly and anticipate events. Tests have shown that a driver in a hurry consumes 40 per cent more fuel (and money) over a 28-km stretch of urban road with 32 sets of traffic lights and saves a mere 7 minutes.

*21 Drive at a constant speed, even on motorways. On a test journey, a fast driver needed 175 litres of fuel for 1550 km, while a slower driver consumed only 125 litres, a saving of 50 litres of fuel and 12.5 kg carbon monoxide emission. The time difference between the two journeys was $1\frac{1}{2}$ hours.

*22 Change gear as soon as possible and use the most economical gear. Use first gear for setting off only and change rapidly into higher gears.

*23 Switch off the engine at traffic lights, level crossings, and so on where waiting time is longer than 30 seconds.

*24 Drive with foresight to make optimum use of synchronized traffic lights.

*25 Do not warm up a cold engine by letting it tick over; set off immediately. The engine actually warms up more quickly when the vehicle is being driven and the automatic choke is then switched off earlier.

26 Do not fill the petrol tank up to the brim.

*27 Use a manual choke carefully. When the outside temperature is 20° C, do not use the choke. At 0° C, push the choke half-way in after 30 seconds, and completely in after 2–3 minutes. When the choke is out, twice as many hydrocarbons and nine times as much carbon dioxide is produced.

28 Switch off fans in traffic jams. When the fan is switched on, up to 25 per cent more carbon monoxide and up to 36 per cent more hydrocarbons find their way into vehicles.

Environmental journey planning

*29 Avoid short journeys. Short journeys consume large amounts of fuel. When the engine is cold, fuel consumption straight after setting off is around 40 litres per 100 km, after 1 km it is still around 20 litres per 100 km, and normal consumption is reached only after travelling 4 km.

*30 Use public transport for shopping expeditions into cities; use 'park and ride' facilities. One motoring association has calculated that on Saturdays during shopping hours, 75 per cent of vehicles driving through city centres are looking for a parking space.

*31 Offer staff training in environmentally aware and economical driving, particularly in companies running lorries or large numbers of cars and vans.

*32 Organize a competition, with prizes for the most economical drivers in the company.

*33 Remove roof-racks when they are not required. The additional fuel consumption of a family saloon travelling at a constant 130 km per hour is over 12 per cent with an empty roof-rack, up to 20 per cent with a loaded roof-rack and covering sheet, and up to 25 per cent with a loaded roof-rack without a covering sheet.

*34 Encourage car-pooling. If 4 people share a car for a daily journey, up to 70 per cent of travelling costs can be saved, in addition to substantially reducing pollution by reducing the number of cars on the road.

EXAMPLES OF GOOD PRACTICE—Facilities issues

The facilities and equipment a company uses are the most visible indication of the concern it has for the environment. These impact staff and neighbours. Many companies have introduced 'greener' factories and offices, making them pleasant places to work and be beside. Efficient transport logistics, as well as use of different modes of transport, help reduce costs and pollution. The examples given here are intended to stimulate ideas.

Landscape and buildings

The packaging manufacturer **Bischof & Klein GmbH & Co.** has developed a biotope in a pond originally designed to provide water in case of fire. To prevent frogs from hopping on to the road running past the pond, a special barrier was erected.

Tarmac Quarrying Products Limited, a UK constructions materials company, restored a worked-out stone quarry in an environmentally responsible way. The landowner and local authority, previously against further work, were so impressed with the restoration and landscaping, that they are now receptive to further quarrying.

In planning a new sales and marketing building and cafeteria, **Hewlett-Packard Gmbh** considered it important that the buildings should blend well with their natural surroundings. In the grounds, native trees were planted to form a habitat for indigenous birds and insects. Parking areas had to blend harmoniously with the countryside and trees were planted to provide shade. The roof of the cafeteria was also given a planted covering.

Manchester Airport has grown rapidly in recent years. The airport company was committed to protecting the surrounding communities and environment from the adverse effect of this growth. Self-imposed restrictions on night flying and fines on noisy jets have been introduced. Landscaping, perimeter structure planting, and nature conservation initiatives have meant that the airport has developed with a minimum of local resistance.

Unternehmensgruppe Rudolf Bohnacker chose a new factory site very close to a railway station so that goods could be directly transported by rail, reducing pollution from the exhaust of lorries. For example, deliveries to and from the factory by rail of 120 000 tonnes of goods saves 20 000 lorry journeys.

The Baxi Partnership, a UK maker of domestic boilers, built and now operates a metal foundry in a residential area near Preston. The company countered local opposition by consulting the community at all stages of its construction. It made every effort to reduce the foundry's impact on the community, and continues to do so. Baxi runs an efficient operation, using clean technology, and the community also benefits economically as it now has a prosperous local employer.

IBM Deutschland has a section entitled 'Ecology in Construction and Use of Buildings' in the firm's own real estate handbook. It covers topics such as sound and heat insulation, use of recycled materials, wood preservatives, roof gardens, as well as water management and waste disposal. Staff working in construction and extension work, and employees involved in the use and maintenance of buildings, all have to work within these guidelines. Any exceptions require permission from both the company's management and the construction department.

In the construction of a new bottling plant, **Staatl, Mineralbrunen GmbH Bad Bruckenau** placed great importance on instituting measures to prevent the ground being polluted by harmful substances used or resulting from its production processes. The ground is sealed with several layers of foil, clay, and concrete. In addition, rainwater is collected at the entrance to the plant and an oil separator is used to remove any dirt originating from lorries and fork-lift trucks. The bottling plant's cleaning solution is run as a closed circuit and, to save water, is purified after every cycle and reused. Ultraviolet rays are used instead of disinfectant to sterilize the fresh water required for rinsing the bottles.

Ecological aspects, particularly in relation to noise, were also taken into consideration in the construction of its filling plant. Preference was given to materials such as cork, wood, sandstone, and linoleum. Laminates, paints, and glues used are solvent-free, and there is no plastic in the wallpaper, which is made from recycled material. Light is provided by large windows and energy-saving lamps. A balanced indoor climate is achieved by having plants inside, on external walls, and on the roof. These help regulate the moisture, oxygen content, and temperature of the buildings.

Noise is minimized by measures to 'avoid, contain, and absorb'. Vibration and impact sounds are dampened by shock absorbers, and machine noise is reduced by the clear plastic covers over them. Special wall and ceiling fitments absorb other sound waves. Thus, only muted production noise is heard outside the bottling plant.

Time/System GmbH took ecologically and biologically orientated construction factors into consideration when building its new administration office. A considerable reduction in the amount of heating energy required was achieved by reducing the external wall surface, using insulating material, ensuring that windows faced south, and exploiting a warehouse on the north side as a climate buffer zone.

Heat generated by a low-temperature gas boiler achieved a high calorie value and this was distributed via panel heater units. The energy-saving design of the building has produced a 30 per cent saving on the average heating requirements of a building this size. The heat-exchange unit brought the requirement down by a further 17 per cent. Even a rainwater installation brought savings as less drinking water was required.

St Thomas's Hospital, London, has reduced its annual energy bill by £70 000 by installing a building energy management system. The system monitors electricity, gas, and oil usage, water consumption, lighting, and room temperatures, and provides information about outside weather conditions.

Vehicles and transport

A Swiss company **Abroll-Container-Service AG**, demonstrates how efficient and environmentally beneficial cargo transport by rail can be. The innovative container service saves over 2000 truck journeys annually.

Oxford City Council has issued bicycles for staff to use on official business in the city.

As with many other companies **Edding AG** has tested the possibility of introducing solar-powered vehicles in the company's own vehicle fleet. The electric car has shown its worth, particularly over short distances, where it gives good service.

Albright & Wilson, a UK chemicals company, has persuaded customers to take chemicals in bulk tanker loads instead of non-returnable drums, which created disposal problems. The company has also reduced the number of tanker movements by about a quarter, by increasing the size of tank trailers from 18 to 23 tonnes.

Up to 1000 heavy trucks pass through the south gate of the Frankfurt-Höchst factory of **Hoechst AG**. Every truck passing through the gates with a dangerous load is subjected to a series of checks carried out by specially trained staff. The checks also enhance drivers' safety awareness and this has led to a clear reduction of the risks associated with transporting dangerous goods by road.

Tesco in the UK has redesigned certain of their distribution vehicles. Moveable, insulated partitions now divide the vehicles into one, two, or three separate compartments, depending on the composition of the load. These compartments can then be set at different controlled temperatures. The result is that where five vehicles were previously needed to supply one Tesco store with all its product lines, now only one is needed.

British Telecom the UK telephone company, runs a fleet of 52 000 petrol-driven commercial vehicles. Following the completion of a conversion programme, all these vehicles will run on unleaded fuel. The programme cost over £3 million, but this will be paid back in 18 months as unleaded petrol is cheaper than leaded petrol.

POLICY EXTRACTS—Facilities issues

ICI UK

'To require all its new plants to be built to standards that will meet the regulations it can reasonably anticipate in the most environmentally demanding country in which it operates that process. This will normally require the use of the best environmental practice within the industry.'

IBM, USA

'Provide a safe and healthful workplace, including avoiding or correcting hazards and ensuring that personnel are properly trained and have appropriate safety and emergency equipment.'

ACRO Chemical Company, USA

'ACRO Chemical Company will manage worldwide businesses and facilities to protect the environment and the health and safety of employees, customers, contractors, and the public.

Build, operate, and maintain worldwide facilities in a manner that uniformly protects the environment, and the health and safety of our employees and the public.'

THORN EMI, UK

'Thorn EMI companies will promote the sensitive siting and design of new facilities, taking into account the efficient use of energy and materials and recognizing the importance of conserving scarce and non-renewable resources.'

Checklists for staff issues

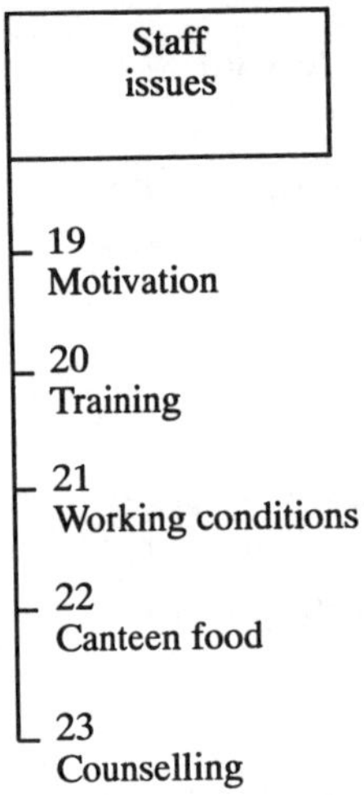

```
┌─────────────┐
│    Staff    │
│    issues   │
└─────────────┘
   │
   ├─ 19
   │  Motivation
   │
   ├─ 20
   │  Training
   │
   ├─ 21
   │  Working conditions
   │
   ├─ 22
   │  Canteen food
   │
   └─ 23
      Counselling
```

FIGURE 9.1   STAFF ISSUES IN THE WINTER MODEL

If a company is to adopt an environmentally aware approach to its activities, the employees are the key to its success or failure. If the employees are not persuaded of its benefits, the project will fail no matter how well it has been otherwise prepared. If they are convinced of the value of environmental management, the project can virtually run itself.

Staff will also become more enthusiastic if, in their daily, routine work, they appear to be safeguarding the environment. No one can put their heart and soul into their work, unless they are sure that they are not destroying their surroundings.

Staff motivation and training (see Checklists 19 and 20 in this chapter) must also reflect the truth that, in the long term, a company can perform to high standards in its efforts to protect the environment only by maintaining consistently high standards of work in its traditional activities. This is because the achievements in this area provide the personnel and equipment to effect its environmental plans and performance.

Concern for environmental standards must, in practice, always progress in step with an increasing awareness of standards of workmanship in the conventional sense, that is an inner commitment to work and ensuring that products are of a high quality.

In addition, environmental management is easier if the management style is cooperative. To impose environmentally aware ideas from above without directly involving the workforce, will not only be ineffective, but nullify the human dimension of the concept from the outset. Where it is proposed to introduce enlightened modes of thought and behaviour, this must always be done in a sensitive manner, showing consideration towards the people concerned.

These objectives might seem impossibly high given the limited time available to give to staff motivation and training in the daily struggle for survival in a competitive world, and, indeed there is a great deal that will not be achieved until environmental problems and public concern have become even more urgent, but failure to set ambitious targets often means that realistic objectives are not achieved either.

Checklists 21 to 23 are concerned with the welfare of staff, both at work and at home. Checklist 21 addresses physical working conditions, Checklist 22 addresses canteen catering and Checklist 23 environmental issues beyond the workplace.

CHECKLIST 19: MOTIVATION

This checklist and Checklist 20, Training, need to be read together as the activities of the two areas often merge.

Two stages are considered:

- developing the concepts—deciding what we want to achieve
- implementation—deciding how we want to achieve it.

In the first, we will look at such issues as:

- how to develop motivation to become environmentally aware, that is who needs to be motivated and trained
- how this can be achieved and whose role it is to effect it.

In the second we will look at specific ways in which to achieve this end, including the means of:

■ information
■ meetings and other gatherings
■ direct involvement
■ introducing incentive schemes
■ recognizing achievements
■ eliminating demotivating elements.

Developing the motivation concepts

1 Decide who is to be motivated and trained:

■ current employees:
  - Senior management (for example, Board of Directors, senior executives, management team)
  - middle management (for example, managers of departments and sections)
  - other white-collar and blue-collar workers and trainees.
■ employees of service companies who work regularly for the company such as painters, plumbers, fitters, and cleaning or waste disposal staff (it may be easier, however, to select service companies that already have a sound environmental approach—see Checklist 8, Materials management).
■ employees' families, by means of environmental counselling for households
■ former workers of the company, such as retired employees, by also providing home counselling.

2 Determine the objectives of the motivation activity. These could include imparting the willingness and ability:

■ to work energetically and creatively towards the attainment of the company's environmental goals
■ to act in an environmentally sound way at the workplace while still doing a fully satisfactory job in the conventional sense
■ to show a proper concern for the environment outside the workplace, at home and in leisure pursuits
■ to exercise one's responsibility for the environment and a quality-and environment-conscious economy as a citizen at local, regional or national level by taking part in elections and other citizens' initiatives
■ to defend an environmental viewpoint at work, at home, in sports clubs or other associations.

3 Clarify, whenever appropriate, the wider objectives of motivation and training. These might be to win over staff to the idea of being environmentally aware by directing motivation and training towards their:

■ feelings—strengthening their emotional attachment to nature
■ intellect—training them to perceive environmental interrelationships, for example, a dwindling bird population encourages insect infestation, hence the use of pesticides, hence the threat to groundwater reserves, each link in the causal chain giving rise to a further series of consequences and multiple interactions
■ sense of responsibility—that they will be demonstrating responsibility for their own health, for that of fellow human beings, plants, and animals, and future generations and their living environment
■ discernment—developing their ability to select, assess, and use information on environmental matters in order to make responsible and purposeful decisions
■ a desire for action—encouraging them to put decisions into practice for the benefit of human beings and the environment.

The ultimate objective, however, should be to develop all these aspects and harness their motivation to produce high-quality work and products while also caring for the environment.

4 Clarify the messages that are to be communicated. These might include such issues as:

■ the world as an interrelated ecological system, the natural basis of all life and, therefore, the precondition for its existence
■ the threat to the ecological equilibrium and, hence, to human beings as result of damage to water, soil, air, and fauna and flora
■ the scope for stopping or preventing damage to the environment by trade and industry, the energy sector, agriculture, and private households.

The points here that need to be thoroughly understood are:

■ how an integrated system of environmentally aware business management works
■ that damage to the environment can be reduced considerably if all businesses adopt such as system
■ that, in the long term, environmentally aware management can be practised and promoted only by companies that maintain their market competitiveness by offering high-quality products or services at appropriate prices

■ that there are many practical opportunities for individuals themselves to stop or prevent damage to the environment or to take other action to preserve the environment:

  – as an employee, by taking precision measurements of pollutants at the workplace and by properly calibrating machines and tools; high-quality work and products help to safeguard the competitive position of the company, and hence, its superior environmental standards

  – as a private person, by saving energy, water, and chemicals in the home

  – as a citizen, by, for example, cooperating with local special-category refuse collection schemes

  – as a propagandist, in word and deed in community associations, such as church groups, sports clubs, gardening clubs, at camp sites, and in touring parties.

5 Clarify the methods of motivation to be used.

■ The gradual, persuasive method. In practice, it has proved effective to proceed in the following ways:

  – arouse the curiosity and interest of the staff about environmental issues by, for example: posting a newspaper report on a local pollution scandal that directly affects the staff there on the company's noticeboard; displaying a catalytic converter together with a description of how it operates and what it does; exhibiting a water butt with the caption: 'This is the amount of water you waste in [period x] by not using water-saving devices in your WC's cistern'

  – gradually raising the level of knowledge about the environment within the company by setting up a special noticeboard entitled 'Environment News' and pinning up-to-date information on it about measures to protect the environment that can be employed inside and outside the company

  – take proactive measures to develop an environmental awareness so that the problems are recognized by the staff and they seek to make specific contributions to solving them, such as having a forester explain the forest die-back phenomenon to trainees on a field trip

  – providing practical encouragement and guidance for better environmental behaviour at work, at home, and during leisure pursuits, for example by providing, on the company's premises, facilities for collecting used batteries or financing environmental counsellors to visit employees' homes at the request of employees

■ Making the best use of the learning capacity of the employees. Using a teacher's 'rule-of-thumb' approach, select appropriate methods to make the desired impact. People remember about:
  – 10 per cent of what they read (say a column in the company's newspaper)
  – 20 per cent of what they hear (for example, from a cassette from the company's cassette library)
  – 30 per cent of what they see (say, of a demonstration of how to use biological paints given by the company's painters and decorators)
  – 50 per cent of what they hear *and* see (for example, of a lecture and demonstration at an ecology session for trainees)
  – 70 per cent of what they say themselves (such as workers' own descriptions of particular environmental problems at meetings of an environment committee)
  – 90 per cent of what they do themselves (such as, using powder in a washing machine economically after having been instructed by the home counsellor).
■ Appealing to the typical needs of staff. The needs most easily appealed to are:
  – the need for material earnings to meet the cost of living and satisfy a wide range of requirements (bonuses could be given to those attaining the company's environmental objectives or who suggest ecological improvements)
  – the need for safety (information could be provided on, for example, toxins present in certain foods or by stressing the importance of wearing any necessary protective clothing at work)
  – the need for a sense of belonging (educative activities, such as trainees' environmental seminars extending over several days, can foster the development of a team spirit)
  – the need for status (thanking employees, praising them, recognizing their efforts, giving them awards for exemplary conduct are all positive ways of boosting employees' self-esteem)
  – the need for self-realization (asking the staff to participate in formulating the company's environmental objectives is an excellent way to satisfy this need).

Implementation

6 Decide who is to be responsible for the motivation and training of staff. Depending on the objectives and arrangements, implementing the policies decided on for this area may be made the responsibility of:

- the person responsible for environmental matters at senior management level
- others who may be contracted or persuaded to undertake educational work, for example:
  - representatives from agencies responsible for enforcing the laws and obligations laid down regarding protecting the environment
  - scientists (say, environmentally concerned doctors, chemists, physicists, home economists and nutritional scientists, and ecologists)
- environmental counsellors for households and local authorities taking part in schemes introduced in a number of the EU's member states
- specially trained teachers from vocational training organizations or colleges
- representatives from consumer's associations
- representatives from waste disposal companies, manufacturers of environment-related products or from companies that set an example in pollution abatement technology
- craftsmen who exercise their trade in such a way as to minimize damage to the environment, for example, by returning to traditional methods, and who are able to give practical demonstrations
- inventors of technical solutions to environmental problems
- specialist journalists
- representatives from ecological citizens' initiatives or students' associations
- 'victims' who can report at first hand how their health or property has suffered as a result of damage to the environment
- public figures (with whom the workers may identify) who can speak about their own commitment to ecologically sound behaviour and, thus, set an example.

7 Disseminating environmental information. Activities which effectively spread information include:

- press articles dealing with environmental matters circulated or displayed on noticeboards
- informing employees, in good time, of forthcoming press, radio, or television reports on the company's activities aimed at protecting the environment
- having a regular environmental column in the company newspaper or a special issue on the environment or both
- a special issue on leisure activities, including ecological pastimes, with articles by employees on, for example, organic gardening, protection

of birds, bicycle tours, nature conservation, and encourage other employees to take up these activities

■ using the in-house newspaper to conduct competitions with prizes about some aspect of the environment, such as 'My best nature photograph', 'Trees and woodland—a drawing and painting competition for everyone', 'Young animals painted by our children'

■ awarding prizes connected with the environment, such as a one-week holiday in a scenic part of the country

■ publishing prize-winning entries in the newspaper (consider enlarging them to decorate walls at the plant, too)

■ if the company is part of an international group, involving the foreign branches in the competition, too; this not only introduces greater diversity of entries, but also helps to bring the members of the group closer together and spreads the idea of protecting the environment beyond national boundaries

■ displaying in-house and external environmental information on the official noticeboard

■ creating a special noticeboard for environmental information to highlight its importance in relation to the company and how it operates

■ distributing material from external sources dealing with the environment, such as material published by the Department of the Environment

■ setting up a company environment library (books, charts, environmental games), an audio library (cassettes, records) or video library (slides, video, and cine films) for staff use

■ installing an electronic noticeboard in the canteen with, for example, new tips each week for caring better for the environment (for example, 'Don't forget to use our paper recycling bank')

■ at Christmas, issue appropriate posters of birds, plants, and so on to be used as wall decorations

■ at regular works and information meetings for management, report briefly on successes and shortcomings in measures implemented to protect the environment at the plant or in offices.

8 Use all kinds of social occasions to spread the environmental message:

■ refer to the question of protecting the environment in annual reports and other official addresses or statements

■ hold an 'environmental quiz' in all departments, with such prizes as bird tables, seeds and bulbs, and unbleached items of clothing

■ organize attractively presented consumer counselling shows during works outings

- organize an 'environmental raffle' at works or office parties, with, perhaps, a bicycle as the main prize
- whenever the occasion presents itself, hold a raffle for books, cassettes, and videos covering environmental matters or for subscriptions to nature magazines
- organize a cycle ride or rally for staff to help them rediscover the health benefits of cycling
- organize an open day to inform staff's relatives or the wider public about the company's achievements in implementing measures to protect the environment
- at a party for employees' families, arrange for environmental counsellors or representatives of consumer organizations to demonstrate environmentally friendly children's toys and offer healthy confectionery instead of sugary confectionaries to show parents what alternative toys and foods are available
- before children's parties, open days, and similar functions, check whether it is possible to invite families living in the neighbourhood as well as employees and their families (this not only serves to spread the message that we need to protect the environment but also, and particularly in small communities, has a very beneficial effect on the company's public image)
- realize that social functions bringing together employees' and the neighbourhood's children under the environmental banner are less expensive and more effective than major public relations exercises, especially as an original idea may well attract reporters who will give the company free, positive publicity
- arrange for environmental counsellors to speak at senior citizens' functions as old people are generally very eager to act ecologically and they can help spread the message to others during their, usually, large amounts of free time.

9 Involve staff directly. The senior environmental manager in any organization should have the opportunity to involve others. Here are some ways in which this could be achieved:

- before the beginning of each financial year, all designated staff should prepare a list of realistic environmental objectives for their departments
- discuss these objectives with them and ensure that they are consistent with the firm's philosophy and aims, the department's other financial objectives, and quantified, for example:
- to reduce energy and water consumption by x per cent with no loss of

output and y per cent increase in recycled input materials as a proportion of total purchases

■ encourage staff to use the checklist approach to look for possible cost-cutting ecological measures and setting objectives, and do not forget to congratulate them if they are successful

■ ensure that the economic objectives are specified with the same degree of thoroughness as the ecological objectives, and that the employee is equally determined to attain both

■ agree on a binding final version of the list with the employees concerned and strengthen their conviction that they have, for the most part, set their *own* objectives

■ stress the importance of results and replace management monitoring with self-monitoring to encourage staff to develop more initiative and, thus, gain greater job satisfaction

■ hold an end-of-year check with each employee to see whether or not they have achieved the goals jointly set and accepted, and to account for any shortcomings.

10 Introduce incentive schemes. These can involve monetary or other rewards, such as bonuses for reaching agreed targets for cutting costs and making other savings. Regarding bonuses:

■ they create incentive for attaining or exceeding economic and ecological objectives

■ consider a scheme whereby the bonus for attaining economic objectives is reduced if the ecological objectives are not attained at the same time

■ ensure that the bonus formula does not allow below-target ecological performance to be offset by above-target economic performance, and vice versa.

Suggestions schemes can also create incentive:

■ introduce a company suggestions scheme, that gives workers a share of the savings made as a result of their proposal

■ lay down in the rules governing the scheme that a higher payment than usual will be made for suggestions that cut costs, and at the same time, save energy, water, or raw materials or help protect the environment in some other, specifically defined way

■ Install special 'suggestions for protecting the environment' boxes to encourage staff to make other suggestions of this type as they do not necessarily save money and so would not generally be rewarded under the company suggestions scheme

- acknowledge acceptable environmental suggestions with thanks, praise, mention in the staff newspaper or, where the suggestion is a particularly good one or someone has made several such suggestions, with a badge of honour
- make an automatic cash bonus award for any environmental suggestions that are found to reduce costs
- ensure that members of 'quality circles', in which employees make suggestions for improvements in a creative, competitive atmosphere without management constraint or departmental boundaries, address themselves to ways of improving the environment as well and, thus, demonstrate that environmental protection is an aspect of quality
- consider setting up special 'environmental circles' for particular problem areas
- make use of other creativity techniques, such as brainstorming, to find solutions to environmental problems
- select a social function—say, during the Christmas period—to recognize those employees who have distinguished themselves by coming up with good suggestions (for example, through the suggestions scheme or in the quality circles)
- consider inviting spouses to 'inventors' celebrations' event so as to give awardwinners the chance to gain status in the eyes of their spouses and, also, to win their support for the company's efforts to protect the environment.

Other kinds of incentive schemes:

- announce that employees' salaries and promotion prospects will depend not only on their economic performance but also on whether or not they attain their environmental objectives
- in all incentive schemes, take particular care to ensure that the criteria on which rewards are based are clearly defined and uniformly and equitably administered.

11 Recognize achievements.

- give praise, thanks, and recognition for environmental awareness to motivate all employees at all levels to continue their efforts to protect the environment
- ensure that exceptional performance in the area of caring for the environment is rewarded in the same way as achievements in the traditional fields of, say, sales and production
- recognize company employees who have distinguished themselves in

their efforts to protect the environment by putting their names forward for awards from outside organizations

■ through public relations, ensure that reports on the company's activities to protect the environment appear in the media as this gives staff a feeling of being successful and strengthens their bonds with each other and the company *vis-à-vis* the environment

■ supply the media with a selection of information so that they will use at least some of it and give coverage to advances in environmental technology, such as savings in energy and water consumption (many engineers and technicians feel that the media in general treat them as scapegoats, so they are likely to be motivated by positive media response)

■ include details of quality products and services in press releases dealing with the company's activities with regard to protecting the environment as the media may also publish some of these details and thereby provide publicity, at the same time giving credit to staff for their performance in their normal fields of activity.

12 Eliminate demotivating factors. Recognize that psychological preparation, moral support, and rewards for success are as important to the ecologically aware manager as a rope is to a mountain climber.

■ psychological preparation:
   – do not present employees with a *fait accompli* or proceed without consulting them, as this may come as too much of a shock and will be demotivating, but inform them in good time what has been decided and why
   – try to acknowledge and use their expertise, say by consulting them to find the quickest, most effective, and most economical way of implementing whatever has been decided.

■ Moral support:
   – provide moral support if a particular measure requires a change of habit (such as driving smoothly and avoiding short journeys to save petrol) or if habitually accepted standards are lowered (the recycled paper is not as white as the paper used before) or extra effort is required (the paper bank is 40 paces away)
   – be patient and persevere to ensure that new methods are not eroded by a return to old habits, such as throwing used batteries into wastepaper baskets.

■ Reward success:
   – be generous with thanks and praise for a measure to protect the environment that has been carried out well

- act on the principle that recognition given in the presence of others is not only twice as effective, but also motivates the others present to seek recognition by the same means.

Work on eliminating opposition to implementing measures to protect the environment:

- find out why environmental measures that have been agreed to are being postponed, 'forgotten', or blocked (opposition is rarely based on objective reasons, but stems mostly from errors in personal relations)
- if personal efforts and objective arguments fail, act on the principle that an acceptable compromise can be more useful than an order imposed from above, which demotivates employees and leaves them intractable.

13   Encourage staff involvement in environmental projects:

- adopt 'selfless' measures to protect the environment and make very clear within the company, and particularly to any works councils or staff representatives, that the company or the shareholders have contributed some of their earnings in the interests of the environment
- on the basis that the 'first step is the most difficult', encourage every member of staff to make a small voluntary contribution, such as by paying a penny a day into an environmental fund and announce that, at the end of the year, the company will pay into the fund an amount equal to the amount they have collected, and manage the fund jointly, that is by giving management and staff equal voting rights
- for example, decide jointly to support a farm for the purpose of supplying the company canteen or staff with organically grown foodstuffs
- if employees wish to undertake voluntary work to protect the environment that is connected with the company outside working hours—such as establishing a wetland habitat on company land, respond by providing money for the necessary materials, expertise, and catering
- with a particularly well-motivated workforce, consider holding a secret ballot to determine whether part of the company's budget earmarked for staff bonuses should be used for a popular environmental project that will be of immediate benefit to the employees, such as the purchase of a company sports and recreation centre that is environmentally sound in design and would then belong to the employees who became members

■ use environmental projects made possible by joint sacrifices on the part of shareholders and staff to show that, nationally also, progress in protecting the environment can best be achieved through material restraints made by all sections of the community

■ celebrate the success of joint projects to protect the environment with social functions, such as a garden party at the sports and recreation ground bought with bonuses, with a view to encouraging the staff to take part in future projects and other companies to undertake similar projects.

CHECKLIST 20: TRAINING

In this checklist, we will look at training activities for:

■ new staff and trainees (apprentices)
■ more experienced staff.

Training apprentices

This section is influenced by the existence in Germany, the home country of the author, of a comprehensive system of apprenticeship in industry and commerce. While this is less common elsewhere, training of junior staff still occurs, so the points made in this section are important whatever system operates in your company.

Training given to apprentices can be geared towards respect for the environment as trainees are particularly receptive to ecological ideas and transmitting this to the new generation of employees can influence the future course of industry for the better.

1 Establish and maintain a balance between economic and ecological effort by:

   ■ designing the training programme so that the trainees can identify with the company's economic and ecological objectives, exercise initiative and work hard in both fields

   ■ in their practical work, encouraging trainees to develop the same degree of application, thoroughness, self-discipline and quality awareness in conventional fields (such as measuring the tolerances of the items they are working on) as in the environmental field (such as measuring harmful substances)

   ■ in the classroom, convincing trainees that their responses to problems involving opposing aspects of economics and ecology should not be a negative 'either/or' but a positive 'one-and-the-other' (that is, rather than take the easy way out in one direction or the other, they should make special efforts to do justice to both aspects)

■ ensuring that this principle is seen to run like a thread through all lessons

■ using imagery to get the message across, for example, 'the economic and ecological ends of the bow both have to move equally if we are to hit the target'

■ eradicating the misconception that gearing the training of apprentices towards environmental issues makes it a soft option, leaving no one in any doubt that the complexity of the work actually makes it harder, but its usefulness makes it more rewarding.

2 Make environmental protection an integral part of the training pro-gramme. Here are some ideas:

■ organize visits or field trips under the following three main headings:
  – 'discovering and exploring nature'—visits to a forestry department, wildlife park, nature trail, bird sanctuary, or nature reserve.
  – 'discovering and experiencing environmental devastation'—an 'alternative' trip around a port, identifying the major polluters' outlet pipes, a visit to a special-category waste tip or a visit to an intensive feedlot unit.
  – 'discovering and testing possible solutions'—a visit to a model sewage treatment plant, a phosphate removal plant, a desulphuriza-tion plant or an organic farm; alternatively, collect mixed refuse and sort it, under the heading 'Camping refuse and how it can be avoided'.

■ undertake 'learning-by-doing' projects, such as conducting simple soil, water, and air analyses, helping with the planting and seeding of the works site under expert instruction, testing silencer equipment on their own motorbikes, mopeds, or cars

■ organize longer environmental seminars, which each trainee can attend perhaps once during their apprenticeship, where they are addressed by experts in different fields in order to ensure that a balanced picture is presented

■ at intervals, perhaps every eight weeks, have an 'environment Friday'

■ extend theory teaching at a vocational school by prevailing on the governors to devote more time in the syllabus to looking at environmentally sound behaviour in the workplace

■ incorporate environmental objectives into workshop teaching, for example, for lathe operators and toolmakers structuring the course to include, in the first year, basic concepts of the trade and environmentally sound usage of materials and consumables; in the second year, making equipment for in-house use and constructing small devices to protect the environment; in the third year transferring to the actual workplace and exploring what constitutes environmentally sound behaviour there

■ try to get the examination regulations adapted accordingly, so that for the above example of trainee lathe operators and toolmakers:

- try to ensure that the written examination taken at the vocational school includes questions beyond those about the different types of lathe, forms of gear and varieties of thread, measurement techniques, production tolerances, and so on to include such things as typical hazards to the environment posed by lubricants and so on
- try to ensure that the marking system for the practical examination takes into account any work relevant to the environment, in addition to appearance, dimensional accuracy, surface quality, and operational skills
- try to ensure that the subject of protecting the environment is covered in the oral examination before the Chamber of Commerce and Industry examination committee.
- make sure that teachers and examiners have received the necessary training in protecting the environment.

Training adults

1 Develop in-house and external training programmes to bring not only standards of workmanship, but also employees' knowledge of business ecology and skills in this area up to a level where they can cope with the latest technical and other requirements so that they can meet the highest economic objectives at all times.

2 Ensure that a balance is maintained between conventional and ecological teaching.

3 Prevent training in ecological matters from becoming a separate course that seems to have no obvious links with occupational training; make it an essential component of normal training courses:

■ do not isolate the ecological components of the usual courses, but instead bring out any ecological points as they become relevant with each normal learning step (for example, teach about the judicious use of oil and oil cans when these are being used, instead of merely showing a video film on tanker disasters as an adjunct to the practical work)

■ make all employees aware of the functional and ecological consequences of every work step and give them practical instruction and
training so as to optimize these aspects throughout the course (this
will ensure that all operational aspects are considered from an
environmental perspective as well from a quality perspective, leading
to them being fully integrated in the employees' work practice).

4 Take great care when training the training supervisors, such as the
master craftsmen, who often combine an innate honesty with a
craftsman's pride and whose sense of responsibility can be relied on.

5 Make full use of the services offered by existing institutions. For example:

■ employ environmental counsellors or representatives from consumer's organizations to give talks after working hours on subjects of
interest, such as environmentally sound household management and
nutrition

■ encourage employees to go on environmental courses at a university
or other establishment, the fees being paid by the company, if the
subject-matter can be applied in the company

■ encourage employees to take correspondence and distance learning
courses on business and the environment.

CHECKLIST 21: WORKING CONDITIONS

Staff can hardly be expected to be enthusiastic about the environment if
they themselves are required to work in unsatisfactory conditions or under
physical or mental stress. Such conditions can cause physical problems
when, for example, equipment or lighting is poorly designed, badly installed,
or maintained. They can also cause stress, when say, computer programs are
illogically designed or described.

Industrial and office regulations often cover many of the issues mentioned
in this checklist and these should, of course, be complied with.

The basic approach

■ Implement measures to avoid stress by changing working processes or
production conditions.

■ If this is not possible, isolate and contain stress-producing conditions.

■ Where change and isolation are not feasible, ensure that protective
measures are taken in the workplace to limit stress. Stress is defined in
the following sections.

Eight causes of stress are considered: noise, lighting, climate, dangerous materials, poor design, safety and computer programs.

Stress factor 1: noise and vibration

■ Reduce noise by carefully selecting suitable equipment and following the appropriate procedures for its use.
■ Reduce noise from subsidiary activities.
■ Shield off sources of major noise.
■ Demarcate noisy areas.
■ Provide and ensure that equipment to protect staff from noise is used.
■ Provide regular medical check-ups for staff exposed to noise.

Stress factor 2: lighting and colour

■ Match lighting intensity to the type of work being performed, paying attention to aspects such as distribution, avoiding dazzle, the colour of the light and its direction.
■ Use lighting the spectrum of which is close to that of normal daylight.
■ Use electronic devices or three phase switches to avoid flickering in fluorescent lights.
■ Employ indirect lighting at computer workstations to avoid reflections and, thus, eye strain.
■ Select colour schemes on the basis of:
    – features of the room (size, machines installed, windows, pillars, ceiling design, and various access points)
    – existing colours (of carpets, curtains, machines, products, or other materials)
    – division of work and rest areas
    – the number of people and the work they perform
    – the working time spent in the facility.

Colour can have a marked impact on the feel of the working environment. For example a light colour on the ceiling will make a low ceiling appear higher and a dark ceiling lower. Green gives the impression of reducing noise and gives maximum light in dim conditions.

Stress factor 3: room climate

■ Adjust the air temperature, humidity, air speed, and radiant heat to acceptable comfort levels.

■ Take action against any draughts. These are caused by differences in local air speeds and floors that are either too hot or too cold.

■ Avoid excessive differences in temperature between head and foot levels.

Stress factor 4: dangerous materials

■ Minimize the use of dangerous substances or materials by selecting suitable processes and materials and optimizing operating parameters.

■ Demarcate those areas where hazardous substances are emitted or used.

■ Measure hazardous substances produced and ensure that they are within the limits set down by appropriate regulations.

■ Take measures to eliminate or reduce the impact of emissions, such as those from building fabrics and waste materials.

■ Ensure that personal protective equipment is available and used where necessary.

■ Ensure that there is adequate ventilation and, thus, avoid the long-term effects of low levels of emissions of dangerous substances.

■ Give regular medical check-ups to people exposed to hazardous substances.

Stress factor 5: equipment and workplace design

■ Design workplace space, controls, and displays in human, not machine, terms. Pay special attention to ensuring that there is headroom, space for knees and feet, and to carry out the sequence of operations required, seating, as necessary, and that the field of vision is adequate to avoid forced and uncomfortable postures. As a general rule, static work, one-sided and excessive muscular exertion should be avoided.

■ Make sure that equipment and components operate reliably and are easy to use.

■ Ensure that emergency shut-off switches are clearly marked and easily accessible.

■ Ensure that computer screens (VDUs) have adequate luminance, do not flicker excessively, have a stable image, are free from reflections, that the angle can be adequately adjusted and have enough contrast.

Stress factor 6: safety

■ Ensure that all safety regulations are observed, including the wearing of personal protective equipment where this is necessary.

■ Install safety barriers so that staff do not enter danger areas around automatic machines (such as digital machine equipment and industrial robots) and that if stray objects are thrown out by the machine, they do not endanger people's safety.

■ Provide anti-dazzle equipment and splatter protection where required.
■ Ensure that emergency shut-off equipment can be operated quickly, easily and safely, and that it operates automatically to pre-set limits.
■ Demarcate and clearly mark access routes.
■ Ensure that safety signs (coloured symbols) are always clearly visible.
■ Take additional precautions when safety equipment is not yet installed during commissioning or removed during maintenance.

Stress factor 7: computer software programs

With almost all office and many industrial staff now operating computers, the quality and dependability of the software programs greatly affects the working patterns and the quality of time spent at the job. Confirm that the programs:

■ are suited to the tasks to be done (the user should not have to carry the burden of the idiosyncrasies of the system)
■ do not require the active involvement of the computer user to organize input data
■ ensure that the system is self-explanatory
■ match the level of input to the knowledge of the user
■ make error displays readily understood for correction purposes
■ provide training to familiarize staff with any new systems or procedures.

Other issues concerning working conditions

The quality of life at work can be enhanced in a positive way by improving the ways in which people are asked to perform. Thus:

■ match staff to the demands of the job
■ avoid monotony and a rigid working pace
■ organize the work in such a way that the staff have the freedom to carry out their tasks
■ avoid social isolation
■ organize things to include opportunities for teamwork, such as quality circles and training workshops.

CHECKLIST 22: CANTEEN FOOD

Despite scientists' and doctors' warnings, bad press and television publicity, people still eat:

■ too much, too quickly, and chew too little
■ too much animal and not enough vegetable fat
■ white bread, tinned food, sugar and salt, and not enough fresh vegetables, salads, potatoes, and pulses.

Illness can cause a great deal of suffering, for both the sick and their families. It lowers the quality of life and may cause other, sometimes serious problems. Working hours lost through illness seriously affect productivity and, of course, lead to higher costs in contributions to health insurance schemes and other related expenditures.

Many doctors consider that a change of eating habits is the fundamental therapy for a whole host of illnesses and, indeed, it is often sufficient in itself to relieve or cure many of them.

Millions of workers eat at work every day. The canteen and the food it serves offers a unique opportunity to serve healthy and tasty food. In can also be habit-forming, in that good dietary habits acquired at work may spill over into the home.

In purely business terms, a healthy worker should be a productive one, but a sick worker still has to be paid while absent from work. This is a point worth stressing when attempting to revise canteen menus to include more balanced and wholesome dishes.

Nutrition is an area riddled with preconceived ideas. It can only be influenced for the better by relying on specific and, as far as possible, objective and scientifically well-founded information. If you wish to eat healthily and enjoy your food at the same time, you need information on what your body requires, on essential nutrients and on what goes to make up your food.

Provide information

1 Inform staff about the effects of poor eating habits via information in bulletins, circulars or posters on noticeboards.
2 Use short questionnaires to find out what interest there would be in alternative menus.
3 All major changes in menu pattern should be preceded by information about the changes and the benefits of them.
4 Enlist the help of the personnel department, the works council, and the works doctor in organizing the information process.
5 Check the canteen food presently served.

   ■ If the food is not cooked on the premises, check with the supplier how much time elapses between its preparation and delivery (the longer

the time-lag between when the food is cooked and when it is eaten, the greater the loss of vitamins and minerals
■ The quality of the food:
  – check whether or not the menus provide sufficient quantities of mineral, vitamin, and trace elements
  – check on the percentages of carbohydrates, fats, and proteins of the meals
  – determine how much sugar and salt each menu contains
  – determine what food additives are used
  – ensure that no irradiated foodstuffs are eaten
  – urge the use of higher quality foodstuffs.
  – encourage the use of products grown according to controlled cultivation methods, even if the costs are higher than for mass-produced food.

6 Prepare wholefood menus. By 'wholefood' is meant food prepared in such a way that as many vitamins, minerals, and essential nutrients as possible are preserved. To achieve this, food must be carefully prepared, cooking times should be short so as not to overcook the food, and it should be served to diners quickly.
7 Indicate the fat and salt content and number of joules or calories on menus.

Expand and improve the range of dishes and drinks
8 Offer alternative dishes such as:
  ■ raw vegetable salads
  ■ vegetarian meals.

9 Check whether or not it would be beneficial for the canteen to have its own kitchen if meals are bought in.
10 Contact nearby restaurants and cafés where staff eat and encourage them to pay more attention to 'healthy eating' when producing their menus.
11 Check the contents of the drinks dispensers and replace certain drinks with a high sugar content with mineral water, fruit juices without added sugar and similar healthy drinks.
12 Check other dispensing machines and replace unhealthy foodstuffs with more healthy ones or extend the range of healthier foods (such as fruit, wholemeal biscuits, fruit slices, muesli bars, and so on).

Stimulate interest in healthy eating

13 On special occasions—such as parties and outings—provide healthfoods, at least as an alternative. Wholemeal products can provide very tasty and healthy snacks, between-meal nibbles, and menus.

14 Do not attempt to do everything at once, but, rather, make a simple and unobtrusive start, such as including wholemeal pasta, brown rice, and fresh salads daily.

15 Offer alternative breakfast foods, where served, such as wholemeal rolls, yogurt, and muesli.

16 Provide honey instead of sugar for sweetening.

17 Whenever possible, offer non-alcoholic in preference to alcoholic drinks at works and office social occasions. Make mineral water and no-added-sugar fruit juices available instead.

18 At business conferences and meetings, offer nuts, dried fruits, and fresh fruit, together with wholemeal biscuits, as an alternative to the customary sugary biscuits made with white flour.

19 Provide pleasant surroundings for staff to eat in. Plants and other greenery, the right lighting, and carefully laid tables all make important contributions to creating a pleasant and relaxed atmosphere.

CHECKLIST 23: ENVIRONMENTAL COUNSELLING

Environmentalists have calculated that, in developed countries, private households can account for up to 30 per cent of the total pollution of the environment. Examples of the kinds of 'contributions' made are as follows:

- household refuse—approximately 250 kg per person per year
- using too much water—140 to 150 litres per person, per day
- consuming too much energy
- creating effluent pollution by flushing washing powders, household cleaning agents and various other products into the sewage system
- polluting the air with harmful solvents and propellant gases by using paints and varnishes, thinners, adhesives, and sprays
- producing harmful exhaust gases from cars
- polluting gardens with pesticides and fertilizers
- using salt in winter to thaw ice.

We can all help protect rather than damage the environment in our daily lives by:

- saving many litres of water each day by using it carefully
- making do with less packaging and without plastic bags
- using returnable bottles instead of disposable bottles or tins
- using fewer chemicals in and around the house
- being more environmentally aware when driving
- purchasing items that help to protect or, at least, do not harm, the environment and avoiding those that positively harm it
- refusing to use pesticides in the garden.

If more people around the world were to do this, there could be a major improvement in the state of the environment and in the quality of life everywhere. However, there is frequently a lack of understanding of the impact wasteful practices have on the environment and little advice available on what people can do.

Employers can provide assistance here, by giving their staff access to environmental advice on issues concerning their own homes.

Provide environmental counselling for employees

1 Appoint environmental counsellors whose role will be to advise staff. Alternatively, support this through an independent service, contributing financial support where appropriate. Otherwise, a joint counsellor for two or more companies may be possible where such cooperation exists. Contact local environmental organizations and encourage the appointment of environmental counsellors.

2 Counsellors should be appropriately qualified, politically neutral, and objective.

3 Introduce the counsellor service to staff and explain in detail the objective and value of environmental counselling.

4 Collect information about any financial assistance (for example, financial support is sometimes available through official job creation schemes).

5 Organize meetings and discussions with environmental counsellors and workers. Topics might include:

- the use of chemicals in the household
- how to avoid creating waste
- how to save water and energy
- environmentally benign buildings
- do-it-yourself principles.

6 Draw up rules and objective advice on the environment:

- make advice unbiased and avoid negative criticism

- recommend only those products or services that have been tested by neutral, reliable experts and are proven to be environmentally safe
- make no claims that are untrue or be proven incorrect
- praise ecologically beneficial products or services rather than criticize those that harm the environment.

7 Ensure that any information on staff made available to counsellors is handled confidentially.

8 Influence the city or local authorities to appoint environmental counsellors for their various activities.

9 Make staff more aware of environmental problems by providing information geared to their specific domestic needs.

Provide information about environmentally aware practices

10 Save energy:

- maintain appropriate room temperatures; 1°C less saves 6 per cent energy
- do not use tumble dryers or, if you must, use machines with low power consumption figures
- install thermostatic radiator valves (up to 15 per cent energy can be saved)
- seal or double-glaze windows
- do not cover radiators
- install boilers with low power consumption figures.

11 Reduce water consumption:

- install flow restrictors on taps
- install water-saving devices in the cisterns of toilets
- install single-lever mixer taps
- repair leaking taps and toilet cisterns
- shower instead of having a bath.

Combined, these measures can easily yield a saving of 10 000 litres of water per person per year in the home.

12 Be more pollution-conscious when using a washing machine:

- buy washing machines with lower water and power consumption figures
- do not use the pre-wash facility
- wash at 60°C instead of boiling
- use one-third less washing powder per cycle

- wait until you can wash full loads
- use washing powder for delicate fabrics rather than heavy duty detergents
- treat stains separately.

13 Use household cleaning products more sparingly:

- use 'green' soap or a mild, all-purpose cleanser rather than WC or bathroom cleansers
- treat scale deposits with acetic acid
- do not use deodorant blocks in toilet pans or cisterns
- unblock pipes and U-bends with plungers or specially designed rods rather than with chemical agents
- wash non-greasy dishes in hot water, without washing-up liquid
- avoid cleansers containing bleach or disinfectant
- clean windows with water and a dash of vinegar or alcohol rather than proprietary window-cleaning products
- clean floors that are not particularly dirty with clear water only; if they are more heavily soiled, use a little green soap or a mild all-purpose cleanser
- protect untreated furniture with beeswax, linseed oil, or shellac.

14 Avoid creating waste:

- do not buy products with excessive packaging
- wherever possible, use reusable packaging, such as returnable bottles
- avoid plastic packaging
- reuse or collect paper to recycle
- collect glass for recycling
- put kitchen waste on a compost heap
- take used car oil to special collecting points
- in your community, support the setting up of collecting points for paper, glass, special category refuse, and used oil.

15 Use biological paints, dyes, and wood preservatives:

- In the home, use natural resin latex paints or synthetic resin latex paints that are low in pollutants
- Inside, avoid using chemical wood preservatives as much as possible.

16 Do not use poisons in the garden:

- avoid chemical pesticides
- treat pesticide residues as special waste and do not put them in the dustbin

- use natural manure whenever possible, such as compost, green manure, or vegetable fertilizer
- compost organic waste
- Do not use peat—bark humus and compost are effective alternatives.

All these and many more practical tips can:

- save a great deal of money
- protect family health
- make a personal contribution to improving the environment.

EXAMPLES OF GOOD PRACTICE—Staff issues

As has been mentioned in the checklists, employees can feel involved in environmental issues if motivated to do so. This can be done by providing information and giving staff a role to play in the formulation and practice of environmental measures. Making them aware of environmental issues away from work also helps spread the message of sustainable development.

Motivation and training

The computer firm **Atari** introduced a special holiday allowance to workers who gave up taking smoking breaks. This can be taken as a half day per month or accumulated to make an extra six days holiday leave annually.

Tesco, the UK supermarket chain, has over 300 people involved in greening the company. It also publishes a series of customer information sheets on environmental issues.

Elida Gibbs GmbH keeps its workforce up to date with a special 'green report' containing information about environmental measures taken by the firm, plus praise and criticism from both within and outside the company. Contributions relating to improving the environment are sought from any of the employees.

Neckermann raised the level of its workforce's environmental awareness through information and further training. To achieve this, the company set up 'environment letter boxes', an environment newspaper, ran seminars on the environment, and sponsored correspondence courses were run on how to become a home environmental adviser.

Otto Versand GmbH & Co. believes that increasing the awareness and knowledge of the workforce is a central part of any environmental policy.

Their staff is kept up to date with developments in protecting the environment by means of in-house reports, a staff newspaper, video bulletins, news reports, and an environmental telephone line. Further, the company's training courses place emphasis on 'green' activities during lectures, discussion groups, and workshops.

On a practical note, in the workplace, there are battery collection points, waste is collected and separated by sorting, and there are even special offers on public transport tickets.

The company gives every employee a copy of its own environmental publication containing numerous ideas for 'green' awareness in daily life.

IBM UK operates a programme called 'Local Environment Action Teams'. This gives grants to encourage IBM's employees and their families to get involved in local environmental projects and activities.

Canteen food

The **Evangelischen Akademie Bad Boll** has set certain basic guidelines for the running of its canteen. It purchases regional and seasonal, wholefood, natural, and fresh foods from ecologically aware growers, and uses energy-saving methods of transport and kitchen management.

Hewlett-Packard GmbH brought environmental awareness into its canteen by sorting and recycling waste. Suppliers were requested to reduce packaging, and a 15 per cent saving in cleaning products has been made by changing from liquid to powder detergents. Switching to using smaller kitchen machines has reduced the amount of energy consumed, as has the use of heat recovery units in the dishwashers.

Otto Versand GmbH & Co has a canteen motto that reads 're-usable, not disposable', and has reduced the amount of waste created considerably. Porcelain replaced plastic, drinks were made available 'on tap' rather than in cans, 90 per cent of the bottles used are returnable, and bulk food is bought only in reusable containers. A healthfood menu is available every day, and non-smoking dining areas ensure a pleasant atmosphere.

In addition, water-saving units and biodegradable cleaning products have led to a reduction in water consumption and less polluted waste water.

Staff counselling

Procter & Gamble GmbH issues a staff newspaper about the environment and product safety. Items include ideas from the WWF about washing laundry, which are also printed on their packets of washing powder, plus the WWF's address and bank number for donations.

POLICY EXTRACTS—Staff issues

ESKOM, South Africa: policy regarding employees

'ESKOM will encourage employee involvement as an important part of our commitment to improve the environment. We will:

- communicate and reinforce environmental values throughout Eskom
- train responsible personnel in sound environmental management practice
- assign and establish clearly defined accountability for environmental management performance at all levels
- motivate employees to reduce electricity consumption at all Eskom facilities and to make greater use of environmentally preferred materials and products.'

ACRO Chemical Company

'ACRO Chemical Company will manage worldwide businesses and facilities to protect the environment and the health and safety of employees, customers, contractors, and the public.

To accomplish this we:

- educate and train each employee, and hold each employee responsible for compliance with this policy and accountable for measured performance relative to our standards of manufacturing excellence.
- establish and promote programmes that help employees achieve a safer and healthier lifestyle.'

Checklists for finance and legal issues

10

Finance
and legal
issues

- 24
  Public subsidies

- 25
  Insurance

- 26
  Legal aspects

- 27
  Damage liability

- 28
  Criminal liability

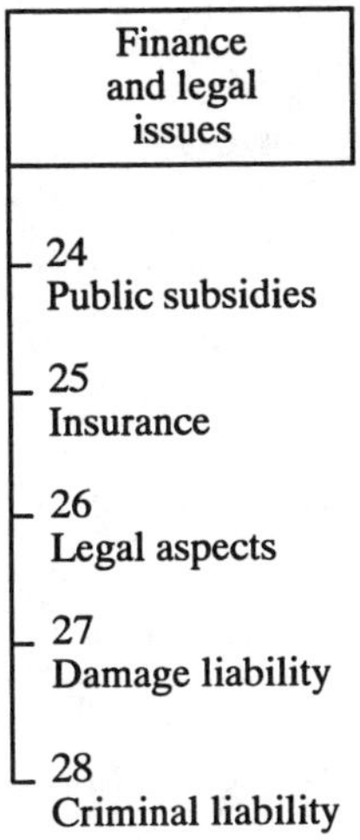

FIGURE 10.1   FINANCE AND LEGAL ISSUES IN THE WINTER MODEL

This chapter covers the roles of the finance department and legal advisers in the business. Most smaller business will not have a legal department, but depend on trade associations or consultants to help them monitor and comply with legal and regulatory requirements.

As we have mentioned before, the sequence of the checklists in this book is not an indication of the order of priority of issues for all business. Indeed, for certain businessmen and managers, Checklist 28, Criminal liability, in this chapter may be the aspect of this area that they will want to consider first.

CHECKLIST 24: SUBSIDIES

For any firm committed to the concept of sound environmental management, the availability and proper use of finance is an important key to success. Thus, the finance department's role is important in the research and monitoring of:

■ the costings for and financing of developing new technology or purchasing environmentally beneficial equipment
■ the availability of and procedures for receiving government aid, either directly through grants or loans, or indirectly through fiscal allowances granted for environmentally related projects
■ trends in the costs involved in protecting the environment and ensuring that these are incorporated into the calculations made regarding investment projects and decision making concerning them.

Researching the financial implications of environment-related expenditures

1 Define what is understood by investment in protecting the environment. Think about the type and amount of investment that is expected to bring about a required reduction in:

■ the volume and noxiousness of solid waste and waste water or air emissions
■ avoiding damage to the soil or of removing any damage that has already occurred.

The point of reference for these calculations is that which exists before the requisite planned investment is made.

2 So if investment is planned, decide whether or not:

■ it may relate to protecting the environment
■ it is intended exclusively as such or might merely enhance production capacity under the guise of integrated environmental protection.

3 Before investing in plant to protect the environment, investigate whether or not similar, or even better, benefits could be obtained by installing new non-polluting machinery in all existing plants. Agencies working to protect the environment are often prepared to grant a longer stay of execution to facilitate a more integrated approach. Some tenacity may be required to achieve this. These agencies tend to prefer conventional solutions.

4 If a particular proposed project is likely to increase pollution, ensure that

all costs arising as a result of this have been properly taken into account in the costing for this project. Such increased costs could include:

■ the cost of disposing of special-category waste
■ changes in environmental threshold limits
■ new constraints on future investment.

However, there may be:

■ savings on raw materials and other consumables through recycling the waste internally
■ savings in energy
■ savings in dumping costs as a result of introducing recycling measures.

Use appropriate capital investment and costing methods

5 When evaluating investment projects, ensure that all appropriate methods are considered and that these do not prejudice the long-term investment projects, which may only bear financial benefits in later years.

6 Introduce specific costing methods for environmental issues. Consider the 'cost follows cause' philosophy. A sharp increase in costs is not necessarily caused by higher protection requirements, but often by an overconventional approach to adapting to these requirements. The most common mistakes are:

■ relying exclusively on 'end-of-pipe' solutions
■ focusing only on the area of the operation where the problem arises.

Take advantage of state schemes and other benefits given to encourage the protection of the environment

7 Take advantage of national schemes to support or promote protection of the environment. Examples of projects for which financial assistance is available in certain countries include:

■ developing technology where the project would not otherwise be economically feasible
■ recycling waste
■ counselling services on protecting the environment and on market opportunities for environmentally friendly equipment
■ waste water treatment installations
■ demonstration installations.

8 Financial assistance may take the form of low-interest loans in subsidies. Finance and investment project managers should investigate all such

state assistance as large sums of money can be saved on 'acceptable' projects, such as those for technology to reduce and treat hazardous waste. In the USA, it is possible to 'bank' the sale or any part of emissions reduction that goes beyond the government requirement.

9 For organizations operating within the European Union, the Commission and the European Investment Bank offer loans and other forms of assistance for suitable projects.

10 Companies with subsidiaries in foreign countries should investigate what assistance is available in each of them. For example, the kinds of tax-deductible depreciation rates that can be claimed for environment-related investments can differ in each country. A tax planning strategy may find savings.

A byproduct of all this research is that the finance division itself can become as aware of the environment as it is of the need to be cost conscious. For example, a German water authority pays farmers in its catchment area compensation for lost subsidies to encourage the use of environmentally sound farming practices. It also employs an agricultural adviser to consult with the farmers. It hopes that this programme will make expensive purification plants unnecessary.

Other publicly financed or supported ventures include:

■ an international and private-sector joint venture for processing used batteries
■ a joint venture between a private-sector company and a university to improve the quality of recycled paper.

CHECKLIST 25: INSURANCE

The purpose of managing environmental risks is to:

■ recognize quantifiable as well as unquantifiable factors
■ determine which risks can be avoided or reduced, either technically or by other means
■ determine which risks can and should be insured against
■ help protect commercial organizational entities from unquantifiable risks.

Thus, insurance is only one possible option in reducing risks, but the main strategy is to avoid risks in the first place.

The insurance markets are only gradually adapting to environmental risk issues and policies. Insurance cover for certain environmental risks, particularly gradual pollution as opposed to rapid pollution is still in its infancy.

Organizations' exposure to environmental risks
Environmental damages may affect the lives and health of staff, as well as the assets of the company.

1 Check current health, accident, and life insurance policies. Injury to the respiratory tract, the eyes, skin or, indeed, any organ may develop slowly and get worse. Illnesses such as asbestosis and pneumoconiosis can often lead to occupational incapacity and early death. Such illnesses may occur after accidents, like at Bophal, Seveso, and Chernobyl. Injuries described as 'temporary' at the time now appear equally serious. Most countries of the Western world have a certain basic protection provided by their national social security systems, but in high-risk industries such as asbestos, mining, and chemicals, management should accept that *they* have a social responsibility towards their employees and, if necessary, provide supplementary company insurance schemes for them. For countries that have little or no such infrastructure, this becomes almost a 'moral obligation'.

2 Review all forms of insurance, including that for fire, boilers and machinery, and business interruption insurance. The release of acids, gases, vapours, or soot may cause damage to property and buildings covered by fire insurance, even though machinery itself is not destroyed by a fire. Contaminated water, air containing aggressive particles, polluted oils or coolants may cause damage to machinery. This applies particularly to water pumps and filter installations. Contamination from toxic substances caused by a fire can also greatly increase the cost of cleaning up. These may be covered by boiler and machinery insurance or by some form of all-risk policy. Property insurances are required in some countries but are optional in others. The cost of this type of insurance must be based on the correct valuation of the property or asset concerned. Important assets should be insured not only against loss in value, but also against business interruption in case assets are unusable as a result of damage. Self-insurance might be considered under certain circumstances if these are smaller or widely dispersed risks.

3 Check insurance with regard to soil contamination. In the future, ordinary liability insurance will probably not cover the cost of decontaminating soil. This should, therefore, be included in property insurance contracts as far as possible, whether it be fire, boilers and machinery or

electronics insurance. Preservation of the existing environment, including water, air, and soil resources, is not insurable.

Environmental risks from third parties

An even greater risk for a company is the possibility of being held liable by third parties for environmental damage. Protection against this becomes increasingly important as the question of placing liability (fault) for such damage is now more accepted throughout the world. Practically all countries now have written or case laws that impose a strict liability on a polluter of the environment. The necessity for the plaintiff to prove a causal link has been diminished. Because the rising awareness of environmental isues and, consequently, environmental liability are fairly recent developments, insurances to protect companies from liability for environmental damage are still available but they are becoming more limited. Thus, the following advice holds.

1 Maintain existing insurances. Normally, existing insurance schemes give fuller coverage than the newer ones. Existing schemes should, therefore, be maintained as long as the insurers agree. If change is unavoidable, particular attention should be paid to the 'time gap'—the length of time any old claims and any new claims can be made. When changing from an old to a new insurance scheme, the existing risks should be laid down in detail, to clearly distinguish the claims against the former insurer from those against the new.

2 Recognize and analyse the risks. Environmental risks should be approached on the basis of avoid, reduce, limit, control, and delegate. Insurance schemes transfer risk. However, the company should proceed through the other stages first, via a risk management process. Any serious environmental liability insurance is based on a thorough risk analysis, which should not only comprise the (not insurable) losses that have previously occurred, but the current and future risks arising from operational procedures and products. As insurance becomes less available, the risk analysis sometimes becomes more of an 'alternative' than the basis for risk transfer.

3 Minimize risks—make use of insurers' experience. The recognized risks can often be diminished by simply altering operational procedures or the production process. Make use of the experience insurers have had of risks their other clients have experienced in similar industries.

4 Consider liability limits, deductibles, and self-insurance. The risk analysis process could identify what level of exposure to damages arising from operational procedures or products the company is currently

risking. Limits to the liability the company can cope with should be defined in accordance with any findings and consideration given to the danger of accumulation. The maximum liability limit, which is part of some environmental impairment liability laws, is, however, of minor importance for this decision. Furthermore, the ability to undertake the obligation will depend on whether or not the insurers' are able to meet it. National insurers depend on international reinsurance companies for this. Knowledge of the insurance premiums that need to be paid for cover make management and staff more aware of risks. Last, it should be noted that environmental liability insurance cover will often not match legal liability requirements. Uninsured or, indeed, uninsurable risks may remain.

CHECKLIST 26: LEGAL ASPECTS

Any legal system gives businesses a wide range of opportunities to incorporate their own policies of environmental management within binding agreements. Such agreements may be negotiated with partners, shareholders, employees, suppliers, or customers. Examples of these are:

■ inclusion of measures to protect the environment in the strategic goals of the company within its Articles of Association
■ adoption of internal guidelines and instructions to implement such measures in a practical way
■ agreements with the works council or trade unions
■ decision to manufacture, purchase, use or market products that are environmentally sound at all stages, including disposal.

Naturally, all businesses are required to comply with environmental laws and regulations, which are becoming ever more detailed and strict. Liability law has, thus, become a key issue in these more recent times. Internationally, the principle of strict liability (that is, liability disregarding intent or negligence) has been adopted. This applies to anyone who has caused damage or injury. The consequences of violation of the laws may be:

■ production bans
■ shutting down of machinery
■ shutting down of production plants
■ criminal prosecution
■ fines
■ payment of damages and other penalties.

The competence of the EU in matters concerning the protection of the environment was already stipulated in the Treaty of Rome, which established the Community. Further, the Single European Act explicitly and comprehensively sets out the legal basis for the Union's environmental policy and for the status of protecting the environment. However, the laws concerning protecting the environment still fall mostly within the confines of national law for most companies at the present time.

The following checklist is influenced by the situation in Germany as this is the home country of the author, but much of the advice will also be relevant in other countries.

Four main aspects are considered in this checklist:

- meeting official requirements
- minimizing damage to the environment and liability risks
- care taken when acquiring a new company and property
- care when advertising and promoting.

Take steps to meet all statutory and official requirements

1 Plan, implement, and supervise measures to protect the environment. A decision to include protecting the environment in the corporate goals can promote a willingness on the part of the entire workforce to do as much as possible to achieve this. This can help the company in any legal action that may arise and may avert liability and damage claims. The following steps are recommended:

- include the desire to protect the environment in corporate goals, by
  - adding these to the company's Articles of Association
  - providing written notification of these to employees, suppliers, and customers
- allocate overall responsibility for protecting the environment to senior management
- appoint a member of the Board to be responsible for measures to protect the environment (the person appointed will be responsible for talking to third parties about complying with environmental legislation and the associated administrative regulations), but the overall responsibility of all members of top management or the Board should remain unaffected by this appointment
- appoint an environmental officer, whose functions and responsibilities should include:
  - keeping abreast of all environmental legislation and government/local authority regulations that affect the company's operations
  - supervising compliance with these regulations by carrying out on-

site inspections, and, in particular, by observing and measuring the impact of the plant's operations on the environment

- advising the company on the development, introduction, and application of environmentally sound processes, especially those that avoid or reduce residual substances resulting from the company's operations
- informing and safeguarding all company employees from environmental risks at work
- reporting to senior management when required and at regular intervals on environmental issues

■ setting up a company suggestions scheme to help reduce environmental pollution and similar risks.

2 Set up an environmental committee in each major plant or establishment. The role of this committee is to ensure that the rules and regulations for preventing damage to the environment and pollution of it are respected. Steps to take to make this committee effective include:

■ creating a written organizational framework for protecting the environment (this should set out what the environmental responsibilities are for product planning and development, testing, and production activities as well as the related purchasing, sales, and advertising

■ creating a supervision and control system.

3 Notify the responsible authority of the company's planning, execution, and control of measures to protect the environment. This may be a statutory duty.

4 Comply with all environmental laws and regulations concerning the plant's operations, such as those for:

■ discharging or releasing of substances in water, air, or soil
■ vibrations, noise, pressure, gases, heat
■ collecting, transporting, handling, storing, and depositing waste materials
■ recycling of waste for recovery of materials and energy
■ producing, marketing, and utilizing substances and products
■ transporting dangerous substances.

5 Before starting up operations and/or before completion of the plant:

■ eliminate any dangers that might cause death, physical injury, or damage to health or property by holding trial runs or demonstration of processes during installation

- obtain all the necessary permits and, when modifying the plant, check whether permits are needed and, if necessary, obtain them.

6 After any interruption of operations or shutdown of a dangerous plant, take action to eliminate the cause of the problem including checking that procedures are in place to ensure maintenance and proper operation of measuring devices and that no unauthorized persons have access to the plant's controls.

Minimize damage to the environment and liability risks

7 Label all substances that are hazardous to people, animals, and plants and keep them stored separately (see also Checklists 8, 'Materials management, and 11, Waste management). Record the origins of all dangerous substances.

8 Operate production and plant in accordance with instructions. Keep within the specified emission values and maintain regular records of these:

- obtain all the necessary permits
- ensure that inspections prescribed by law or stipulated by the authorities are recorded and changes implemented
- in the event of any unusual findings, take immediate action and record all relevant facts of the action taken.

It is essential to maintain proper records, as this is the only way to prove that operations were conducted in accordance with requirements, and they may be necessary evidence, showing that there has been no breach of regulations.

9 Prepare emergency plans specifying action to be taken in the event of environmental mishaps or accidents, and specify these in written procedures. For example, specify the procedures to be followed if:

- sulphur dioxide emissions in a coal-fired power station exceed limits
- noise from aircraft maintenance or repair systems exceeds limits
- levels of phosphates exceed limits when discharging effluent into a public sewer.

10 Establish rules and procedures for:

- shutting down the plant in an emergency
- minimizing damage
- recording causes of damage
- providing information to responsible authorities and the general public

- consulting the legal department or a lawyer regarding possible liability claims or investigations by the public prosecutor.

11 Avoid the chance of product liability action being taken against the company for damage to the environment, such as:

- detergents that are above the maximum stipulated limits for phosphates
- defects in design and manufacture of the product
- improper handling
- lack of a recall system
- lack of information about materials purchased and used in the manufacture of a product.

12 Include in contracts with the company's suppliers, building contractors, forwarding agents, and so on, obligations to:

- supply environmentally sound products
- provide information on any environmentally dangerous characteristics
- provide information on emergency measures to be taken in the event of environmental damage, particularly action to neutralize the damage
- dispose of the product after use, or take back the residues remaining after the product has been used
- take back the packaging in which the product was delivered.

13 Check the waste materials with a view to recycling. If it is not possible to recycle them:

- ensure that waste disposal is within legal requirements
- obtain any permits needed
- if disposal is subcontracted, check first that the company's business practices and economic position are satisfactory.

Take care when acquiring another company or property

14 Undertake an environmental risk analysis (environmental audit) of the industrial activity of the company or real estate to be acquired if there is anything to suggest that this might be necessary. Questions to ask include the following:

- Do the existing machines and systems meet today's legal and technological requirements?
  - Have the necessary permits been obtained for all machinery in its present state?

- Are official proceedings pending? Were there any in the past or are they likely to be any in the future?
- Does the production process cause problems or have there been problems in the past?
- Does the appearance of the company site in itself give reason for concern?
- Has a soil survey been conducted?

■ What contamination is there on the site (is there anything to suggest the presence of environmentally hazardous substances, such as rusty drums, leaky tanks, and so on)?

■ Are there any records of previous activities on the site, or records of former owners or tenants and their activities? Do these refer to problems such as asbestos, PCBs, trichloroethylene, heavy metals, landfill activities or other such substances or activities?

■ Is there any history of disputes with neighbours?

■ What tightening up of regulations is expected in the future, and how will this affect operational costs?

■ What risks of accidents are there in, for example, the handling of hazardous substances?

■ What arrangements are made for liability issues, in particular:
  - product liability
  - liability in the case of negligence or intent
  - establishing the burden of proof.

■ Is the company aware of any EU directives regarding contaminated sites and what conclusions should be drawn in this case? Contaminated sites are those that have accumulations of harmful substances in the soil and ground water, due to:
  - environmentally hazardous after-effects of industrial production
  - warfare, particularly in continental Europe after the two World Wars
  - where there is sufficient reason to suppose that the intended use of the real estate by a purchaser will give rise to consequences that have, or will have, serious effects on safety and public order.

15 Any risks identified during an environmental risk analysis need to be corrected or limited, particularly the following types of risk:

■ those to the operator
■ of clean-up costs being required
■ of hazard investigations being necessary
■ of the need for waste to be disposed of
■ of criminal liability

- of interruption or shutdown of operations
- of building land being unusable
- of building time being increased because extra work needs to be done to make the site safe
- of building costs increasing as a result
- of action in tort being brought against the company by third parties.

16 Examples of possible agreements that can be made with sellers include:

- contractual warranty (declaration) on existing operating permits or the absence of contamination on the site or a declaration that no contamination is known to exist on the site
- warranty by the seller for the existence of all necessary operating permits and freedom of the land from environmentally hazardous contamination
- agreement by the seller to indemnify the purchaser for any operating or contamination risks under law
- reduction in the purchase price after identifying existing or suspected contamination of the site
- deferment of the payment date until any necessary clean-up of the site has been completed and after its safety has been confirmed by expert assessment
- postponement of the transfer of the title until the risk of site contamination has been clarified
- agreement on unlimited or limited liability for risks
- assignment of the seller's claims under the law of tort against third-party polluters responsible for damage
- regulation of burden of proof, for example, in the event of a dispute, for the seller to bear the burden of proof that he and his agents and servants had no knowledge of circumstances indicating the presence of contamination on the site
- extension of periods under any statute of limitations, increasing the period of warranty for contamination from one year to three or five years from the date of transfer of the site.

Take a responsible attitude to advertising regarding environmental issues

Terms indicating that a product contributes to protecting the environment are often used indiscriminately in advertising or promoting a company or a product. Thus, avoid using terms such as 'environmentally friendly', 'environmentally sound', 'environmental awareness', 'organic' or 'eco' or phrases such as 'Our watchword is environmental awareness', or 'We sell only environmentally friendly products'. If terms such as 'environmentally friendly' or 'environmentally sound', *are* used in advertising, indicate clearly and accurately what exactly it is that makes the product 'environmentally friendly'. The information given must, of course, be true and must not be misleading in any way. For example, the statement 'This washing machine is environmentally sound because its washing cycle requires only 50 per cent of the water normally required by washing machines in the past' implements these principles.

17 Do not use recognized environmental logos, such the recycling symbol, in isolation in your advertising. Indicate why the symbol is used, for example, it is a glass bottle and can be taken to a bottle bank for recycling.

CHECKLIST 27: DAMAGE LIABILITY

Any examination of environmental safety undertaken by companies requires a knowledge of the risks of claims and any ensuing legal liability. If a liability should arise as a result of third-party claims against a company, it can, in certain material circumstances, lead to the company closing down. All companies, therefore, should assess the risks of such claims being brought against them.

This checklist is in nine parts:

■ knowing the bases of legal liability
■ enhancing employees' awareness of liabilities
■ avoiding breaches of regulations
■ creating management structures to deal with risks
■ workplace risks
■ monitoring risks of liability arising from production
■ waste disposal risks
■ post-delivery liability risks
■ preventative measures.

Know the bases of liability

Each country has inherited its own legal systems. Some, such as the United Kingdom and many of its former colonies, are based on common law, a main feature of this system being judical law making. For many of the rest of the countries belonging to the EU, the legal system is based on written laws and takes the form of codes. In the UK's legal framework, the concept of 'reasonable skill and care' is preferred to the 'strict liability' concept exercised in the EU. Strict liability means that it is not necessary to prove that you intended a particular harmful event to occur. It is thus often described as 'no fault liability'. Therefore, the acts may not be criminal in any real sense, but are judged to require penalties to be paid.

The following checklist has been drawn up on the assumption that strict liability applies, but you must apply the rules and directions of your country where these differ.

Liability based on fault (not applying reasonable skill and care) is conditional on wrongful, culpable behaviour on the part of the person causing the damage. Strict liability can attach to the owner or operator of a plant regardless of fault, such as:

■ liability for water pollution that contravenes a water law
■ liability for damage to third parties arising from pollution of water, ground, and air.

1 Know the legal bases of claims for damage or threat to the environment (acts or conditions causing damage) particularly concerning toxic waste and other factors that are potentially dangerous or damaging to the environment.
2 Produce a comprehensive study of the legal framework in which the enterprise operates, detailing:

   ■ the laws, regulations, and ordinances
   ■ conditions necessary for certain approval to be given
   ■ other regulations, such as technical instructions for the preservation of air quality, storage, chemo-physical treatment, incineration and disposal of waste requiring special supervision, and general technical regulations.

3 Constantly review and revise this framework in close cooperation with the legal department or outside counsel, noting any recent relevant legal decisions and legislation.
4 Continually update information concerning risks peculiar to your industry by means of

   ■ reviewing the relevant technical periodicals
   ■ sharing experiences with companies in the same industry.

5 Guarantee that financial costs will be recoverable from subcontractors in the event of a claim being made.
6 Carry out systematic studies of on-site risks and review details of preventative measures being taken regularly concerning:

- employees' safety
- protecting the environment.

7 When drafting a company manual, include regulations for the conduct of non-company personnel.
8 Protect company premises from being entered by unauthorized personnel.

Enhance employees' awareness of legal liability

9 Inform employees in all departments about the risks and available preventative measures.
10 Give regular training and updates to employees.
11 In the company manual, include guidelines for both normal operations and for sudden and accidental situations, in particular:

- accident prevention measures
- regulations relating to dangerous substances
- conditions for which certain approvals are required.

Avoid breaking regulations

12 Allocate duties to ensure company safety and conformance to regulations:

- clearly define duties and responsibilities
- ensure that the work of individual work areas is coordinated with the others
- examine and clarify all reporting and notification procedures.

13 Select employees with the appropriate qualifications:

- who understand the legal requirements of the job
- who are aware of the risks to employees if they do not follow best practice.

14 Provide comprehensive instruction and training of employees.
15 Ensure that security duties are appropriately supervised.
16 Involve in decision making those people who are responsible for maintaining safety, such as those with:

- control duties
- participatory duties
- reporting duties
- involvement in investment measures.

17 Provide information on structures and procedures by means of:

- organization charts
- lists of by-laws and business plans
- task and job descriptions
- company procedures manual
- a safety handbook.

Create management structures and methods to deal with risks

18 Create, where appropriate, a crisis management team with:

- the authority to make decisions
- coordinating duties
- public relations responsibilities in the event of a crisis.

19 Pinpoint potential risks losses by looking at worst case scenarios (what if this or that happened?)
20 Produce an action plan with guidelines for 'on site' employees.
21 Review installations and procedures with regard to early warning and notification procedures.
22 Provide regular maintenance of equipment to protect staff in case of fire.
23 Nominate a fire prevention officer for each major site.

Avoid workplace risks

24 Analyse and keep under constant review the impact and effects on employees and the environment of workplace activities and equipment.
25 Control access to the site:

- check people by name
- establish clear access routes for delivery vehicles
- check materials arriving at the site.

26 Control the identity of materials brought on to the site, paying particular attention to:

- security documentation
- classification, as described in the dangerous goods regulations.

27 Research the possibilities of finding substitutes for environmentally difficult substances.
28 Ensure compliance with legal requirements concerning storage of materials, paying particular attention to:

- requirements relating to water laws
- regulations regarding inflammable liquids
- regulations regarding dangerous materials, in particular the technical regulations regarding inflammable liquids and dangerous materials

- the conditions subject to which any approval has been granted by an authority.

29 Keep up-to-date delivery and stores records of all materials held on site.

Monitor risks of liability arising from production

30 Document the location and movement of materials within the production areas.

31 Maintain and service transportation systems:

- check pipes for permeability
- inspect containers used for the storage of liquids that could pollute water if they leaked out.

32 Document maintenance and inspection measures.

33 Apply for extensions of any permits before important changes are made to the plant:

- make comprehensive preparation so as to accelerate approval procedures
- examine existing permits regularly so that rights of appeal can be exercised before they become time-barred as a result of any statute of limitations.

34 Comply with any duties to notify any authorities of the company's systems and organization, such as:

- notifying them of the name of the person having personal responsibility for the plant
- of conformance with the instructions from authorities concerning the measures the company should take to comply with emission protection law.

35 Definite emissions in the context of:

- a declaration of substances being emitted
- recordings of data made for special reasons
- recurrent or continuous recordings of data.

36 Appoint one or more emission protection officers.

Avoid waste disposal risks

37 Systematically try to avoid the production of waste and encourage the recycling of materials.

38 Ensure that a central collection point for waste is provided.

39 Avoid using unauthorized intermediary waste dumps.

40 Respect legal requirements concerning the disposal of waste requiring special attention ('special waste'), particularly:

- classify it in accordance with the Waste Definition Ordinance
- follow the correct procedures for collection and disposal of waste
- follow the correct approval procedures.

41 Comply with dangerous goods regulations concerning the transportation of waste.

42 Ensure that contractors hired to transport waste are chosen carefully and supervised.

43 Maintain or initiate methods for promptly disposing of waste.

44 Appoint a waste disposal officer.

Avoid post-delivery liability risks

45 Collect and make use of any information relating to the impact of products on the environment by:

- passing on product information to all departments in the company
- observing the effects of the same or similar products.

46 Ensure that products can be disposed of by:

- substituting different materials
- creating a system to recall products
- making products recyclable.

47 Check the reliability of subcontracted transportation companies.

48 Ensure that packaging complies with legal requirements, particularly the dangerous goods regulations.

Preventative measures

49 Ensure that there is continuous dialogue between experts from all of the company's departments.

50 Share and agree data gathering systems with the relevant authorities.

51 Cooperate with liability insurers:

- inform them about all changes in the company's operations, product range, waste disposal arrangements or the workplace itself that would affect liability
- adapt insurance coverage to take account of any new legal demands that arise

- adjust sums assured in accordance with any changes in exposure to liability.

52 Cooperate with competent consulting institutes:

- to analyse the company's technical and organizational risks
- to produce suitable fire prevention and security measures
- to establish suitable security management
- to take stock of the legal position of the company and its insurance cover
- to review the company's risk management policy.

CHECKLIST 28: CRIMINAL LIABILITY

Unlike *civil* liability, which can attach to an inanimate body like a company, *criminal* proceedings can only be brought against people.

Where environmental negligence is concerned, management is often implicated under the heading of 'organizational fault'. Company directors and managers are increasingly being included in investigation for alleged failures to fulfil their duties (of surveillance, supervision, and control). With the increase in the number of environmental laws for which criminal liability suits can be brought, some European countries have seen a ten-fold increase in prosecutions against management.

In addition to the obvious risks of loss to the business, criminal proceedings against company officials can have other unsettling consequences:

- negative publicity that tarnishes the company's image, increases protests from public pressure groups and may make recruitment of new staff difficult
- an unsettling effect on employees who suffer direct or indirect blame
- the convicted employees are tainted with a criminal record, which can have a serious impact on their future careers
- a general decline in employees' willingness to take risks and make decisions
- a weakening of employees' identification with the company, known as 'mental resignation'
- additional costs arising from the criminal proceedings, such as salary costs incurred for deputizing for managers and staff who are involved in the court proceedings.

Wherever people work, mistakes, carelessness, and inattention can never be eradicated. The risk of any resulting criminal liability following from this can, however, be reduced by:

■ carefully selecting staff
■ ensuring adequate supervision and training
■ defining everyone's responsibilities and the procedures to be followed
■ cooperating with staff representatives.

Select employees with care

1 A well-defined job description clearly stating the personal and professional responsibilities of the job should be used when interviewing job applicants and given to the person chosen. When making internal transfers, ensure that the same procedure is applied. Any unskilled workers should demonstrate the same degree of involvement in their duties as the managing director.

Ensure adequate supervision and training

2 Include environmental awareness as one of the responsibilities of the job of every employee.

3 Ensure staff have up-to-date information and training on changing security and environmental issues. Ignorance of existing legislation will be no defence if an employee is prosecuted. All training should be carried out by the same person wherever possible. In this way, the training officer can take advantage of accumulated know-how and experience, as well as getting to know the staff and their abilities.

4 Knowledge gained by those attending outside seminars should be analysed and passed on to other staff. Seminars run by insurers or professional associations may be particularly helpful and rewarding.

5 Check employees' knowledge at regular intervals and make sure that they follow the training courses seriously.

Define responsibilities and procedures

6 Prepare written instructions and guidance on safe working procedures in high-risk areas and check that these are being followed.

7 Clearly define the areas of individual responsibility. Examine internal organization charts and structures to ensure that all aspects are covered.

8 Produce a detailed security, catastrophe, and risk minimization plan and keep it continually up to date. It can be developed with the cooperation of local authorities (the police, fire services, and so on), who should have

copies of this document. In certain cases, simulations of the 'real thing' should be enacted to test the security plan.

9 Employ a legal adviser, either from in-house or an outside consultant, who should:

- keep the company up to date on all relevant legal issues
- address and settle legal problems at an early stage, reducing the company's exposure to risk and administrative costs
- be aware of the company's security plans
- be accessible to the company when required.

10 Inform employees about their rights and duties. This gives them guidance should it happen for real. This is important as employees may be required to assist the police or other officers with their enquiries. As this situation will not be familiar to them, a short information document should be produced when necessary.

11 Plan how best to inform the public in the event of an environmental accident. Any statement should be factual and show that it has been carefully considered. This ensures that the media do not have to rely on the police or public prosecutors office alone for information.

Cooperate with staff representatives

12 Seek the cooperation of the union or employees' representatives regarding all aspects the protective measures drawn up within the organization. The representatives should be encouraged to identify positively with the measures in force. The environmental officer or managers responsible should keep the representatives informed of all major developments and changes and invite them to attend training events and briefings.

13 Consider taking out insurance policies to cover the legal and other costs of individual executives, managers, and employees. These costs could be incurred if individuals are accused of criminal liability for environmental damage or for producing dangerous products. This insurance gives employees a certain confidence that the company does not intend to leave them to their own resources if personal liability cases are brought against them. This provision should not, of course, reduce the need for employees to take due care. Fines imposed are not usually covered by such insurance.

Experience has shown that environmental damage is often not caused by deliberate intent or gross negligence, but, rather, as a result of ignorance of the regulations and legal liability. Corporate indifference can also be a contributory factor.

EXAMPLES OF GOOD PRACTICE—Finance and legal issues

Assisting public bodies and associations is another way in which business can contribute to protecting the environment and show their environmental credentials. The ways in which this can be done are by funding research, directly financing environmental projects or by exercising its buying power to environmental ends.

The Munich firm, **Pfanni-Werke Otto Ernst KG** took precautions to protect consumers by ordering the 1300 farmers under contract to the company not to use sewage-treatment sludge as fertilizer. This came shortly after the German Government's Ministry of the Environment advised that sludge, suspected of contamination with dioxins and heavy metals, should not be spread as fertilizer.

As part of its secondment programme, **IBM Deutschland GmbH** puts managers at the disposal of charitable organizations for periods of two to three years to work on projects to protect the environment. IBM cover the cost of their salaries and expenses during this period.

The **German Ministry of the Environment** has financed a private-sector project to dispose of used refrigerators. Some 30 workers dismantle the fridges into their component parts, the oil and cooling liquids are syphoned off, and 90 per cent of the CFC content of the insulating foam is removed.

The **German Research Ministry** has granted major financial assistance to the large German motorcar manufacturer Daimler-Benz AG to develop a hydrogen-powered vehicle, producing as exhaust pure steam, containing no carbon dioxide at all.

The major German bank **Deutsche Bank AG** has developed a databank which provides companies and self-employed people with access to information on funding programmes for environmental and other projects. Such funding is provided by state, federal, and EU sources. Over 100 programmes are aimed at investments in the field of protecting the environment.

The industrial insurance company **Colonia Versicherung AG** offers environmental advice to its clients on action they can take to ensure that they do not breach laws protecting the environment.

POLICY EXTRACTS—Finance and legal issues

IBM, USA
'Meet or exceed all applicable government requirements. Where none exist, set and adhere to stringent standards of our own and continually improve these standards in the light of technological advances and new environmental data.'

Philips, Netherlands
'Philips is committed to complying with all applicable environmental laws and regulations and emphasizes the necessity of international harmonization of environmental regulations.

Philips will cooperate with governments, regulatory bodies, industries and consumers' organizations and will take the initiative, where necessary, to promote workable and improved codes of practice and effective laws and regulations.'

Digital, USA
'We shall consider full compliance with the law as being the minimum acceptable standard. In support of this principle, Digital will:

■ implement programmes to ensure full compliance with applicable laws and regulations
■ conduct environmental, health, and safety programme evaluations to ensure all facilities are in compliance with government regulations and company policies and procedures
■ participate with governments and public interest groups in the development of sound environmental, health, and safety public policy
■ monitor environmental, health, and safety legal and policy developments in each country and integrate prospective new compliance requirements into business plans and ongoing operations.'

Current and future developments

Checklists are extremely useful and effective in getting things moving, but they are no substitute for formal systems and policies. Use them as tools to help identify the matters that need attention, to motivate the development and introduction of dedicated systems of environmental management for key functions.

In this final chapter, we will review some of the next steps you can take towards a full, active recognition of the environment as a key element in business planning and success. By taking these, you are making a very positive commitment to environmental issues.

In this chapter, we will look at:

- eco controlling and accounting
- environmental auditing and verification
- environmental reporting

Eco controlling and accounting are still in the experimental stages of development, but environmental auditing and reporting are very much part of life today.

ECO CONTROLLING

Eco controlling is a term used to describe that part of the management system which provides information for the ongoing planning and control of ecological issues at all levels of management. Eco-controlling is still in its infancy in many companies. The process of setting accepted standards of performance and information collection methods in individual industries, is one that is only beginning to be developed.

The responsibility for eco controlling can be given to a separate environment department or retained by an existing monitoring/controlling function within the company. Equally, it could be an interdisciplinary function, with line responsibility for aspects such as materials management, where material inputs are high and complicated processes are involved.

Eco controlling covers the following.

1 Planning and coordination

- Defining goals and operational objectives by area and management level.
- Establishing environmental information systems for the collection of ecological data for departments needing information on the environment.
- Recommending action regarding capital expenditure, substitution, recycling, product improvement, product elimination, and so on.
- Being involved in decisions about staff training, creation of environmental circles, analysing environmental weaknesses, and the finding of alternatives.

2 Analysis

- Identifying ecological weaknesses using checklists, product and process balance sheets, and ecological accounting and balance sheets.
- Preparing and using selected ecological assessments and having a summary of findings for each sector, then drawing up priority lists by product, area, material or location to assist management when making decisions.

3 Monitoring and control

- Discussion and critical assessment of the impact on the environment of the company's products.
- Regular comparisons being made between targets set and actual achievements.
- Carrying out voluntary internal environmental audits.
- Finding and correcting problems and errors.
- Avoiding the occurrence of new environmental problems.
- Updating ecological weakness analysis databases.

Acquiring the necessary environmental information

Eco controlling requires information. Conventional accounting systems do not provide sufficient information for this kind of analysis. They can provide certain of the information needed, on such issues as the costs of energy and raw materials, the depreciation on filter systems or the cost of waste disposal. However, these are only part of a company's impact on the environment.

Conventional accounting is based on the actual costs incurred. In addition, it mainly provides cost and price information retrospectively and is influenced by short-term supply and demand. In addition, with some ecological information it is not possible to put a monetary value on it. For example, what is the 'value' of the natural world as a whole or the 'value' of a particular species of butterfly or a beautiful landscape? Judgements relating to these sorts of issues involve taking an ethical standpoint and thinking of the impact on the quality of life of future generations.

Environmental information is very varied. It includes facts and issues from the fields of biology, geology, physics, and chemistry, among others, and often these are uncertain and highly complicated disciplines.

Thus, if ecological performance is to be measured and controlled efficiently, it is necessary to do the following:

- allow time to identify ecological weaknesses and, thus, avoid any risks to and safeguard the company's competitive position
- reduce the complexity of the environmental problem, making information comprehensible to management, but still scientifically accurate
- ensure that indicators are applicable to the different sectors and types of business
- recognize the company's strengths and weaknesses and stage of progress it has reached in its commitment to the environment.

Ecological weakness analyses may be applied to:

- products and their packaging
- processes, including energy efficiency
- materials and issues of eco-toxicity
- polluted sites
- office supplies, and so on.

The results of studying these areas can be used to draw up action plans to correct weaknesses. The company's environmental group can use this information to compile an ecology report, which should identify the major environmental achievements and weaknesses in a form of an eco balance sheet.

Total analysis involves a different approach. The objective here is to record all significant impacts on the environment made by a company from its inception—a system that shadows the company's financial accounts.

ECOLOGICAL ACCOUNTING

This is an advanced method of eco controlling. The concepts and approaches involved are interesting to appreciate the total accountability of a company's activities.

In ecological accounting, 'environmentally relevant' activities of the company are recorded in physical units, such as kilograms, cubic metres or joules. By 'environmentally relevant' is meant all the inputs of materials and energy from the natural environment required by the company.

Inputs and waste materials are given equivalence coefficients (or eco factors) depending on the extent to which they are a burden on the natural environment. For example, the depletion of natural resources or pollution of the environment would be highlighted.

This provides an index—expressed in units of account (UA)—for wasted heat, consumption of non-renewable raw materials and production of waste. The UA total indicates the overall environmental pollution produced by a company.

The equivalence coefficients takes account of two different concepts, such as 'capacity scarcity' (that is, the limited capacity of the atmosphere to absorb pollution) and 'cumulative scarcity' (meaning, the depletion of non-renewable resources).

Provided the same equivalence coefficients are used, this system also allows a company to compare *its* impact on the environment with that of another company in the same industry or region. However, its main purpose is to help companies make rational decisions and channel the available resources into those areas where the benefit to the environment will be greatest.

Ecological accounting has the following benefits:

- it shows to management the environmental impact of its entire range of products or individual products and production methods
- it identifies the ecological weaknesses of a company and focuses management attention on problem areas
- it enables management to increase the company's real net output without increasing ecological problems, but rather, hopefully decreasing them—a 'qualitative growth strategy'
- it can operate as an effective shadow accounting system alongside financial accounting, without mixing monetary values and real values
- it can provide a tangible base for cooperation with authorities in the area as well as valuable information about the measures taken by the company to protect the environment

- it can improve the credibility of public relations work and help to provide an objective basis for advertising.

Perhaps some time in the future, the results of financial accounting will run parallel to those of ecological accounting.
This system has clear benefits but also raises some problems:

- it lacks flexibility as it aims to set a standard with equivalence coefficients for *all* companies, which would permit external auditing and government control
- presently it does not cover issues such as noise, toxicity, radioactivity, elimination of species, upstream and downstream pollution (or, in the more recent version, depletion of raw materials), as well as other factors such as vehicle fleets, buildings, and storerooms
- it uses numerical expressions in absolute terms, which tends to give an impression of scientific precision and expert decision-making structures
- it fails to consider existing and expected environmental risks, tougher legislation, and the greater acceptance of environmental measures and sensitivity to such issues on the part of the general public.

THE ECO BALANCE SHEET

The eco balance sheet is another approach to systematic and comprehensive ecological weakness analysis.
   This system analyses the company's environmental impact and reports by means of four statements:

- operating statement
- product line statement
- process statement
- site statement.

An operating statement
This records:

- all inputs—raw materials and auxiliary materials, bought-in materials, and trade products
- tangible and intangible emissions—effluent, extracted air, solid waste, noise, radioactivity
- energy losses
- outputs—products, including joint and byproducts, giving the most accurate data on quantities as possible.

A product line statement

This statement tracks the environmental impact of representative products, from raw material stage through transportation to the company and intermediate processing stages to marketing, consumption, and post-consumption phases (waste disposal). This approach is often referred to as the 'cradle-to-grave' or even 'cradle-to-cradle' approach.

A process statement

This statement analyses the input/output flows of materials and energy in the company's production processes showing a breakdown of the production processes and specific areas.

Site statement

This statement analyses all other environmentally relevant factors and activities at the site or sites. The use of space, buildings, the existence of contaminated land, including the inventory situation, infrastructure, consumption of materials and inventory in administrative departments are all considered.

Using the statements

By analysing these four statements, environmental problems and issues can be identified. This permits comparisons to be made between polluting products, materials, or machines, showing the effects of concentration and accumulation, such as a concentration of material-induced emissions resulting from the use of certain products or processes.

Management can then refer to formulas or parts lists to identify which environmentally hazardous substances are used in different products. It may find that by substituting one specific substance for another, a whole series of ecological problems in product application, storage, production, and waste disposal can be solved or, alternatively, that harmful emissions can be eliminated by changing work flow (say, by subcontracting certain operations).

The ecological problems identified during the analysis are then classified to help decide whether action is needed and when. The classifications can include:

■ legal and political requirements, national and/or regional
■ social acceptance, such as the demands of various groups within society, or, 'ecology pull'
■ hazard/accident potential of normal operation and malfunction
■ internalized environmental cost, that is, the cost to the environment and

the cost of environment-induced loss of business appearing in company accounts

■ external costs along the product line, such as contamination of soil, air, and water and the impact on species/upstream and downstream of the site of production

■ depletion of non-renewable resources or the overexploitation of renewable resources, for example, consider the extent of reserves of raw materials used by the company, whether or not potentially renewable raw materials of vegetable or animal origin are overused or exploited or whether they are derived from monocultures/mass livestock production.

These criteria may be used together and put in order of relative urgency, to give priority to planned fields of action and time horizons.

The classifications are simple, provide environmental information and avoid quantification in numerical and, above all, monetary terms. At the same time, the combination of ABC (qualitative) analysis and XYZ (quantitative) analysis enables management to handle a mass of environmental data, providing transparency, condensing it, and separating the essential from the non-essential.

This method avoids confusing subjective value judgements with the arbitrary preferences of individual companies; it presents different environmental impacts in a way that helps strategic decision making (product/sector portfolio, investment/product planning) and decision making about operations (choice of processes, make-or-buy decisions, design improvements). Either of the two foremost priorities (A or B) may be selected, depending on the progress the company has made in implementing its environmental measures and depending on the strengths and weaknesses of the company, its competitive situation and other relevant aspects of strategic planning. This enables the company to balance ecological priorities with its other social and business objectives.

By including an XYZ analysis, the relevance of materials/processes can be analysed, permitting a comparison to be made between different degrees of harmful effects on the environment, for example, by using 'critical consumption quantities'.

Identifying ecological weaknesses is in the company's own interest, and is done on a voluntary basis. It mainly serves internal company purposes, namely:

■ it provides information on the environmental soundness of materials, processes, products, systems, and other company activities

■ it facilitates management's control of measures to protect the environment acting like an environmental audit

- it monitors the success of corporate environmental goals and compliance with the official requirements
- it makes staff aware of measures taken to protect the environment and their responsibilities in this area and involves them in collecting environmental data, searching for alternatives during environment committees, and workshops
- it identifies productivity losses (waste materials), environmental risks, and acute and impending competitive disadvantages
- it provides invaluable information for accident or emergency situations (such as a warehouse fire).

Ecological weakness analysis also provides a solid basis for credible public relations work and is helpful in other ways:

- by providing authorities with proof of the environmental soundness of processes, the promotion of integrated environmental measures (rather than 'end-of-the-pipe' technologies), information on current environmental data, and so on
- in dealings with insurance companies, as it is easier to obtain insurance cover for environmental risk, product liability, and accident risk when it is clear that efforts are being made to avoid these occurring
- with consumers as it presents the measures to protect the environment the company is already implementing, plans to implement in the future, and shows how carefully they have been considered and that they are well-founded.

The individual statements of the eco balance sheet are constantly updated (if possible in a computerized system). This permits changes in ecological weaknesses ('A' cases of substances, products, processes, and so on), due to measures taken and changes in external parameters, to be monitored. This provides management with the latest environmental data for internal eco auditing and for guiding the decision-making process.

ENVIRONMENTAL RATIOS

The planning and control process can be improved by developing a system of appropriate environmental ratios. These are designed and calculated to assist the various sectors, departments, and levels of management. They permit comparisons to be made between:

- target and actual values achieved
- performances over periods of time

■ performance of other companies or divisions.

The ratios use numbers or measures. Typical numbers are for quantities and volumes, money, number of employees, time, and space measurements. In environmental issues, the elements being compared might also be waste, recycling, energy, water usage or emissions. For example, the following selected environmental ratios might be used by an industrial company:

■ waste volume/weight (sorted) per annum/per day
■ waste as a ratio of product earnings from sales per annum
■ amount of returnable/disposable items of packing in incoming goods to total amount of incoming goods
■ waste disposal cost (toxic waste/household waste) as a ratio of total manufacturing costs
■ actual recycling quantity as a ratio of budgeted recycling quantity
■ rejects as a ratio of good production
■ water charges paid in relation to units produced per annum
■ volume and structure of tangible or non-tangible emissions in relation to units produced by an activity
■ energy consumption as a ratio of net units to production units.

ENVIRONMENTAL AUDITING

The final stages of any accountability process is an audit. All managers are familiar with financial audits, during which an independent person undertakes an examination of the financial records of a company and expresses an opinion on these. Their statement is communicated to shareholders or owners on the financial statements produced by the enterprise.

Within businesses themselves, internal auditors are often employed to undertake similar examinations of the performance of various functions, but reporting to senior management.

Environmental audits are closer to this latter form of audit than they are to the first. The International Chamber of Commerce (ICC) has defined (ICC, *Environmental Auditing*, Paris 1989) an environmental audit as:

> a management tool for systematic, documented, regular and objective assessment of how well environmental protection organization, management, and facilities are working in order to promote the protection of the environment.

The European Union has a similar definition.

Such audits are presently voluntary and auditors can be employees of the company, but independent of the activity or function being audited. Some companies have appointed external auditors to ensure complete independence from the operations they are auditing.

The European Union's 'Eco Management and Audit Scheme' (No 1836/93) has introduced another level of review, called a 'validation'. In this process, a totally independent verifier examines the policies, programmes, management systems, audits undertaken, and the environmental statement to verify that they comply with the European regulations.

ENVIRONMENTAL REPORTING

In the last few years, there has been an increase in the number of reports on the environmental performance of companies that have been published.

This trend started with references being made to environmental matters in the directors' or managers' reports within the annual financial report. Information about the impacts and expenditure on environmental issues was commonly the content of these reports. Certain companies followed this by publishing newsletters and one-off special reports on their company's activities and efforts.

As environmental management and eco accounting systems have developed, companies have started to report on their plans and targets they have set, and how they are performing in relation to these.

After defining their current environmental policies and strategies, the kinds of issues commonly reported, often quantified with comparative figures and targets, include:

- expenditure, both capital and revenue, on environmental issues, such as the
  - cost of safety and protecting the environment
  - research and development costs of new 'greener' products, including life cycle analysis studies
  - cost of cleaning up contaminated sites
  - environmentally related costs involved in the construction of new buildings and plant
  - cost of adapting transport vehicles
  - supplier analysis and improvements in the environmental purchasing chain
  - management of energy and water resources and conservation efforts made

- recycling of various materials and the financial saving that has resulted
- necessary measures to control and reduce emissions into the air, water, and land
- achievements in reducing waste
- new products and their environmental qualities
- eco labels or equivalent recognitions granted
- awards and public recognition of environmental good practice
- community services, such as the development of nature parks and local school projects
- financial contributions to local environmental study groups
- environmentally related staff training events and attendances
- environmentally related grants and financial assistance received
- environmental audits undertaken and their findings
- fines and prosecutions against the company for breaches of regulations
- future goals and plans.

For the companies that have developed an eco accounting system, an ecological balance sheet is the final output of such a report. These are still rare.

Epilogue

THE WAY FORWARD IN ACTION AND THINKING

Boldness and imagination are needed in environmentally minded entrepreneurs and managers. The more dramatically the environmental situation of our planet deteriorates, the bolder and more unconventional will be the decisions they have to make.

They also need the courage to critically rethink the habits of a lifetime. They have to think about the meaning and ecological soundness of what they are doing; if necessary they must be willing to change to a more environmentally acceptable line of business.

Entrepreneurs who, with their staff, produce a high standard of products or services, and has to survive in competition with other companies, has a hard job to do. Working for environmental management required additional efforts—and in certain sectors and certain economic situations, they almost go beyond the bounds of human endeavour.

We entrepreneurs and managers have a long and uphill path ahead of us. At the end of the day, we will only achieve real success in environmental management if this springs from a lifestyle derived from our innermost attitudes to life.

Appendix A

THE WORK OF THE INTERNATIONAL NETWORK FOR ENVIRONMENTAL MANAGEMENT

The International Network for Environmental Management (INEM) is the world federation of non-profit business organizations for environmental management and sustainable development. INEM was established on 19 February 1991 when three existing business associations for environmental management in Germany (founded in 1985), Austria (founded in 1989), and Sweden (founded in 1990) decided to link themselves in a more formal registered network and provide assistance to new associations in the process of being created around the world. As of September 1994, INEM had members and affiliated associations in 21 countries on 5 continents. The INEM association represents more than 5000 companies.

The purpose of INEM and its member associations is to promote, disseminate, develop, and apply the principles and methods of environmental management. INEM is not a lobbying body, but a group of business associations, which are devoted to helping their member companies implement *practical* solutions to environmental problems. It is our experience that these solutions are also economically advantageous, if they are applied as part of a holistic plan to integrate the environment into a company's operations.

INEM's goals are to:

- reduce the negative environmental impacts of industry worldwide
- show that proactive environmental policies are a condition for market success
- promote cleaner production and cleaner technologies, rather than end-of-the-pipe approaches
- help business to integrate environmental management into its culture, operations, and methods

- help, in particular, small- and medium-sized enterprises
- assist businesses in developing countries and Eastern Europe.

In general the INEM associations receive support for their activities for environmental management and sustainable development. This support may vary depending on their needs. Following are some of the specific benefits:

Information
- receiving up-to-date-information about environmental management in other countries
- having access to experts from other countries
- obtaining an information advantage via quick access to ongoing ISO international environmental standards work
- meeting peers from other countries to exchange know-how and experiences

Activities
- obtaining publishing rights to environmental management literature
- receiving help in developing national and international strategies to strengthen activities
- having the possibility to obtain environmental management project-related sub-contracts from INEM Main Secretariat and research/training contracts from other member associations.
- participating in working seminars of international institutions (e.g. OECD, UNEP, EBRD etc.)
- participating in the work of international organizations, such as the ISO

Financing
- meeting potential donors first hand
- benefiting from Main Secretariat fund-raising activities
- obtaining discounts on events organized by all other associations in network
- benefiting from donor funding to participate in international events

Public relations
- gaining international publicity for achievements of the associations and of member companies
- disseminating information on environmental technology of member companies
- obtaining support in international dissemination of national environmental management case studies

INEM's main guiding principles are innovation, prevention, partnerships, capacity building, and decentralization. INEM is accredited to the United Nations' Commission on Sustainable Development (CSD) and works with several other UN bodies, including the United Nations Environment Programme (UNEP), United Nations Industrial Development Organization (UNIDO), and United Nations Conference on Trade and Development (UNCTAD). In addition, INEM works with other international organizations, such as the International Organization for Standardization (ISO), the Organization for Economic Cooperation and Development (OECD), the European Bank for Reconstruction and Development (EBRD), and the International Council of Local Environmental Initiatives (ICLEI). INEM advises the OECD on the 'greening' of Official Development Assistance, and the EBRD on the training of bankers in Central and Eastern Europe.

INEM develops innovative concepts to solve the environmental problems of industry and offers these to interested parties to implement with national associations. National associations cooperating in a network is one of the most cost-effective ways to promote the application of environmental management in any country.

Each year, the most important international conference organized by an INEM association is the International Industry Conferences for Sustainable Development (IICSD) of that year. The IICSD provides a public forum for discussion of the latest practical applications of environmental management. The first IICSD, organized by the INEM main secretariat and SIGA, the Brazilian member of INEM, was held as part of the 1992 Global Forum of the UN Conference on Environment and Development in Rio. The International Conference on Eco Management, held in Tokyo in 1993, and organized by the Japan Eco-Life Center, INEM's Japanese affiliate, and the United Nations' University Headquarters in collaboration with INEM, was the 1993 IICSD. The 1994 conference in the series was the Second Southern African International Conference on Environmental Management (SAICEM II), organized by the IEF and the EFZ, the INEM member associations in Southern Africa and Zimbabwe.

National associations rooted in the cultural and economic life of their home country are best placed to reach small- and medium-sized enterprises. Such companies account for the majority of the world's business community. This is why another major element of INEM's work is the creation of new business associations for environmental management around the world. The main secretariat helps new associations to apply the methods that have been proven effective by established associations in both environmental management and organizational areas. For example, in 1992 and 1993, the main secretariat of INEM helped to create new associations in Argentina,

France, Israel, and Slovenia. In 1994, assistance was also provided to Belgium, Chile, Hungary, and Russia.

Also in 1994, INEM member associations agreed to create two new associated networks: the INEM Educational and Research Network (for management and business schools as well as technical universities and research institutes) and the INEM Environmental Industry Network. Members of these networks will benefit from synergies with each other and with the member/affiliated associations.

Although individual companies cannot be direct members of INEM, they can, nevertheless, become sponsors of INEM, thereby supporting the development and implementation of environmental management on a global scale. Specific company sponsorship can take the form of capacity-building support, project support, or support for the activities of a member association in a developing country.

Since the Earth Summit in Rio de Janeiro in 1992, INEM has developed specific programmes in accordance with United Nations' Agenda 21. These programmes fall under the umbrella of Industry 21, which is the private sector's first major post-Rio initiative for the implementation of the business portion of the Agenda 21. The first project initiated under Industry 21 is the Global Environmental Management Survey (GEMS). The goal of GEMS is to create a baseline study of the state of, and the problems that are hindering, the implementation of environmental management in each country. The pilot study for GEMS was carried out by the INEM association in Argentina. The next countries planning to implement GEMS are Brazil, South Africa, and Malaysia. INEM is working with UNCTAD to extend the survey to another 20 countries in the next few years.

INEM has also launched Industrial Agenda 21, which involves individual companies making statements setting themselves environmental performance targets. The members of INEM believe that setting concrete environmental performance goals is key to measuring, monitoring, and improving environmental performance. Such public Industrial Agendas 21 are the necessary next step for industry to track its progress towards sustainable development, after the establishment of policies and the signing of environmental codes of conduct.

APPENDIX B:

MEMBERS AND AFFILIATES OF INEM

Country and address	Full name and contacts
INEM Bahnhofstrasse 36 D–22880 Wedel (Holstein) Germany *Tel*: 49–4103–84019 *Fax*: 49–4103–13699	*Chairman*: Dr Georg Winter *Executive Director*: Mr Troy Davis
Argentina ADEGA c/o CINSA Legal Counsel Av. Belgrano 367, piso 7 AR–1092 Buenos Aires *Tel*: 54–1–331–0259 *Fax (Tel)*: 54–1–343–6557	Associatión para Desarrollo dela Gestion Ambiental
Australia EMIAA GPO Box 2231 Brisbane Queensland 4001 *Tel*: 61–7–229–8522 *Fax*: 61–7–229–8577	Environmental Management Industry Association of Australia

Country and address	Full name and contacts
Austria BAUM Lohnsteinstrasse 36 A–2380 Perchtoldsdorf *Tel*: 43–1–865–0614 *Fax*: 43–1–865–3893	Bundesweiter Arbeitskreis für unweltbewusstes Management *Chairman*: Dr Walter Seeböck *Executive Director*: Dr Thomas Gutwinski
Brazil SIGA c/o Sistema Globo de Radio Rua do Russel, 434 22210–010 Rio de Janeiro, RJ *Tel*: 55–21–205–5103 *Fax*: 55–21–205–4386	Sociedade para o Incentivo ao gerenciamento Ambiental *Chairman*: Mr José Roberto Marinho *Secretary General*: Mr Haroldo Mattos
Canada The Canadian Chamber of Commerce Focus 2000 Project 1160–55 Metcalfe Ottawa, Ontario K1P 6N4 *Tel*: 1–613–238–4000 *Fax*: 1–613–238–7643 *e-mail*: INET JD BARRY	*President and CEO*: Mr Tim Reid *Coordinator*: Mr Jean-Denis Barry
China NICEST No. 13 Xue Yuan Lane Xi Cheng District Beijing 100032 P.R. China *Tel*: 86–1–839–3934 *Fax*: 86–1–839–3245	National Information Center of Environmental Science and Technology *Director*: Mr Cao Fengzhong *Director, Foreign Affairs*: Mr Zhao Feng

Country and address	Full name and contacts

Columbia

Propel
Transversal 18 No 101–76
Bogotá

Tel: 57–1–257–4363
Fax: 57–1–218–7328

Promocion de la Pequeña Empresa

President: Dr Ernst A Brugger
General Manager: Mr Jaime Ospina

Denmark

ELM Danmark
c/o Brødrene Hartmann A/S
203 Klampenborgvej
DK–2800 Lyngby

Tel: 45–45–875–030
Fax: 45–45–873–321

Erhvervslivets Ledelsesforum for
Miljøfremme

Chairman: Mr Vagn Genter
Coordinator: Ms Anna Lise Mortensen

France

Orée
11, rue d'Uzès
75002 Paris

Tel: 33–1–4221–9686
Fax: 33–1–4221–9685

Partenariat Entreprises
Collectivités Environnement

President: Mr Alain Mamou-Mani
International Liaison: Professor
Philippe Bernard

Germany

BAUM
Tinsdaler Kirchenweg 211
D–22559 Hamburg

Tel: 49–40–810101
Fax: 49–40–810126

Bundesdeutscher Arbeitskreis für
umweltbewußtes Management

Chairman: Dr Georg Winter
Executive Director: Dr Maximilian
Gege

Ireland

IPC
IPC House
35/39 Shelbourne Road
Ballsbridge
Gallagher
IRL-Dublin 4

Tel: 353–16–686244
Fax: 353–16–686525

Irish Productivity Centre

Chief Executive: Mr E. A. Cahill
Director European Affairs: Mr Norbert
Gallagher

Country and address	Full name and contacts
Israel ALVA PO Box 68 70650 Yavne *Tel*: 972–8–433777 *Fax*: 972–8–439901	Society of Industry for Ecology *Chairman*: Mr Lucien Bronicki *Coordinator*: Mr Michael Gill
Japan JECL Mitani Building, 4th Floor 2–13–6 Nishi-Shinbashi Minato-ku, Tokyo 105 *Tel*: 81–3–3580–8221 *Fax*: 81–3–3580–8265	Japan Eco-Life Center *Chairs*: Mr Eiji Tanaka Dr Kunio Saeki Mr Tokutaro Hirose
Malaysia ENSEARCH 38A Jln SS21/58 Damansara Utama 47400 Petaling Jaya *Tel*: 60–3–717–7588 *Fax:* 60–3–7177–596	Environmental Management and Research Association of Malaysia *Chairman*: Mr Ir K. Kumarasivam *Director*: Mr Goh Kiam Seng
Netherlands CE Oude Delft 180 NL–2611 HH Delft *Tel*: 31–15–150150 *Fax*: 31–15–150151	Centre for Energy Conservation and Clean Technology *Director*: Mr Jan-Paul van Soest *International Liaison*: Ms Connie Aarsbergen

Country and address	Full name and contacts
Philippines	
Philippine Business for the Environment	*Chairman*: Mr Washington SyCip
Ground Floor/Padilla Building	*President*: Mr Leonardo B. Alejandrino
Emerald Avenue	*International Liaison*: Dr Corazon P. B.
Pasig/Metro Manila	Claudio (Founding Trustee)
	Executive Director: Ms Grace Favila

Postal address
PO Box 12228, Ortigas Center
Post Office 1600

Tel: 63–2–631–3138
Fax: 63–2–631–5714

Slovenia
DREVO
c/o MANAGER
Dunajska 106
61000 Ljubljiana

Tel: 386–61–168–1169
Fax: 386–61–168–3106

Drustvo Poslovodnih Delavcev
Slovenije

Chairman: Dr Tone Krasovec
Executive Manager: Mr Bogo Seme
International Liaison: Ms Polona
Smonig

South Africa
IEF of Southern Africa
c/o ESKOM
Location 01T40
PO Box 1091
RSA–2000 Johannesburg

Tel: 27–11–800–5401
Fax: 27–11–800–4360

Industrial Environmental Forum of
Southern Africa

Chairman: Dr John Maree
Director: Mr Jon Hobbs
Deputy Director: Ms Karin Ireton

Sweden
Svenska BAUM
Artillerigatan 38
S–11445 Stockholm

Tel: 46–8–662–0388
Fax: 46–8–662-0-1496

Näringslivets Miljöforum

Acting Chairman: Mr Rolf Henriksson
International Liaison: Mr Edwin
Krzesinski

Country and address	Full name and contacts
Switzerland Ö.B.U./A.S.I.E.G.E. Im Stieg 7 CH–8134 Adliswil *Tel*: 41–1–7090980 *Fax*: 41–1–7090981	Schweizerische Vereinigung für ökologisch bewusste Unternehmungsführung/Association Suisse pour l'Intégration de l'Ecologie dans la Gestion d'Entreprises *Chairman*: Mr Stephan Baer *Executive Director*: Dr Arthur Braunschweig
Zimbabwe EFZ PO Box BW 294 Harare *Tel*: 263–4–883865 *Fax*: 263–4–883864	The Environmental Forum of Zimbabwe *Chairman*: Mr J. P. Rooney *Group Secretary*: Mr H. D. Gaitskell

Index

Successful Practices